IRISH
UNIVERSITY
REVIEW

A JOURNAL OF IRISH STUDIES

EDITOR
John Branniga

ASSISTANT EDITOR
Emilie Pine

SPECIAL ISSUE
Irish Experimental Poetry

GUEST EDITOR
David Lloyd

Volume 46 Number 1   Spring/Summer 2016

Subscription rates for 2016

Two issues per year, published in May and November

		Tier	UK	EUR	RoW	N. America
Institutions	Print & online	1	£53.50	£60.80	£65.40	$111.00
		2	£67.50	£74.80	£79.40	$135.00
		3	£83.50	£90.80	£95.40	$162.00
		4	£101.00	£108.30	£112.90	$192.00
		5	£114.50	£121.80	£126.40	$215.00
	Online	1	£45.00	£45.00	£45.00	$76.50
		2	£56.50	£56.50	£56.50	$96.00
		3	£71.00	£71.00	£71.00	$120.50
		4	£85.50	£85.50	£85.50	$145.50
		5	£97.00	£97.00	£97.00	$165.00
	Additional print volumes		£47.50	£55.00	£59.50	$101.00
	Single issues		£37.00	£40.50	£43.00	$73.00
Individuals	Print		£31.00	£38.50	£43.00	$73.00
	Online		£31.00	£31.00	£31.00	$52.50
	Print & online		£38.50	£46.00	£50.50	$86.00
	Back issues/single copies		£17.00	£20.50	£23.00	$39.00

How to order

Subscriptions can be accepted for complete volumes only. Print prices include packing and airmail for subscribers outside the UK. Volumes back to the year 2000 are included in online prices. Print back volumes will be charged at the current volume subscription rate.

All orders must be accompanied by the correct payment. You can pay by cheque in Pounds Sterling or US Dollars, bank transfer, Direct Debit or Credit/Debit Card. The individual rate applies only when a subscription is paid for with a personal cheque or credit card. Please make your cheques payable to Edinburgh University Press Ltd. Sterling cheques must be drawn on a UK bank account.

Orders for subscriptions and back issues can be placed by telephone, on +44(0)131 650 4196, by fax on +44(0)131 662 3286, using your Visa or Mastercard credit cards, or by email on journals@eup.ed.ac.uk. Don't forget to include the expiry date of your card, and the address that the card is registered to. Alternatively, you can use the online order form at www.euppublishing.com/iur/page/subscribe.

Requests for sample copies, subscription enquiries, and changes of address should be sent to Journals Department, Edinburgh University Press Ltd, The Tun – Holyrood Road, 12(2f) Jackson's Entry, Edinburgh EH8 8PJ, UK; email: journals@eup.ed.ac.uk

IASIL MEMBERSHIP

Subscription to the journal comes with membership of the International Association for the Study of Irish Literatures (IASIL). Details of IASIL membership can be found at www.iasil.org

Advertising Advertisements are welcomed and rates are available on our website at www.euppublishing.com. Advertisers should send their enquiries to the Journals Marketing Manager at the address above.

Two new translations of Máirtín Ó Cadhain's radically original
Cré na Cille

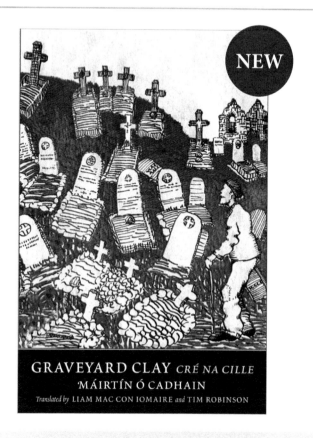

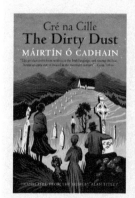

Also available

Translated from the Irish by Alan Titley

The Dirty Dust
Cré na Cille

Máirtín Ó Cadhain

This lilting translation of Máirtín Ó Cadhain's internationally admired satiric novel is full of the brio and guts of the Irish author's original. Alan Titley captures the absurdity of human behaviour, the rhythm of Irish gab and the nasty, deceptive magic of human connection that takes place even beneath the cemetery's sod.

'[An] earthy, poetic, and darkly comic masterpiece ... with its exhilaratingly free-wheeling celebration of all that is worst in human nature.' – *Sunday Times*

The Margellos World Republic of Letters

New in paperback ISBN 978-0-300-21982-1 €11.50

NEW

GRAVEYARD CLAY CRÉ NA CILLE
MÁIRTÍN Ó CADHAIN
Translated by LIAM MAC CON IOMAIRE and TIM ROBINSON

Graveyard Clay *Cré na Cille*
by Máirtín Ó Cadhain

In critical opinion and popular polls, Máirtín Ó Cadhain's *Graveyard Clay* is invariably ranked the most important prose work in modern Irish. This bold new translation of his radically original *Cré na Cille* is the shared project of two fluent speakers of the Irish of Ó Cadhain's native region, Liam Mac Con Iomaire and Tim Robinson. They have achieved a lofty goal: to convey Ó Cadhain's meaning accurately and to meet his towering literary standards.

Graveyard Clay is a novel of black humour, reminiscent of the work of Synge and Beckett. The story unfolds entirely in dialogue as the newly dead arrive in the graveyard, bringing news of recent local happenings to those already confined in their coffins. Avalanches of gossip, backbiting, flirting, feuds and scandal-mongering ensue, while the absurdity of human nature becomes ever clearer. This edition of Ó Cadhain's masterpiece is enriched with footnotes, bibliography, publication and reception history, and other materials that invite further study and deeper enjoyment of his most engaging and challenging work.

Máirtín Ó Cadhain (1906–1970) is widely acknowledged as one of the most significant writers in the Irish language and a giant among 20th-century authors. A lifelong language-rights activist, he invigorated the Irish language and Irish literature with his imaginative genius.

Liam Mac Con Iomaire is a lecturer, broadcaster, translator and biographer.

Tim Robinson is a writer, artist and cartographer.

The Margellos World Republic of Letters

HB ISBN 978-0-300-20376-9
RRP €18.00

ORDER FORM **To receive this title, send this form to:**
Yale University Press, 'Direct Mail Department', 47 Bedford Square, London WC1B 3DP   Tel: 020 7079 4900   email: sales@yaleup.co.uk

OR ORDER ON-LINE *www.yalebooks.co.uk*

Please send me .... copies of:
Graveyard Clay

HB ISBN 978-0-300-20376-9   at   €18.00

Subtotal ....
Delivery: Free in the UK
Delivery (outside UK*)   ....

Total order amount   ....
Your order will be processed by John Wiley

Send to (please print): Name ....
Address ....
....

Payment method: ☐ Cheque enclosed (payable to Yale University Press)
☐ Visa   ☐ American Express   ☐ Mastercard
Please supply billing address of credit card if different from address above:
....
....

Credit card no. ....
Expiry date .... Start date .... Security code ....
Signature ....

*DELIVERY Add the following to your order for delivery if outside UK:
European customers (EU/non-EU) add £5.35 surface mail; £12.75 airmail
All other countries add £7.75 surface mail; £14.95 airmail

☐ Tick here if you wish to receive notifications from Yale about related books

YaleBooks
www.yalebooks.co.uk

Y1591

Contents

Poetry

This publication is available as a book (ISBN: 9781474415323) or as a single issue or part of a subscription to *Irish University Review*, Volume 46 (ISSN: 0021-1427). Please visit www.euppublishing.com/journal/iur for more information.

Abstracts

Francis Hutton-Williams, Against Irish Modernism: Towards an Analysis of Experimental Irish Poetry

This essay rewrites the history of Irish poetic experiment away from modernism, or at least from contemporary industry-driven senses of the term which have multiplied to the point of overuse as a catch-all category. It is divided into two parts. The first part of the essay focuses on questions of literary history, defining some of the key trends of literary production and reception in Ireland during the 1920s and 30s. By surveying the negative impact of religion and censorship on literary development within the Irish Free State (1922–1937), the essay challenges the concept of Ireland as a place of widespread modernist assertion. The second part of the essay steers the discussion towards an 'avant-garde' trio of Irish writers, offering an extended and detailed characterisation of their poetry. It traces the emergence of an experimental Irish poetry with a selection of examples taken from Denis Devlin's *Intercessions* (1937), Thomas McGreevy's *Poems* (1934) and Samuel Beckett's *Echo's Bones and Other Precipitates* (1935), showing how poetic experiments of the 1930s challenge the lyric as a versifying form after Irish independence.

Geoffrey Squires, Modernism, Empiricism, and Rationalism

Modernism is usually defined historically as the composite movement at the beginning of the twentieth century which led to a radical break with what had gone before in literature and the other arts. Given the problems of the continuing use of the concept to cover subsequent writing, this essay proposes an alternative, philosophical perspective which explores the impact of rationalism (what we bring to the world) on the prevailing empiricism (what we take from the world) of modern poetry, which leads to a concern with consciousness rather than experience. This in turn involves a re-conceptualisation of the lyric or narrative I, of language itself as a phenomenon, and of other poetic themes such as nature, culture, history, and art. Against the background of the dominant empiricism of modern Irish poetry as

Irish University Review 46.1 (2016): v–x
DOI: 10.3366/iur.2016.0193
© Edinburgh University Press
www.euppublishing.com/journal/iur

presented in Crotty's anthology, the essay explores these ideas in terms of a small number of poets who may be considered modernist in various ways. This does not rule out modernist elements in some other poets and the initial distinction between a poetics of experience and one of consciousness is better seen as a multi-dimensional spectrum that requires further, more detailed analysis than is possible here.

J.C.C. Mays, The Third Walker

A review of the two most recent collections by Billy Mills and Catherine Walsh: namely, *Imaginary Gardens* and *Astonished Birds/Cara, Jane, Bob and James*, both published by hardPressed poetry in 2012. An attempt is made to describe how both authors are concerned to write a different kind of poetry than that which achieves greater public success in our time, as represented by recent collections by Harry Clifton.

Alex Davis, Paper & Place: The Poetry of Billy Mills

This essay discusses the issue of place and its representation in the work of the contemporary Irish experimental poet, Billy Mills. It considers the ontological priority Mills's poetry and related critical work grant the object world, and the necessarily provisional quality of the 'mapping' of the environment in verbal art. Mills's ecopoetics are contrasted with the pastoral poetic tradition, as he construes it, with the poetry of Seamus Heaney, and with Language Writing. In conclusion, Mills's practice as a translator is shown to display an attentiveness to nonlinear form that, as a critic, he identifies in the work of contemporaries including Maurice Scully, Geoffrey Squires, and Catherine Walsh.

Claire Bracken, Nomadic Ethics: Gender and Class in Catherine Walsh's *City West*

This essay argues that a feminist ethics of emplaced nomadism underpins Catherine Walsh's *City West*. It examines Walsh's engagement with the politics of contemporary neo-liberal Ireland, and argues that her experimentation with nomadism is an attempt to navigate through the environs of late capitalism.

Kit Fryatt, The Poetics of Elegy in Maurice Scully's *Humming*

Maurice Scully published *Humming* (2009), a single, self-contained work, after the completion of the monumental eight-book 'set' *Things That Happen* (1987–2008). *Humming* is an elegy, dedicated to the poet's brother, who died in 2004. This article explores *Humming* as a poem of mourning, assessing the extent to which it expresses and subverts some of the traditional characteristics and functions of elegy. Elegies often include pastoral motifs, repetitions (particularly repeated questions), an element of imprecation, multivocal performance, commentary on the elegist's ambition and achievement, and enact a general movement from grief to consolation; this essay considers the forms these take. For Scully, whose poetic practice advocates self-effacement, the egoistical nature of elegy, its emphasis on accomplishment and aspiration, presents a problem which is perhaps only partially overcome by the formal strategies discussed here. Poetry without designs upon its subjects or readers remains a goal to be achieved: 'it is hard/ work whichever way/ you look at it.' In conclusion, however, it might be said that *Humming*, like many elegies, enacts a transition between different phases of the poet's work.

Romana Huk, 'Out Past / Self-Dramatization': Maurice Scully's *Several Dances*

What has lyric to do with any radical phenomenology's choreography? Maurice Scully in *Several Dances* asks that question, as he has for years now, alongside other poets of Ireland's avant-garde whose 'distinguishing (not inhibiting) feature', as Sarah Bennett writes (acknowledging the work of Alex Davis and Eric Falci before her) is that in it 'the lyric subject persists' – in tandem with, this essay argues, what she names 'an interest in perception ... [which] is perhaps the most compelling commonality in these poets' work'. What distinguishes Scully's from the lyric phenomenology of American poets from William Carlos Williams (invoked throughout the volume) to George Oppen (also invoked) is that he queries existentialism's 'singular' approach to phenomena, achieved as Heidegger thought through the phenomenological 'bracketing' of individual (and communal) preconceptions from the perception of things. Cosmic – even theological – speculation enters in as Scully's poems move out past both self-centered lyric *and* twentieth-century cancellations of all preconceptions in the 'limit-thinking' and *being-toward-death* that phenomenology proposed for seeing past the self. Yet Scully works with mortality always in his sights too as he sings 'the

Huuuman / Limit-at-tation Blues' (p.118) and, more vertiginously, considers both the undelimitability and the fragility of us.

Niamh O'Mahony, 'Releasing the Chaos of Energies': Communicating the Concurrences in Trevor Joyce's Appropriative Poems

This essay addresses appropriation in the poetry of Trevor Joyce. The author analyses the function and impact of textual borrowing in a number of recent poems by Joyce, comparing and contrasting Joyce's appropriative practice to that of a number of contemporary poets.

Marthine Satris, Codex Vitae: The Material Poetics of Randolph Healy's 'Arbor Vitae'

Randolph Healy's 1997 poem 'Arbor Vitae' connects formally experimental poetry with an Irish tradition of politically engaged literature. Eschewing questions of national boundaries or authenticity, Healy instead develops a poetics and ethics of intersection. His apparently depersonalized poem is composed of essayistic fragments that address the role of the deaf in Irish society. This essay argues that Healy's formal choices refuse the oral basis of the lyric, and instead align his poem with nonverbal forms of communication. This challenge to the authenticity of speech also questions the language policies of the Republic of Ireland and reveals the role of the state in disciplining citizens, particularly through education. In addition to the accumulation of disparate pieces in the poem, Healy's formal innovation continues in the poem's paratextual apparatus, contributing to his development of an alternative to the epic and the lyric. As Healy incorporates references to the material basis for all communication in this poem, he establishes the lived body as key to connecting the hearing with the deaf. By fracturing poetic expectations in 'Arbor Vitae', Healy reconnects language deeply to the material and social world of contemporary Ireland, offering a path for conceptual poetry to be also a public and political poetry.

Kenneth Keating, Repetition and Alterity: Geoffrey Squires's 'texts for screen'

This essay examines a number of Geoffrey Squires's recent digital texts which were released in various forms online and later standardised and published together in the Kindle Book *Abstract Lyrics and other poems: 2006–2012*. It is contended that Squires embraces computer technology to compose texts which inhabit the screen, but which refuse to adhere to the recently established norms of any of the recognised forms of electronic literature while simultaneously representing something more than the digital conversion of a print text to an ebook. It is argued that these 'texts for screen' thus hold an uneasy position in relation to emerging electronic literature and the more conventional ebook, occupying a problematizing middle ground which at the same time promotes and undermines stability and the author's control over the text. Close readings of a number of these texts reveal that this challenging destabilisation is supported through Squires's utilisation of techniques of repetition which complicates the nature of reproduction and disrupts the critical location of singular meaning in favour of embracing the progressively troubling force of indeterminacy.

James Cummins, 'The history of Ireland he knew before he went to school': The Irish Tom Raworth

In an interview in 1971 Tom Raworth states 'I don't really see any reason for a term like "English poet"' and throughout his career Raworth has resisted such simple national classifications. His work is often discussed in relation to the strong relationship he fostered with American poets and poetics. Raworth, for many, exemplifies the transatlantic conversation that flourished during the 1960s onward. He was influenced by numerous schools of American poetry and would in turn act as an influence to many American writers. As Ted Berrigan states 'he's as good as we are, & rude a thing as it is to say, we don't expect that, from English poets today, (I wonder is he better?)'. However, considering Raworth's mother was Irish and that since 1990 Raworth himself has travelled under an Irish passport this simple duality of British / American does not go far enough in exploring Raworth's complex national poetic identity. Using a combination of contextual and biographical information alongside close readings of a number of collected and uncollected poems this essay explores the influence Ireland, its culture, religion and history, has had on Raworth's upbringing, his sense of national identity and his poetry.

Rachel Warriner, Image and Witness in Maggie O'Sullivan's *A Natural History in 3 Incomplete Parts* and *POINT.BLANK.RANGE*

This essay takes as its focus the visual elements in Maggie O'Sullivan's *A Natural History in 3 Incomplete Parts* (1985) and

POINT.BLANK.RANGE (1984). Considering the question of how these visual elements fit in with her wider practice, it explores the images used by O'Sullivan; looking at those included in *A Natural History* for their interaction with language and those included in the purely visual *POINT.BLANK.RANGE* for the way in which meaning is built through poetic technique. Arguing for the political potency of these works, this essay proposes that O'Sullivan acts as a kind of witness, filtering societal violence through her fractured imagery.

Notes on Contributors

DAVID LLOYD, Distinguished Professor of English at the University of California, Riverside, works primarily on Irish culture and on postcolonial and cultural theory. His most recent books are *Irish Times: Temporalities of Irish Modernity* (Dublin: Field Day, 2008) and *Irish Culture and Colonial Modernity: The Transformation of Oral Space* (Cambridge University Press, 2011). His study of Samuel Beckett's visual aesthetics, *Beckett's Thing: Painting and Theatre* is forthcoming from Edinburgh University Press, 2016. He is completing a collection of essays on aesthetics, representation, and race, forthcoming from Living Commons, 2016. His *Arc & Sill: Poems 1979–2009* was published by Shearsman Books in the UK and New Writers' Press, Dublin, 2012 and an online chapbook, *Kodalith*, can be found at Smithereens Press. He has co-published several other books, including *The Politics of Culture in the Shadow of Capital* (1997), with Lisa Lowe, and *The Black and Green Atlantic: Cross-Currents of the African and Irish Diasporas* (2008), edited with Peter D. O'Neill.

FRANCIS HUTTON-WILLIAMS is a postdoctoral research assistant at Oxford University. He completed his DPhil as an Amelia Jackson scholar at Exeter College, Oxford. A graduate also of Cambridge University and Trinity College Dublin, he has published and presented widely on literature and cultural politics in England and Ireland, and is currently preparing his first monograph on Irish literature for Oxford University Press. His teaching and research interests include English and Irish literature since the Act of Union (1801); naturalism, modernism, and postmodernism; practical criticism and reader-response theory.

GEOFFREY SQUIRES is originally from Co. Donegal. After living and working in a number of countries he is now retired and living in Yorkshire. His poetry is gathered into two collections, *Untitled and other poems* (2004) and *Abstract Lyrics and other poems* (2012) both published by Wild Honey Press. Three of his books have been translated into French and widely reviewed there. His translations of the ghazals of the Persian poet *Hafez* won a prize in

Irish University Review 46.1 (2016): xi–xiv
DOI: 10.3366/iur.2016.0194
© Edinburgh University Press
www.euppublishing.com/journal/iur

the United States in 2014 and Shearsman Books have recently published his translations of medieval Irish poetry, *My News for You* (2015).

J.C.C. MAYS retired from UCD in 2004. He assisted Maurice Harmon in the early years of *Irish University Review* and afterwards edited volumes of Coleridge, Yeats, and several other Irish authors. A little book, *N 11 A Musing* (reprinted by Coracle Press, Grange, Co. Tipperary, 2006), is relevant to the present contribution. His *Coleridge's "Ancient Mariner": A Refit* will appear in 2016.

ALEX DAVIS is Professor of English at University College Cork. He is the author of *A Broken Line: Denis Devlin and Irish Poetic Modernism* (2000), and many essays in anglophone poetry from decadence to the present day. He is co-editor, with Lee M. Jenkins, of *Locations of Literary Modernism: Region and Nation in British and American Modernist Poetry* (2000), *The Cambridge Companion to Modernist Poetry* (2007), and *A History of Modernist Poetry* (2015); and, with Patricia Coughlan, of *Modernism and Ireland: The Poetry of the 1930s* (1995). He is currently writing a book on the Edwardian Yeats.

CLAIRE BRACKEN is an Associate Professor in the English Department at Union College, New York, where she teaches courses on Irish literature and film. She has published articles on Irish women's writing, feminist criticism, and Irish cultural studies. She is co-editor of *Anne Enright* (Irish Academic Press, Spring 2011) and *Viewpoints: Theoretical Perspectives on Irish Visual Texts* (Cork University Press, 2013). Her book, *Irish Feminist Futures*, is in production with Routledge and will be published in January 2016.

KIT FRYATT is a lecturer in English at Mater Dei Institute of Education (Dublin City University) and with colleagues there co-ordinates the activities of the Irish Centre for Poetry Studies.

ROMANA HUK is co-editor of *Contemporary British Poetry: Essays in Theory and Criticism* (SUNY Press, 1996), editor of *Assembling Alternatives: Reading Postmodern Poetries Transnationally* (Wesleyan UP, 2003), and author of *Stevie Smith: Between the Lines* (Palgrave Macmillan, 2005). Her current book project, *"Rewriting the word 'God'": In the Arc of Postmodern Theory, Theology and Poetry*, involves reading radical departures in twentieth-century phenomenology, theology, and linguistics alongside developments in transnational avant-garde aesthetics and poetries.

NIAMH O'MAHONY is the editor of *Essays on the Poetry of Trevor Joyce* (Shearsman Press, 2015), and has also authored a special feature on the poet in *Jacket2* (3 February 2014). She completed a PhD at University College Cork on the topic of appropriation in the poetries of Joyce, Alan Halsey, and Susan Howe in 2015, and is the recipient of a Fulbright scholarship.

MARTHINE SATRIS is the associate editor of the humanities at Stanford University Press. She is also a contributing editor of *Golden Handcuffs Review*. She wrote her doctoral dissertation at UC Santa Barbara on contemporary Irish poetry. Her 2009 interviews with Maurice Scully and Trevor Joyce have been published in *Contemporary Literature* and the *Journal of British and Irish Innovative Poetry*, respectively. She regularly reviews contemporary fiction and poetry and recently contributed an essay to *Essays on the Poetry of Trevor Joyce*, edited by Niamh O'Mahony (Shearsman Books, 2015).

KENNETH KEATING is a postdoctoral researcher at University College Dublin contributing to the Digital Platform for Contemporary Irish Writing. He completed his doctoral research on Jacques Derrida and contemporary Irish poetry in 2014 and has published articles and reviews on a number of Irish poets. He is the editor of Smithereens Press.

JAMES CUMMINS is currently based in Cork having recently completed a PhD on the work of Tom Raworth at UCC. Previously he has written on British, Irish and American art and literature. Also a poet, his books include *speaking off centre*, *Warbler*, *Origins of Process* and *FLASH/BANG*. He co-organises the SoundEye Poetry Festival and occasional blogs at returntodefault.wordpress.

RACHEL WARRINER is a PhD candidate in History of Art, University College Cork, researching the work of Nancy Spero. She has published on Raymond Pettibon and Spero, is on the editorial board of the Irish Association of Art Historian's *Artefact* Journal, co-founded the Modernisms Research Centre, UCC and is co-curator with Pluck Projects. She is a key organiser in the SoundEye Poetry Festival and has published poetry including *Fine Lament* (Critical Documents, 2012) and *Eleven Days* (RunAmok Press, 2011).

In Memory of Michael Smith, 1942–2014

Photo © Niall Hartnett

Trevor Joyce

Michael Smith: A Brief Tribute

Mike was my oldest friend. He was my companion for so many years, in so many ways, that it's very hard to know what to say here. We founded New Writers Press together, wrote together, translated together, drank, walked, and argued together for going on fifty years. But as everyone who knew him was well aware, Mike always loved a yarn, so let me try to tell one that brings together some of these things.

I first met Mike in the spring of 1966. I'd met Irene where I worked in my first job, at Dominick A. Dolan and Son, wholesale chemists, in Bolton Street. From the beginning, Irene and myself argued like cat and dog, about religion, politics, art, poetry, you name it. Always, though, just when I thought I'd had the better of it, she'd say, 'Just you wait until my boyfriend gets back from England, and he'll sort you out.' The boyfriend, of course, was Mike, and he was working in England, raising enough money to keep himself going in college.

Well, he finally came back in March, I think it was, and then there were three of us to argue. It was great fun. Mike already had some poems published in journals, which impressed me greatly. I'd been trying to 'crack' poetry for a couple of years, but without thought of publication, but Mike tore my stuff apart, and sent me off to read the best poetry and criticism of the previous fifty years. It was like an ice-cold shower.

Soon, writing constantly, and critiquing one another's work, we each had enough to fill a small book, and in the summer of '67 we founded New Writers Press to publish them. We were both happy with the progress we'd made, but I don't think either of us was totally convinced that what we were writing was yet the genuine article.

Fast forward a year to late summer of '68. Mike and Irene had got married, and were living in Irene's family home in Warrenmount Place, in the Liberties, with her father. Mike was starting off as a secondary-school teacher, and I was in the Dublin Corporation Planning Department. We both had paid holidays, and a few quid in our pockets.

Irish University Review 46.1 (2016): 1–3
DOI: 10.3366/iur.2016.0195
© Edinburgh University Press
www.euppublishing.com/journal/iur

The three of us knew central Dublin pretty well, but each was most familiar with a particular area. Mike was from the flats in Sherriff Street, Irene from the Liberties, and I was from Mary Street. That summer we set off rambling around the city, sometimes the three of us, sometimes just Mike and myself, each showing off our favourite secret places. We wandered through derelict areas where abandoned cars lay rusting among piles of rotting brick, and we learned to identify the common city weeds: scarlet pimpernel, greater celandine, groundsel. Our world and our language grew together.

One day Mike and myself rambled to the Grand Canal Harbour, and found a break in the boundary fence through which we got in. Inside the decaying wooden sheds, we found old barges mouldering, and we climbed over them and into them, exploring and exclaiming, filling our souls with the tastes and smells and colours of the rotting timbers. We stayed there for many hours.

When we got back to Warrenmount Place, we told Irene what we'd been at, each of us adding detail on detail, until at last we looked at one another, realizing the day was for both of us something exceptional. We agreed both to try writing poetry out of it, there in Irene's kitchen, as she always insisted we call it, that night. We laboured and laboured, but nothing came. We were both mute. I went home disappointed, but still somehow exalted.

But when I saw Mike again, two days later, he had two new poems to show me, about ten lines each, in five short equal verses, and with a use of language that was new in his work. Over the next two weeks, he kept adding, until he had approaching a dozen, all written in the same bright rich idiom. It was the sequence he later published, with the addition of one other final poem, under the title *Dedications*.

As far as I'm concerned that was the moment, a slightly suspended and enlarged one, when Mike became a poet, and I believe I was similarly transformed, though I didn't produce any new work until several months later. I was changed by the experience of seeing Mike transmute the sights and sounds and all the other sense particulars of that withering city, and of his childhood memories, into something new and wonderful. From then on, I never needed to consult books or inquire of experts to know what poetry, the genuine article, was. I had experienced it in the making, and I knew it in my bones.

I'll read just two poems from that sequence of Mike's. The first one, and then a later one to which he afterwards gave the title, 'The Gift'.

Too soon put up for the wind that blew it down,
   Hope became despair,
And despair was the sea on which my ship had sailed.

The rain became the city, the city became the rain,
And the unnested fledgling that ancient playful dog.

Barbara, Barbara, my canal-bank pinkeen girl,
Your curls are in the water with the barge,
And I am sailing down a purple Nile
Across the mill's aluminium-silver dome

From where the knacker's leans against the sky
And a solitary lilac weeps in its concrete yard.

The Gift

Through no imperial portals, but rusty bars on broken hinges,
To this kingdom of black earth like dampened dust

Where my green knight evades the black-shawled witch's eye,
The dragon's teeth and the sly pervasive worm.

Bells beyond the kingdom toll the significant hour
And the streets are silent, the squares empty.

In his gaslit room of the golden birds
Roosting quiet as the small rain of summer,

The old man receives the boy's green gift,
And the green knight hears his golden song in wonder.

About this last poem, Mike once wrote to me: 'This is my English grandfather again. A chore he often gave me to do was to collect chickweed for his songbirds. In college I had read *Sir Gawain and The Green Knight*, though how that relates to this poem I am not sure. I had to gather the chickweed from the little gardens of nearby cottages. In retrospect, an innocent enough chore but, for the child, one fraught with the danger of trespass, dogs and theft. There is a price to be paid for the writing of poetry and there is also a reward.'

Michael Smith

Translation & Reality: A Letter to the Poet Trevor Joyce

Let me say at the outset, what I think you already know, that I am not terribly knowledgeable about the modern linguistics that have undermined confidence in the use of language. Nevertheless, my doubtless simplistic understanding is that language must now be seen as a human creation with a most uncertain relationship with a postulated 'reality'. This is the 'disjuncture' to which Beckett refers and on which you yourself, quite rightly, place so much importance. Even the most precisely 'descriptive' writing – as, for example, in science – is not a 'window' through which we perceive 'reality' and to which it purports to refer. For years now I have understood this dilemma in terms of the solipsistic position. And I still do now, if only tentatively. How tentatively can clearly be seen in my latest collection of poems (*Prayers for the Dead & Other Poems*, Shearsman Books, 2014).

Substituting 'consciousness' for 'language', one may ask the question, 'How can one know what exists beyond language?' And yet all languages postulate a 'reality', although the nature of that reality will differ from language to language. There is the 'reality' of ancient Greek and of Homer, and there is the 'reality' of 19th-century Russian as we experience it in the novelists of the period. And so it would go on. For instance, the 'reality' of English of the 18th century with all its 'definiteness' and 'precision' as in Pope or Addison. As we engage with these languages and literatures we are conscious of their subjectivity, their historicity. We recognise that their 'realities' or 'worlds' are different from ours and we interpret them into the language of our own postulated 'reality'. This is what Borges means in saying that we can never read the texts of the past as these were understood by their authors and their contemporaries. It is the main point he makes in his famous story 'Pierre Menard, Author of the Quijote'. Pierre Menard's 'translation' of Cervantes text exists only in his own reading of the text, not in any inter-lingual exercise. Borges's *restoration* of many English authors such as Robert Louis Stevenson and Kipling, long considered by English critics as 'dated', derives from

Irish University Review 46.1 (2016): 4–9
DOI: 10.3366/iur.2016.0196
© Edinburgh University Press
www.euppublishing.com/journal/iur

his own special reading of these authors. Despite that, Borges himself has translated many authors in the usual manner.

When we say that language mediates, do we mean that 'reality' is mediated by language? How different is this from saying that 'reality' is mediated by consciousness? How closer are we to knowing 'the facts' by postulating rather than asserting the existence of 'reality'? Do you remember the following from Russell's *The Problems of Philosophy* (Chapter II, on 'The Existence of Matter')?:

> ... it is not by argument that we originally come by our belief in an independent external world. We find this belief ready in ourselves as soon as we begin to reflect: it is what may be called an *instinctive* belief. We should never have been led to question this belief but for the fact that, at any rate in the case of sight, it seems as if the sense-datum were instinctively believed to be the independent object, whereas argument shows that the object cannot be identical with the sense-datum. This discovery, however – which is not at all paradoxical in the case of taste and smell and sound, and only slightly so in the case of touch – leaves undiminished our instinctive belief that there *are* objects *corresponding* to our sense-data. Since this belief does not lead to any difficulties, but on the contrary tends to simplify and systematise our account of our experiences, there seems no good reason for rejecting it. We may therefore admit – though with a slight doubt derived from dreams – that the external world does really exist, and is not wholly dependent for its existence upon our continuing to perceive it.

In the second chapter of his little book, Russell takes things a little further, summing up as follows:

> We may therefore sum up as follows what has been said concerning acquaintance with things that exist. We have acquaintance in sensation with the data of the outer senses, and in introspection with the data of what may be called the inner sense – thoughts, feelings, desires, etc.; we have acquaintance in memory with things which have been data either of the outer senses or of the inner sense. Further, it is probable, though not certain, that we have acquaintance with Self, as that which is aware of things or has desires towards things.

Now this is all very basic stuff and yet it seems to me still to make a great deal of sense and to have important relevance to the question of the nature of the relationship between language and 'reality' (or, as Russell calls it, 'the external world'). If we examine Russell's language closely, we can see that for all Russell's empiricism he is prepared to accept the dubiety of a free-standing reality. What it all comes down to for Russell is that the 'reality' postulated by empirical science seems to 'work' and that there is little profit in denying its existence.

What has all this to do with experimentalism in the use of language in poetic discourse? Well, it seems to me that some 'experimentalists', and not just those of recent times, but also the early Surrealists and Dadaists, reject 'external reality' as postulated in their time, and the language 'corresponding' to that reality, and they opt instead for a private solipsistic world and a language descriptive or expressive of that world. It is as if they invent games that make no sense to anyone else, since no one knows the 'rules' of the game. But there is another kind of experimentalism, such as that of Beckett, for example, or your own for that matter, which is concerned with tackling a perceived discrepancy between language usage and the reality to which it purports to refer. This sort of experimentation is worthwhile in so far as it attempts to liberate consciousness from the straitjacket of the paradigmatic thinking (rationality) and feeling which others have come to accept as the only kind of thinking and feeling that has any validity. This kind of experimentation is genuinely exploratory and positive in its drive. It pushes towards an enhancement of consciousness and a profounder and 'truer' understanding of the 'world', and is a corrective to the limiting world of, say, logical positivism.

Is this making any sense?

How should we 'decode' the 'ravings' of a lunatic? Various psychologies offer their own 'decoders'. There is even the 'decoder' of bio-chemical medicine: the ingestion of lithium as a means of escape from the prison of schizophrenia. How do we define lunacy? A definition such as 'sickness of mind' gets us nowhere since we are left with the problem of defining 'sickness'. An anti-Nazi could have been considered lunatic in Hitler's Germany, or an anti-Stalinist in Stalin's Russia: hence the concentration camp and the gulag. Even Freud has difficulty with this. If one defines a neurotic as mentally sick, in Freudian terms what one means is that he or she is maladjusted to 'reality' as postulated by Freud. But Freud has difficulty dealing with what we should understand by 'reality'. Would he, for instance, describe as neurotic an efficiently functioning guard in the hellish world of a concentration camp? That guard may be well adjusted to the world in which he finds himself. We are really back to the question of who is sane, the patients of the mental asylum or their visitors from outside or their guardians? To talk about infantilism doesn't solve this problem, either, since societies which we would describe as infantile have survived quite well for centuries, and perhaps just as contentedly as many societies we would describe as 'mature' or 'highly civilised'.

Back now to something more relevant ... How does one go about explaining the difficulty or obscurity or inaccessibility of, say, Mallarmé's poetry, or that of Brian Coffey? Isn't it the case that they use language in a way to which we are unaccustomed? But in what way? Surely it is not a simple matter of mere allusions? If that were so, the problem would have been resolved long ago. The Chilean poet, Vicente Huidobro, clearly spelled out his own position: language is not merely referential but also creative; language can create 'entities' – we would probably describe them as aesthetic – which have an existence independent of the external world, and which are nonetheless real on that account. The 'reality status' of such entities, of course, is a matter of dispute. Figments of the imagination? Illusions? Fancies? The 'realism' of the Medieval Scholastics. And how is one supposed to make sense of such entities?

Let me take a poem by Mallarmé to focus the problem. I have chosen it because it has been translated by Brian Coffey and we can look at that translation to see what Brian made of it.

Here's the literal (from the *Penguin* selection of Anthony Hartley):

> Some solitude or other without swan or bank mirrors its disuse in the glance I renounced here of the vainglory, so high as not to be touched, with which man a sky bedecks itself in sunset's gold, but some fleeting bird coasts languorously like white linen taken off if there plunge exultantly beside it in the wave yourself become your naked rejoicing.

Now here's Brian's version:

SLIGHT SONG

What you will a wild
without swan and nor quay
trains its disuse
at gazing I foreswore

Here from the vaingold
high beyond touching
in which man a sky dolls up
with sun-down golds

> but languorously coasts
> like white linen cast off
> some fleeting bird if dives
> exultant sideling
>
> into water you become
> your jubilance nude

Now here's a combination of both which I made to see if I could find out what Brian was doing:

> Whatever you may wish to call it, for example, a wild (or wilderness) without a swan, or a bank (quay), it mirrors (trains) its disuse in the gazing which I foreswore (renounced) from the vaingold (vainglory) that is high beyond touching, in which many a sky dolls itself up (bedecks itself) with sundown golds, but languorously there coasts, like white linen cast off, some fleeting bird if you, become your nude jubilance (your naked rejoicing), dive exultantly beside it (sideling) into water (in the wave).

What are we to 'make' of this? A colourful sky reflected on the surface of a stretch of still water which is without the romantic presence of the swan until the naked person to whom the poem refers dives into the water. A poem in praise of human beauty, the human nude replacing the conventional swan? If not this, then what? If we say that the text exists as a thing in its own right, that is to say without referential meaning, what kind of thing is it? What 'sense' are we to make of it, albeit in the way we might make sense of an abstract painting? Can a text induce a response that stays exclusively within language? Imagine whiteness without imagining anything white.

Does that make sense?

Now back to the question of a readership or an audience. Speaking for myself, I wrote (note the past tense) for literate readers with some knowledge and a love of poetry written in the past at different times and in different cultures. My ambition, if that's not too grand a word, was to record my explorations of my own life, my efforts to make 'sense' of being in the world, through the medium of poetry, that is to say through the resources of language as discovered and exploited by poetry of the past, and, of course, with a preparedness to go beyond these if necessary. It would have been my hope that others would find these explorations meaningful in terms of their own lives. I never thought of poetry as a 'game' in the sense of amusement or entertainment, though I was prepared to see it as a 'game' in the sense of accidentality, unaccountability (Would I be right in thinking that this is how you primarily see poetry?). Remember Brian Coffey's often repeated rejection of the notion of foreknowledge in writing poems. This was not Romanticism (poetry as inspiration) but his core idea that poetry was concerned with discovery, and discovery implies the unknown. For Brian, his latest poem could very well have been his last. Hence, too, Brian's refusal to be called a poet, meaning a special kind of human being, either as the Audenesque 'antenna of the race' or the Shelleyan 'legislator of the world'. For Brian, a poet was only a poet in the act of writing a poem, unlike a carpenter who can count on bring able to produce more works of carpentry, granted the continuance of his acquired skills.

David Lloyd

Introduction: On Irish Experimental Poetry

This issue of the *Irish University Review*, 'Irish Experimental Poetry', is dedicated to Irish poet Michael Smith, who passed away even in the course of its preparation. Probably no one in Ireland did more, in a lifetime devoted to poetry, poetic translation, and publishing, to maintain the connection between contemporary Irish poets and the modernist generation of the 1930s that Alex Davis so aptly dubbed 'a broken line'.[1] This was not only a matter of the editing and reprinting of (then) largely forgotten and unavailable poets like Brian Coffey and Thomas MacGreevy in those volumes that introduced so many of us to possibilities that had seemed occluded in what passed for Irish poetry at the time. From the foundation of the New Writers Press in 1967 and the journal *The Lace Curtain* in 1969 to the monumental translations of the Peruvian modernist César Vallejo and his own late volume *Prayers for the Dead* (2014), Mike never wavered in his commitment to continuing that modernist and innovative dimension of Irish writing which drew its resources from a wide-ranging and inquisitive engagement with international currents that have always, if not always prominently, coursed through Irish writing. As Trevor Joyce testifies in his tribute, Mike introduced many of us to poets who might never otherwise have appeared on our horizons, whether Irish or, as it generally was, Spanish and Latin American. In my own case, it was by Mike that I was stimulated to discover – almost simultaneously – James Clarence Mangan, Charles Donnelly, and the Spanish Civil War poet, Miguel Hernandez.

Such a passionate catholicity of taste kept alive a sense also of alternative modernities, those not forged in the metropolitan centres, but in what Vallejo termed the 'semicolonial', in peripheries that could be those of Latin America or Spain or Greece as they could be of the Liberties of Dublin that Mike so loved. That some notion of rural Ireland – or of a 'backward' Spain or Peru – could monopolize the matter of poetry and confine it to certain conventional forms or

Irish University Review 46.1 (2016): 10–19
DOI: 10.3366/iur.2016.0197
© Edinburgh University Press
www.euppublishing.com/journal/iur

predictable anecdotal fodder always irked him. Translation, and its prompting of other possibilities than those already known and tested, was always for Mike an opening into the unfamiliar, into unanticipated ways of using language or figure, of apprehending a world. It could not be, therefore, a means to forging a substitute set of conventions and Mike's engagement with modernism was always sceptical, testing, and even suspicious, as the brief 'Translation & Reality' (published for the first time in this issue) indicates.

This issue commemorates Mike's life and work most appropriately in carrying forward that spirit of openness and testing. To categorize the poetries that emanate from such a spirit has not proven easy: the current volume might have been titled 'Irish Innovative Poetry', to emphasize the aspect of formal invention that is a shared characteristic of the work discussed here; it might have been called 'The Irish Modernist Tradition', to stress the interrupted lines that connect contemporary writers fitfully to the generation of the 1930s; or drawn on the notion of the avant-garde, a notion that Frank Hutton-Williams here persuasively argues should be used for the group of Irish writers that briefly associated with Samuel Beckett. As opposed to modernism, too often seen as a movement in the arts that sought to find the forms in which the chaos and entropy of modernity could be contained, the avant-garde suggests rather – in words Hutton-Williams cites from Beckett – an art of 'pure interrogation, rhetorical question less the rhetoric'. Apt as that may have been for Beckett and his peers, it is perhaps all the more so for the contemporary poets considered in this issue. The conception of the 'experimental' that informs the essays gathered here refers at once to the formal aspects of the poems discussed and to the relation to language and to the phenomenal world of perception or sensation that they manifest. That distinction, useful in some regards, remains suspect: the experimental in poetry is defined by the condition that the form does not precede the material, but is determined and continually transformed by the very process of the poem's engagement with the things of its world.

Beckett, in his early book review 'Recent Irish Poetry', distinguished between a poetry of convention and a poetry of the actual, the latter having apprehended 'the new thing that has happened', that is, 'the breakdown of the object' or 'breakdown of the subject' and the 'rupture of the lines of communication'.[2] His remarks suggest at least one line of continuity between his modernist moment and our present. 'Conventional' poetry gives the impression that its materials have been processed to furnish a convenient metaphorical or anecdotal vehicle – a 'theme' – for the expression of a subject secure in its self-possession: one is all too familiar with the happy procedure of the poem that commences with a 'vividly realized' experience, draws from it some metaphoric thread, and winds up with a moral payload, validated by a nice turn of phrase, that brings metaphor and experience into graceful concord again. The procedure of the 'well-made poem' is handily available for recycling and the world yields ample material for exploitation in this mode. The experimental, on the other hand, is paradoxically quite the opposite of what a scientific analogy might imply: where the scientific experiment must be repeatable in order to be tested, the poetic experiment cannot in principle be repeated nor can its forms be adopted as conventions for future writing. As Jim Mays suggests in his essay here, it may be this constitutive unavailability to easy and practiced consumption – and not only the material unavailablity of small press volumes – that accounts for the limited circulation to date of Irish experimental poetry. Its open and – in Roland Barthes' terms – 'writable' (*scriptible*) forms place demands on readerly engagement and active alertness that do not make such work apt for classroom teaching or casual acquaintance.

These very general characteristics of experimental poetry set it at odds with conventional critical assumptions, with what we might call the 'common sense' that governs and hinders its reception. As Marthine Satris notes in her essay on Randolph Healy, 'those skeptical of this branch of the poetry tree have argued that the innovative turn in poetry is solipsistic, in that it separates writing from the material, lived world and from readers'. She goes on to show that this is far from the case, and that a poet like Healy multiplies the frames for apprehending the world rather than closing them off. Multiplicity of perceptual and signifying systems drives the paratactic forms through which his work is assembled. The common sense undergirding the scepticism that she notes is, as Antonio Gramsci observed, the uninterrogated ossification of fragments and traces of past critical systems and philosophies.[3] It can envisage a world rendered only within a certain canon of representation that has become second nature to it. Geoffrey Squires argues here that what we continue to call 'modernism' should be defined less in terms of an epoch or literary period (which raises the issue as to when modernism properly ends) than through a more philosophical distinction between empiricism and rationalism. If empiricism believes in the experiential grounding of our perception, rationalism questions the conventionality of the frames. In poetic terms, a modernist poetic inclines towards that rationalist tendency, in that it is concerned 'with what we bring to our encounter with the world, indeed how that world is constituted or constructed, as against simply perceived or experienced'.

Far from implying a 'solipsistic' closing off from the world of experience, history, and alterity, the experimental character of the poetry addressed in these essays may best be defined by the correlation in them of formal inventiveness and phenomenological attention. Perhaps the most formally inventive of contemporary Irish poets is Trevor Joyce, whose books since the mid-1990s have abandoned what he came, after long silence, to consider the dead end of 'lyrics of description and expression dressed in the most transparent of formal attire; the emphasis being almost entirely on the language as carrier of information, with little heed to other possibilities'.[4] Those 'other possibilities' he discovered through procedures that emphasize construction and assemblage. Writing of Joyce's 'appropriative' poetry, poems that are assembled out of reworked borrowings from a wide variety of source texts, Niamh O'Mahony concludes that 'the appropriation of text is not opposed to expression or meaning but actually enables a more explicit account of both the poet's and the reader's experience of the world'. The resonances and tensions that the disjunctive constellations of texts in a poem like Joyce's 'De Iron Trote' set in play 'provoke language to unfamiliar and even unintentional patterns of association' that productively unleash both the violence and the potentialities embedded in a language that is always saturated with the traces of its past usage. In very different ways, as Romana Huk and Kit Fryatt show in essays that both seem to enact and track the very process of reading his work, Maurice Scully constructs books rather than discrete poems, working with webs or lattices of repeated motifs, perceptual investigations, overheard or cited text, and rhythmic variations. Scully's work constantly explores the constitutive tension between his acute sense of poetic composition, sustained lightly but consistently across book-length constructs, and his perceptual attentiveness to 'things as they happen', to invoke the overall title of the eight-book work he composed between 1987 and 2006. As Fryatt nicely puts it, that long work, *Things That Happen*, 'might be understood as a prolonged wrangle with the idea of and necessity for order in art, with poetic *number* seen as at once "something primal. ... Symmetry" and as an aspect of authoritarian power'. Her essay on Scully's first book since *Things That Happen* was completed, *Humming*, compellingly demonstrates that work's engagement with the elegiac tradition and the perhaps unexpected consequence, that 'the manner is modernist, parodic, and fragmented, but the matter is profoundly traditional'. Fragmentation of quite consciously invoked elegiac motifs subsists with Scully's characteristically self-reflexive writing on the leading edge, so to speak, of compositional process, giving rise to what Fryatt terms *Humming*'s 'simultaneous feeling of containment and dissemination'.

If *Humming* draws on the elegiac tradition, the most recent of his books, *Several Dances*, invokes rather the American Objectivists, in particular William Carlos Williams and George Oppen. Noting Scully's implicit qualification of the 'infamous Objectivist credo "No ideas but in things"', Huk proceeds to explore his no less pervasive, if still implicit, revision of Heideggerian phenomenology in *Several Dances*: 'Scully's is, it seems, an improbably "both/and", *inclusive* phenomenology, one that unfolds in step with the immediately perceived even as it remains attentive to its own artful motions redanced in the light of previous possibilities and offered up as "additions to the world / not representations of it"'. Despite 'the volume's extraordinary lightness of touch', it displays, Huk shows, a remarkable capaciousness of reference and allusion, such that through the weave of its metaphorical and structuring webs 'human limitation itself emerges paradoxically as opening, chance, plumb-line, and intimation of immortality'.

Huk's emphasis on the phenomenological alertness of Scully's poetry is echoed in both Jim Mays's and Alex Davis's responses to Billy Mills's work. Mills's is, nonetheless, poetry of an entirely different kind, even if it has learnt in its own way both from objectivism and from the example of Brian Coffey in particular. Noting how the poems in Mills's recent *Imaginary Gardens* slowly build through 'patient attention to what meets our eyes', Mays's no less patient and attentive readings furnish a model for the kind of reading that such a poetry exacts – and of the pleasures that it offers to the attentive reader. It is a poetry that at once refuses closure and demands a reading willing to return, to reread, to remain suspended before an ambiguity and uncertainty that is also the ground of possibility: 'No page of text in this book will be entirely complete and the hundred pages overall enact a process like a film slowed down to its separate frames: even as they connect while they advance, each one retains a sense of separate omnidirectional possibilities at the time it is encountered.' Mays's metaphor here aptly anticipates Geoffrey Squires recent experiments with 'texts for screen', whose minimalist insistence on repetition and revision, Kenneth Keating argues, 'simultaneously suggests singularity and multiplicity through making moves in and out of certainty and uncertainty in turn to finally leave an openness which welcomes alternative understandings'. More abstract than Mills's work, in their bracketing of objects in favour of an exploration primarily of the modalities of deictics and interrogatives, Squires's texts present 'acts of communication as composed of something other than a reductive meaning, containing an unknowable and irreducible element which inherently complicates any supposed singularity'. The attention of the reader is summoned by both the control of the pace of the appearance of the word on the screen and by the structures of repetition with modification that Squires focuses through his radically reduced language.

The attentiveness experimental poetry demands of the reader is no more, as Davis suggests, than that which the poet exhibits in relation to the phenomenal world: as he puts it of Mills, '[his] poems are *periploi*, approximate "chartings" by a consciousness that is always situated, never omniscient to the "weave of things" in which it is braided'. The ethical and, indeed, ecological reserve of the poet is in part humility, akin to that which Huk describes in Scully, acknowledging the partiality of perception and declining what Beckett once named the 'possessiveness' – one might say imperiousness – of Western art and of its all too sovereign subjects.[5] Davis quotes Mills's remark 'that many things are that have never been perceived, and that for most things that are perceived, the perception is imperfect'. That scrupulous relation to the world and scepticism with regard to the limits of representation are bound up no less with the continuous questioning of the relation of the poetic to the given that gives rise to the constantly shifting sense of the poem that Mays unfolds. Davis remarks on 'the seeming disjunction of "paper" and "place", the incompatibility of poem (or language in general) and the extra-linguistic reality of rooms, rivers, and rocks' that recurs in Mills's work, transforming the poem into a continuing *process* rather than a product.

The modernist legacies that remain legible in Irish experimental poetry are paradoxically coupled with an ethic of writing that we might describe as 'counter-modern': one that in its very modernity abjures the possessive relation to the world that culminates in its all-pervasive commodification, a process in which Ireland's own project of modernization since the 1960s has obediently participated. That moment in post-independence Ireland defines the period in which Irish experimental poetry emerged as surely as the Troubles defined the moment of what is now called 'Northern Irish Poetry'. Mays furnishes that context at some length here, and it is clear that the poets with whom he opens – Catherine Walsh as well as Billy Mills – represent an alternative to a process whose impact on the language that has forged its alibis ('derivatives', 'leverage', 'liquidity') is hardly less deleterious than its aggressive appropriation of the earth. Joyce, indeed, has explicitly related his own procedural experiments with that sense of the heteronomy of language, 'the intent being to simulate in various ways the common experience of seeming to act freely and spontaneously, while even a minimal self-awareness reveals that this freedom is to a great extent generated and governed by forces and concerns in which one has had no hand, act, or part. Without some reframing of this sort, I fear that the language of description, expression, aspiration, is constantly being sucked down the sink of calculated, monetized use. Moreover even our means to refresh it have been appropriated.'[6] Poetic constraint becomes the means to manoeuvre through the social constraints it simulates.

Of the poets discussed in this issue, Catherine Walsh is perhaps the most explicit in her engagement with the social world produced by the modernization process that culminated in the late 'Celtic Tiger'. Mays comments on the anger that Walsh – 'alienated by the exploitation of what should preserve and enhance life's opportunities' – exhibits in *Astonished Birds*, which he describes as a satire facing down 'money, power, and manipulation on equal terms'. The comedy of the diptych *Astonished Birds/Cara, Jane, Bob and James* is not foreign to a tradition in Irish poetry that 'has always hidden its sharpest criticism under the mask of comedy', but it presents its own difficulties: 'It is difficult because it is so exactly poised that we don't know, because the author seems not to know, the answer to the questions she poses: she can only show us how things might balance out in a poem.' This capacity to hold in balance deeply contradictory relations to the world, to negotiate the predicament that 'Wrong life cannot be lived rightly', Walsh exhibits in a different mode in her earlier volume, *City West*.[7] As Claire Bracken describes it, *City West* 'traces an immediacy of living in Tiger postmodernity, harnessing a nomadic paradigm as an ethical navigational model through the environs of late capitalism'. According to Bracken, it does so precisely by counterpointing the high mobility both of late capitalism's processes and of the subjects it displaces with the immobility that afflicts the latter – working-class women in particular – 'as intensely managed and contained sites'. *City West* thus establishes 'the potentialities of swift and creative movements that are co-joined with forms of stasis' in a work that articulates feminist critique with reflection on the devastating impact of capitalist development.

More than any other essay in this issue, Bracken's indicates the extent to which Irish experimental poetry has shown itself capable of inventing forms and languages adequate to Irish conditions a century after the nation's partial decolonization. The plural is critical: the poets considered here do not form a movement any more than they have forged anything like a common voice or set of formal procedures. Although, as Mays briefly relates, certain unofficial institutions, like the annual Sound Eye poetry festival, have eventually followed in the wake of the founding of the New Writers Press, journals like Scully's *The Beau* and *The Lace Curtain*, or other small presses like Healy's Wild Honey or Mills and Walsh's hardPressed poetry, the inter-relations remain for the most part occasional if invaluable. But collectively these poets, for too long at the margins of Irish culture, have succeeded in finding ways to address the predicament of a society whose apparent freedom is, as Joyce suggests, 'to a great extent generated and governed by forces and concerns in which one has had no hand, act, or part'. They do so without purveying nostalgic lyric compensation or affecting the naturalistic 'common language' or common sense that have become the hallmarks of contemporary poetic convention, though for the most part the work is full of colloquialism, overheard speech, the self-assured clichés that pass for collective wisdom, but always suspended in a configuration with multiple other modes of language use or discourse. It bears remarking, indeed, that every one of the poets written about in these essays shows their ease with the Irish language, traditionally the mark of an identitarian nationalism: Scully, for example, was schooled in the Gaeltacht, Joyce is a constant translator from Irish among other languages. It is safe to say that no other Irish poets have so successfully integrated the language into the framework of an innovative poetry and done so with neither condescension nor fetishism. The language stands not as a mark of identity in itself, but as one among the multiple vectors that determine the distinctive if generally unmarked Irishness of the work.

To invoke 'Irishness' is or should be to recall that it is a category that has always been defined by mobility, migration, disjunction, and displacement, even if – in Bracken's terms – it has been from time to time 'co-joined with forms of stasis'. It is fitting, then, that the essays culminate in two that address second-generation Irish poets whose work has largely circulated outside Ireland, yet remains marked at some level by that displacement. Tom Raworth is mostly known as a poet of the British avant-garde that emerged in the mid-sixties and as a poet who is virtually an honorary American, his life and his associations having constantly maintained a transatlantic dimension. As James Cummins shows, however, his work – and in particular the experimental prose memoirs – is quite explicitly marked by his mother's background as an Irish republican who emigrated after the foundation of the Free State. The essay not only provides an unexpected lineage for Raworth's own poetry, but also opens a question that has to date only been fitfully treated in Irish cultural histories and on which Hutton-Williams also touches, which is that of the hidden relations between a dissident Irish republicanism and the communities of aesthetically non-conformist, modernist, or avant-garde writers and artists of the post-independence period. Cummins's essay also provokes reflection on the powerful role that migrations of various kinds play on the formation of Irish experimental poetry, whether in a text like Joyce's 'Trem Neul' or in the echoes of Mills's and Walsh's sojourns in Spain and England: are these the experiential correlatives of the mobile and open fields that their writing sets in play? Rachel Warriner concludes the essays with an examination of the visual aspects of the poetry books of Maggie O'Sullivan, another experimental poet of Irish background whose intense exploratory work with sound has occasionally been connected with her father's *sean nós* singing. Warriner focuses rather on O'Sullivan's work with collaged images that counterpoint the fragmented and disassembled texts of the mid-1980s. These books conjoin and at times partially erase their texts with found images of various kinds that juxtapose, for example, images of the women's anti-militarist protest camp at Greenham Common with images of police violence in Northern Ireland or of the H-block hunger strikes, thus suggesting 'both a subject existing between the personal and the public and the relationship between systems such as the media, the state and militarism'. Their effect is a mode of witnessing, 'a political work that foregrounds the subjective experience of the writer not as a means to examine the individualised subject, but instead in order to interpret broader political and cultural concerns'.

It is perhaps fitting that the essays in this issue should conclude with Warriner's characterization of O'Sullivan's books as 'a work of ever shifting, ever radical poetics'. The comment could serve as a description of the work of virtually any of the poets the essays discuss and could find echoes in any one of the other critics. Taken together, these essays are also the most fitting introduction to the selection of new work that follows them, a selection that includes Maurice Scully, Trevor Joyce, Catherine Walsh, and Billy Mills, as well as work by two poets whose work is gradually emerging into greater recognition, Fergal Gaynor and Sarah Hayden. It is not enough to say that this work stands for itself. It does. But it also calls to be read. As many of the essays collected here suggest, experimental poetry above all provokes reading, it solicits and holds and requires attention. Discussing the various possible categories under which the work of all these poets might be gathered, Fergal Gaynor proposed what is perhaps the most effective and straightforward characterization of all. I leave the reader with its resonances and with its implicit challenge: 'This is poetry from people who read, and who have learned something from the reading (i.e. have gone beyond simply extracting models for imitation, or processing texts for education as industry).'

Reader, read on.

NOTES
1. Alex Davis, *A Broken Line: Denis Devlin and Irish Poetic Modernism* (Dublin: University College Dublin Press, 2000).

2. Samuel Beckett, 'Recent Irish Poetry', in *Disjecta: Miscellaneous Writings and a Dramatic Fragment*, ed. Ruby Cohn (New York: Grove Press, 1984), pp.70–71.
3. Antonio Gramsci, *Selections from the Prison Notebooks*, ed. by Quintin Hoare and Geoffrey Nowell Smith (New York: International Publishers, 1971), pp.323–34.
4. Trevor Joyce, 'The Phantom Quarry: Translating a Renaissance Painting Into Modern Poetry', *Enclave Review* 8 (Summer 2013), p.6.
5. Beckett, 'Three Dialogues with Georges Duthuit', *Disjecta*, pp.141, 144.
6. Joyce, 'Phantom Quarry', p.6.
7. Theodor W. Adorno, *Minima Moralia: Reflections from Damaged Life*, trans. E.F.N. Jephcott (London: Verso, 1978), p.39.

Francis Hutton-Williams

Against Irish Modernism: Towards an Analysis of Experimental Irish Poetry

This essay rewrites the history of Irish poetic experiment away from modernism, or at least from contemporary industry-driven senses of the term which have multiplied to the point of its overuse as a catch-all category.[1] It is divided into two parts. The first part of the essay focuses on questions of literary history, defining some of the key trends of literary production and reception in Ireland during the 1920s and 30s. By surveying the negative impact of religion and censorship on literary development within the Irish Free State (1922–1937), the essay challenges the concept of Ireland as a place of widespread modernist assertion. The second part of the essay steers the discussion towards an 'avant-garde' trio of Irish writers, offering an extended and detailed characterisation of their poetry. It traces the emergence of an experimental Irish poetry with a selection of examples taken from Denis Devlin's *Intercessions* (1937), Thomas McGreevy's *Poems* (1934) and Samuel Beckett's *Echo's Bones and Other Precipitates* (1935), showing how poetic experiments of the 1930s challenge the lyric as a verse form after Irish independence.[2]

Inspecting the term 'Irish modernism', which has been increasingly deployed by literature departments and academies as part of the wider phenomenon of international modernism and postmodernity over the past two decades, raises a number of problems. The first of these arises from the number of Irish writers who decided not to engage fully with modernist experiments in literature; the second from the reception of international modernism by native, continental, and Anglo-American critics who have noted a general apathy in Ireland to the energies of modernist texts. The city of Dublin is rarely mentioned in James MacFarlane and Malcolm Bradbury's classic 1978 study *Modernism: A Guide to European Literature, 1890–1930*, and attracts little coverage in Michael Levenson's *The Cambridge Companion to Modernism* which, revised in 2011, is a standard introduction to the field.[3] Nor is it

Irish University Review 46.1 (2016): 20–37
DOI: 10.3366/iur.2016.0198
© Edinburgh University Press
www.euppublishing.com/journal/iur

discussed as part of the various aesthetic and cultural fields that Christopher Butler explores in *Modernism: A Very Short Introduction*.[4] Terence Brown, a critic with whom I engage frequently here, has been especially critical of the subject in a 1995 essay entitled 'Ireland, Modernism and the 1930s', which features as one of a number of essays compiled in *The Literature of Ireland: Culture and Criticism*.[5]

In that essay, Brown cites Thomas McGreevy's 1931 monograph on T.S. Eliot (the first to be published on the American poet) as 'the most persuasive evidence that Ireland and modernism, were, at this time, antithetical congeries of feeling'.[6] Engaging with what he sees as a protective stance taken up by the Irish poet, Brown finds in McGreevy's study an example of 'that endemic Dublin state of feeling [in which] the dangerous implications for the Christian world-view of the major modernist texts can be rendered anodyne in an oddly Olympian conception of tradition which may be the symptom of a certain self-protective provincialism of mind before the arresting challenge of true and threatening originality'.[7] For Brown, McGreevy's Catholic reading of Eliot rests upon an unalterable structure of canonical approval 'in which the devout reader may find nothing is at variance with the "strictest Christianity"', so that such disruptions as may be registered by modernist experiment can be swiftly absorbed and co-opted.[8] Brown attributes this religious anxiety, or *'nostalgie du divin'*, to the dilution of modernist energies and to the failure of Irish writers at the time to apprehend any really disturbing originality of form.

The emphasis that Brown places on Christianity as part of Ireland's cultural inheritance advances the view that dissent from religious institutions, creeds, and rituals was necessary to modernism. Seamus Deane has developed this view in a series of four lectures entitled 'Religion, Liberalism and Modernism in Europe and Ireland, 1830–1970' in which he advocates that 'Modernism's ruptures with tradition were predominantly ruptures with religious beliefs, claims, and practices'.[9] 'It is largely ignored', Deane argues, 'how important religious issues and confrontation between church and state were in the development of liberalism and in the new idolatries of the state which mark the first appearance of modernism as an ideology'.[10] Widening the field of reference from Dublin to mainland Europe, Deane proposes that the history of the Vatican, the Syllabus of Errors (1864), the Declaration of Infallibility (1870), and the reactions against these ecclesiastical forces are critical moments in the first phases of modernist assertion. For both of these literary critics – Brown and Deane – the strengthening of Ireland's religious authority after independence explains the general reluctance of Irish writers to engage with modernist ideas.

During the 1930s, the power of the Catholic Church became increasingly visible within Ireland's government policy. The Thirty-First International Eucharistic Congress, which was held in Dublin in June 1932, resulted in an unprecedented display of partnership between Rome and the new nation, marking fifteen-hundred years of Christianity on the island. Three years before the Eucharistic Congress, the Irish Free State had set up an Academy of Christian Art, which was spearheaded by Count Plunkett, a former director of the National Museum and an ex-Minister for the Fine Arts.[11] Though the collusion of ecclesiastical and temporal authorities was often challenged by Irish writers (and, in some cases, used enterprisingly to their advantage), it appears to have been largely uninhibited by the kind of critical reflection that was necessary for modernism to be more seriously pursued and developed. 'Irish artists', S.B. Kennedy remarks unequivocally in a reference book designed to accompany a Dublin exhibition entitled *Irish Art and Modernism: 1880–1950*, 'merely reacted to Modernism; they did not help to shape its development'.[12]

The difficulty that Kennedy encounters when attempting to find evidence of a ruling engagement with modernist ideas reveals much about the incomplete reception of the movement in Ireland. Kennedy's awareness of painters reacting to rather than shaping modernism can be extended to a number of short-story writers who decided not to engage fully with modernist experiments in literature. Two such examples are Seán Ó Faoláin and Frank O'Connor, both of whom had their work published in modernist magazines like *The Dial*, though their extensive treatment of the short-story genre reveals no consistent adoption of modernist ideas.[13] As Terence Brown has noted in reference to literary production of the decades that followed on from Joyce's 1914 collection *Dubliners*, 'a debilitating air of anachronism' hangs over the predominance of the short story during the 1920s and 30s.[14]

Perhaps the strongest evidence of what the cultural mainstream in Ireland had come to represent at this time is to be found in the dramaturgy of the Abbey Theatre. After receiving its first official subsidy from the Free State in 1925, the venue became the first state-subsidised playhouse in Europe, otherwise known as the National Theatre of Ireland (*Amharclann Náisiúnta na hÉireann*). This was an arena in which the previous concerns of the Irish Revival continued to express themselves in romance, folklore, heroic narrative, and in highly-politicised renditions of rural life. Thomas Cornelius Murray's theatrical studies of the peasant class in *Birthright* (1910), *Maurice Harte* (1912), and *Autumn Fire* (1924) had made this an attractive subject for the national drama, the recurrent success of which would become known as 'the peasant treadmill'.[15] By highlighting the influence of folklorism as opposed to modernism, I do not mean to ignore the production of more innovative drama during this period. George Bernard Shaw was the most frequently produced Abbey dramatist from 1916 to 1935. An Irish translation of Leo Tolstoy's *Falsely True* [*Fíoraon le Fiarán*] was staged at the Abbey Theatre in 1925. As the years progressed, however, the overall predominance of peasant themes on the national stage began to reflect the hardening of ideological positions. On 5 October 1930, Samuel Beckett wrote to Thomas McGreevy comparing Eileen Crowe's performance as Dervorgilla in Lady Gregory's play of that name to 'Frau Lot petrified into a symbolic condemnation of free trade', noting how the abducted wife of Tiernán O'Rourke had been recast as passive justification for the nation's increasingly isolationist social and economic policy.[16]

The vested political interests that now attached themselves to the national drama were by no means representative of the original force with which the Irish Revival had been conceived by Irish poets, the seeds of which lie, as Roy Foster has shown, in 'the literary societies of the mid 1880s, when the Young Ireland ethos was revived'.[17] While the Irish Revival had provided an important framework for radical politics within the oral tradition of song, the movement appears to have lost its force once it moved away from nationalist ballads towards stage melodramas.[18] What I want to emphasise, here, is the translation, and containment, of an earlier vernacular tradition onto the stage during the 1930s, which echoed a strong sense of nostalgia in a country where the Anglo-Irish gentry had been superseded by the Catholic bourgeoisie; where the imaginative intimacy of revolution had been replaced by the Free State; and where the impact of new technologies had been weakened by the new regime's idealisation of peasant and rural life. The state of affairs for Irish writers at this time seems back to front when compared to the socialist politics of their English contemporaries. As James Mays states in his introduction to Denis Devlin's *Collected Poems*:

> The choice for writers like Beckett and Coffey was ... not between Yeats and Marx but between Yeats and Joyce, not whether to join the Communist Party but whether or not to leave the country, not between art and life but between two different kinds of art, each of which contains implications about the way to live. The dilemma of the Irish writer seems at face value more literary and arcane than the choices insisted upon by Christopher Caldwell and Anthony Blunt in the pages of *Left Review*, or explored by Lionel Trilling in *The Middle of the Journey*, but it is not at all.[19]

Though we may object to the exclusionary intensity of the 'choices' that Mays outlines, the description of these loyalties from an Anglophone perspective is useful for charting the very different balance of culture and politics in the Irish context. If a utopian spirit remained imperative for a don turned Soviet spy of the *Left Review*, the issues of the 1930s appeared for Irish writers in a rear-view mirror, largely unchanged by national liberation, and positively oppressed by the constraints that had accompanied popular revolution. A tendency to drift into satire became all too common among Irish writers compelled to react against the demands of an increasingly regimented civilisation.

Division and constraint in the public sphere only stiffened following the passing of the Censorship of Publications Act in 1929, which effectively split apart the artistic intelligentsia from the state's 'protection' of the people. The acceptance of this bill by the Free State government and the lack of dissent surrounding its imposition is perhaps the most important event concerning Ireland's cultural production at this time. Even before the attempt to broaden the interpretation of obscenity in existing legislature had been brought before the Oireachtas (the Free State's legislative body) in the summer of 1928, a level of unofficial assent to censorship from the publishing industry meant that the leaders of literary periodicals had to twice face down strikes from printers who refused to work on the contents of modernist texts. Seumas O'Sullivan decided to reject an essay by 'Con' Leventhal on James Joyce's *Ulysses* (1922) after the Dollard Printinghouse had threatened strike action, and the editors of the short-lived magazine *To-Morrow* had to turn to a printing house in Manchester after Irish printers refused to work on Lennox Robinson's 'The Madonna of Slieve Dun' (1924) and an anonymous essay by W.B. Yeats that ridiculed contemporary bishops.

Further examples of the way in which the censorship act was popularly and imaginatively reinforced are contained in Brendan Behan's 'Letters from Ireland', which were published by the Parisian magazine that Sindbad Vail edited, *Points*. Referring to the outlook of one prudish bookseller, Behan acknowledges to the Parisian editor that

> I got a Penguin *Plato's Symposium*. With difficulty: The Censorship can hardly get after him at this time of day, but as one bookman (saving your presence) said to me: 'We saw a slight run on it, and the same sort of people looking for it, so we just took it out of circulation ourselves. After all, we don't have to be made decent minded by Act of the Dáil. We have our own way of detecting smut, no matter how ancient.'[20]

Looking back on the Free State's rule from the 1970s, the civil servant and writer Mervyn Wall perceived that the state coordination of the 'masses' had been deep and effective and that its censorious legislature had been imposed 'with the will of the entire people' – an observation that is corroborated by other writers who lived through the 1930s.[21] What is most disturbing about these testimonial accounts of the period is the disappearance of a middle audience between the Free State and the general public. Even the Oireachtas festival (an event that now found an unfortunate namesake in the Free State's legislative body), which had been operating since 1897 as Ireland's first annual festival for the literary and performing arts, was cancelled from 1924 to 1939 due to a lack of public interest.

A more complex example of the impact of censorship on literary development can be discerned from within organisations that sought to capitalise on the restrictive nature of the Free State government. As Lauren Arrington has shown from financial records, government correspondence and minutes from Directors meetings, even the Abbey Theatre, which is usually exempt from accounts of restrictive control during this period, was engaged in strategies of self-constraint that manipulated attempts by government officials to interfere directly in its programme.[22] Though the impact of censorship in this instance evidently exceeds in its complexity the ruling of the censors themselves, my purpose here is simply to illustrate the drastic change that it effected on Ireland's cultural situation. Francis Hackett, whose *The Green Lion* (1936) was banned on grounds of indecency, had maintained prior to the revolution that national independence would not equate to a transfer to papal authority – a situation that had been predicted by unionist counterparts in the north. Two decades later, however, in an article entitled 'A Muzzle Made in Ireland', Hackett argues in a parting shot before leaving for Denmark that 'the Catholic Church is giving the lie to every nationalist who, like myself, insisted day in and day out that Home Rule would not mean Rome Rule. Home Rule, through the action of the Censorship, does mean Rome Rule'.[23]

So far I have argued that the formal and social direction of Ireland's cultural mainstream, which favoured Catholic canons, heroic mythology and conservative treatments of rural life, remained generally impervious to modernist influences. Yet it is debatable whether the Irish literary scene in the 1930s was any *less* modernist than that of Britain or even the USA, both of which saw, from the perspective of formal experiment, a resurgence of traditional styles. In 1930s Britain, the emergence of W.H. Auden and Graham Greene after Eliot signalled a return to more conventional techniques of versification and narration; and in 1930s America, the themes and forms of the naturalist novel, particularly in the aftermath of the Great Depression, found arguably their greatest practitioners in John Dos Passos and John Steinbeck. A wider international context for censorship can also be traced from the beginning of the era of the Motion Picture Production Code in Hollywood. On both sides of the Atlantic, the Catholic Church regulated cultural production and appeals to patriotism by merging its public identity with secular and civic institutions. The overall propensity towards naturalistic modes in Britain and America at this time might point to Ireland being seen less as an outlier detached from global movements than as part of a broader, international reaction against modernism. So there is something altogether more complicated about Irish culture post-1922 than an account of the restrictive forces of religion, provincialism, and censorship can imply. And of course a number of key experimental writers still emerged during the 1930s – Kate O'Brien and Elizabeth Bowen among them – whose aesthetic self-consciousness and self-reflexiveness question the strength of any connection that can be drawn between the official cultural climate in Ireland and the work of Irish writers.

In 'Foreword: Theory of Modernism versus Theory of the Avant-Garde', which introduces the 1984 edition of Peter Bürger's *Theory of the Avant-Garde*, Jochen Schulte-Sasse argues that the subversive intent of avant-garde work is socially as well as technically oppositional. 'Modernism', Schulte-Sasse disputes, 'may be understandable as an attack on traditional writing techniques, but the avant-garde can only be understood as an attack meant to alter the institutionalised commerce with art'.[24] Schulte-Sasse's distinction may be usefully employed to reflect upon the separate existence of an avant-garde circle in Ireland after 1922 where modernism did not emerge on a large or consistent scale as a result of the Free State's ideological commitment to a rural and folk aesthetic. The radicalism of the avant-garde position rests upon the expectation of having to take sides: often (but not always) in opposition to a middle-class audience, government ideology, utilitarian preference, or mainstream of traditional art. By applying the concept of the 'avant-garde' to three Irish poets of the 1930s – Denis Devlin, Samuel Beckett, and Thomas McGreevy – I am therefore referring to a formula that is both socially and technically antagonistic.[25] The history of the concept is helpful in two senses: first, for considering the national culture from which these poets had become alienated; and second, for explaining the centrality of Paris to their work. In the following section, I offer an extended and detailed characterisation of their poetry.

INTERCESSIONS, ECHO'S BONES AND POEMS

Along with Denis Devlin's *Intercessions* (1937), Samuel Beckett's *Echo's Bones and Other Precipitates* (1935) and Thomas McGreevy's *Poems* (1934) represent some of the most innovative attempts by Irish poets of the 1930s to dismantle existing mythological archetypes and to divest them of their idealist accretions. A reading of poems from these collections will highlight their different approaches to lyric. As Devlin writes in 'Now':

> Hail to the Holy Adjective!
> *Three-score and ten.*
> What's beauty, truth, life, love, what's me?
> *Can we get there?*
> Don't know, don't know, don't know.
> *By candle-light?*
> Pull down that gilded rubbish. We
> *Candle-light.*
> In metaphysic, apotheo –
> *How many miles is it?*
> – sise Adjective. Hail Sitwell. We
> *How many?*
> Feed on our own decrease.[26]

Highly-respected ideas about the self, language, and national belonging, together with the metaphysical beliefs that underpin them, are here subjected to poetic revision. The 'I' no longer suffices as the marker of a centralising or utopian force. Even the stability of the subject that would give voice to the lyric is questioned: 'what's me?' In the Romantic period, the lyric had answered to the conception of the national landscape as fulfilment, the idea of the world as an extension of the self's desires, and the location of the 'I' / 'eye' as the demonstrative source of origin. For the poet operating comfortably within this tradition, the outer world is recovered by a contemplative attitude that sustains both the position of the speaking subject and its desires, mirroring them perfectly as the absolute locus of visionary experience. In 'Now', the demands of national revolution have irrevocably altered the landscape of lyric poetry. The association of national fulfilment with song clearly belongs to an outstripped poetic tradition.

For a new generation looking back at the recent literary past, Devlin, Beckett, and McGreevy's approaches to the lyric bear all the hallmarks usually associated with the avant-garde: the problem of disintegrating subjectivity in modernity; the absence of unity between the self and the social world; and a self-conscious pastiche of literary form. However, the manner in which they introduce political tensions to the lyric is complex and is not simply motivated by an impulse towards satire. The inclusion of self-interrogative fragments as a central feature of their verse raises more basic questions about a political relationship with society that is no longer available. Especially revealing of the extent to which Devlin's poetry is unable to engage directly with political issues is his decision not to publish the poem 'Transition: To a Violent Communist', which could have easily been addressed to his college contemporary, Charles Donnelly, who died two years later in the Spanish Civil War, aged just twenty-two. Devlin's euphemistically renamed 'Bacchanal', originally entitled 'News of Revolution', anticipates the march of future citizens through a series of jumbling and discordant registers:

> Forerunners run naked as sharks through water,
>   nose to their prey, have message by heart
> Only envy learnt in feeding the shutfist pistoned
>   right machines
> Canaille, canaille, what red horizons of anger
>   for humbled lives lie
> Tumbled up in the old times, the long-ferment-
>   ing now, canaille![27]

Without developing any single image, the passage proceeds through indented lines of deferral that lend a mocking sense of repetition to the word 'canaille' (a French word for 'riff-raff' or 'rabble': from the Italian *canaglia*, 'pack of dogs'). The loss of spatial and temporal coordinates in this dystopian future allows for a mixture of post and pre-revolutionary perspectives that the poem refuses to distil from the appetites of raw, angular, and malignant figures dispossessed of their conscious history. Passive constructions, dangling modifiers and unpredictable line breaks undermine any prospect of resolution at the level of the poetic form.

Devlin was often conflicted about whether or not to publish his poems because of the position he held within the Department of External Affairs.[28] As he writes to McGreevy after he had sent him 'Bacchanal' on 22 January 1937: 'I'm not risking my job lightly especially as I have other responsibilities besides myself, but I must publish it'.[29] The powerlessness of poetry to effect political change emerges as its own theme in a number of Devlin's poems. One of the most sublime examples of failed agitprop in *Intercessions* is that of 'Daphne Stillorgan', a poem very much written from the perspective of a diplomat. Here, the speaker anticipates the disturbance of a calm pastoral scene, voicing the expectation that the inert locale of a Dublin suburb will soon be blast apart by the mobilisation of international forces, for which the approaching train in the poem provides an allegory of 'Emergency' Ireland amid the advance of Nazi Germany. The far-off trampling and humid pounding of the train in the lyric antagonises the complacent harmonies of the pastoral mode. Heard along the rails (and here Devlin emphasises the spatial dynamics of the poem as a verbal icon), the sound of the train's approach is likened to the 'thud / Of thousand pink-soled apes, no humorous family god // Southward, storm / Smashes the flimsy sky.'[30]

The poem weaves in and out of mythic and futurist modes of recognition, playing on the slow confusion of the passengers on the platform to comprehend the deafening apocalypse that is heralded by the train's oncoming:

> Scared faces lifted up,
> Is the menace bestial or a brusque pleiad
> Of gods of fire vagabond?
> Quick, just in time, quick, just in time; ah!
> Trees in light dryad dresses.[31]

The punctual arrival of the locomotive is marked by its rapid assimilation back into the woodland place spirit of the nymph and faun. The train is distinguished not by its shock tactics but by its failure to unsettle the sleepy indolence of the modest country station. Without alarming the native scene, the sound of the train's arrival signals ('ah!') a return to the anthropomorphosis of the parish pump. The questionable return of the Arcadian imagination ('Trees in light dryad dresses') for which the nymph Daphne serves as an obviously eroticised counterpart is undercut by the final stanza, and the image of the station suddenly evaporates – 'Birds (O unreal whitewashed station!) / Compose no more that invisible architecture' – which brings the poem to a sharp ending on that impulse to de-create.[32]

While Devlin's 'Death and Her Beasts, Ignoble Beasts' enters the birds of prey and the birds of song into accretive juxtaposition, the first poem of Beckett's 1935 collection of verse (though the last to be written) is more emphatic in its departure from the airs of Irish melody and is provocatively entitled 'The Vulture'. As is evident from Beckett's annotated copy of the collection, 'The Vulture' is based on the first five lines of Goethe's *Harzreise im Winter* (1777):

> Dem Geier gleich,
> Der auf schweren Morgenwolken
> Mit sanftem Fittich ruhend
> Nach Beute schaut,
> Schwebe mein Leid.

As a vulture would,
That on heavy clouds of morning
With gentle wings reposing
Seeks for his prey –
Hover, my song.[33]

The opening poem in *Echo's Bones* counters the restorative utterance of
the original source by employing death as a metaphor for artistic
creation. A disembodied 'skull shell of sky and earth' offsets the
transcendent subject of the lyric.[34] Hovering above in the title, 'The
Vulture' is desperate to insert itself into the main textual body, but is
denied by a present participle on two separate occasions: 'dragging...
// stooping...'.[35] The predator waits in spite of these deferrals for the
'tissue' to break down before it can finally enter the carcass, just as the
reader waits impatiently for a main verb that is indefinitely withheld,
and eventually replaced, by the noun 'offal', meaning rubbish.[36] 'The
Vulture' approaches alone in the accusative, unable to enter into the
poem until the very last word.

Where the speaker in *Intercessions* vacillates unpredictably and
is continuously invested in outward phenomena (McGreevy even
compares Devlin to Saint Francis in his review of the collection),
in *Echo's Bones* the verse is much more sharply divided between
perceiving subjects and perceived objects.[37] A sense of repressed
utterance, sexual impotence and failed interpersonal exchange is
registered with extreme irony throughout Beckett's experiment
with the lyric. In 'Alba', the pronominal address is suspended
indefinitely to frustrate a sense of impending arrival ('before
morning you shall be here').[38] The failure of the speaker to unite in
this poem with the second person frustrates the erotic desires of the
self, bringing them back to the point of origin: 'only I and then the
sheet / and bulk dead'.[39] Beckett uses the lyric to characterise an
empty awakening across the embroidered patterns of an absent lover's
nightdress.

'Alba' first appeared in 1931 in the October-December edition
of Seumas O'Sullivan's *Dublin Magazine*. The poem 'Da Tagte Es' ('The
Dawn Comes') was also submitted to O'Sullivan's magazine, but was
not included in any edition.[40] Here, 'the sheet astream in your hand'
is transposed from an autoerotic wipe into a handkerchief being
waved from a death ship.[41] The title of the poem is adapted from the
early medieval German poet Walther von der Vogelweide's 'Nemt,
frowe, disen kranz' (c.893) ('Take, lady, this wreath') and more
specifically from a moment of disillusionment towards the end of
that poem where the poet's awakening from the raptures of love
suddenly transforms the meditation: '*dô taget ez* und nuos ich

wachen'.[42] 'Da Tagte Es' shifts der Vogelweide's words into the present continuous, enabling this brief four-line poem to recast the manner of awakening latent in the original source as a prophetic sign or symbol for the enforced separation through death of a father and son ('the glass unmisted above your eyes').[43]

Throughout *Echo's Bones*, Beckett undermines any strategy of personal deliverance that the speaker might derive from the natural world. At the beginning of 'Serena II', a number of Irish locations (the Pins, Clew Bay, and Croagh Patrick) are recast in a twilight setting that resembles the convulsions of an ageing female dog.[44] In another evening song that Beckett sent to McGreevy, entitled 'Serena III', the division of the speaker from the natural world falls back upon a landscape of sexual insistence free from mythological archetypes: a 'brand-new carnation' of 'mammae', 'Butt Bridge' and 'cock up thy moon'.[45] In 'Sanies II', a poem in which a voluptuous Barfrau enchants her local audience, the lyrical act of apostrophe is again reversed as a form of sexual pleading or broken supplication: 'I break down quite in a titter of despite / hark'.[46] Even the line-breaks of this poem are characterised as extorted utterance, the deliverance of which is synchronised with the flagellant strikes of Madame de la Motte's 'cavaletto supplejacks'.[47]

So far we have seen how Beckett estranges the subject from the object of utterance ('dragging... // stooping... // mocked...'), places the self at the centre of the poem, and redirects the perception of external phenomena towards the inward pursuit of a deeper sexual need. The threshold conditions of this strategy repeatedly deny the culminating visions that the lyric once featured. While Beckett recasts dawn and evening songs based on Provençal genres, McGreevy admits live historical pressures into his verse as *faits sociaux* of Ireland's political turmoil. These pressures are often appended to his poems with an exact date and location. 'Crón Tráth na nDéithe', which is postmarked *Easter Saturday, 1923* (seven years on from the day that the leaders of the Easter Rising had surrendered), is one of the few poems to have been written about the Irish Civil War (1922–23). The Irish title of the poem is an approximation of 'Gotterdämmerung' ['Twilight of the Gods']. Susan Schreibman has noted that 'Cróntráth' ('dark time'), which is usually one word, may have been separated by McGreevy in order to emphasise the 'dark' element.

> When the Custom House took fire[48]
> Hope slipped off her green petticoat
> The Four Courts went up in a spasm
> Moses felt for hope

Folge mir Frau
Come up to Valhalla
To *Gile na gile*
The brightness of brightness
Towering in the sky over Dublin

The dark sloblands below in their glory
Wet glory
Dark night has come down on us, mother
And we
Do not look for a star
Or Valhalla

Our Siegfried was doped by the Gibichungs[49]

Surveying the wreckage from which a new nation has arisen, the
speaker questions what has survived and what has perished. *Folge mir
Frau* (literally, 'follow me wife') is taken from the final scene of
Wagner's *Das Rheingold*, where Wotan invites Fricka to 'Come up to
Valhalla' (the home of the gods). As we follow this ambition to the
Irish *'gile na gile'* ('Brightness of brightness') that Beckett celebrates in
his 1934 review in terms of a moment of 'pure perception', the reader
is interrupted by what is really 'towering in the sky', which is the
smoke rising from the Four Courts, a building that had been occupied
by republicans opposed to the 1921 Anglo-Irish Treaty.[50] With the
visual citation of Wotan's motif, the poem extends Wotan's invitation
to mark the event that started the Irish Civil War.

Rhyme and melody are omitted from the lyric the better to
prise apart the association of national fulfilment with song, which is
essential to the conceit that is set up between Wotan's fortress and the
newly-founded Irish Free State. 'Wet glory' is a surprising, orgiastic
image. The passage is strangely disconcerting in the manner in which
it deploys the standard images of female virtue to undercut the idea of
a heroic struggle, with the apostrophes to wives, goddesses, and the
vacant appeal to 'mother' forestalled until the end of the following
line. What is generated, here, is an idea of political fulfilment that is
predicated on Ireland's ability to rise out of mythological identification

and her simultaneous inability to rise out of it. The reiteration of 'glory' as 'wet glory' on this 'Dark night' continues the image of the fertility goddess that inhibits the historicity of self and world, echoing an earlier, more devious allusion to Robert Browning's 'Love Among The Ruins' (1855).[51] Though the passage subverts the idea of a romantic national heritage, the speaker is still determined to ask questions about where the people might be found and how to restore them to their usurped nationhood ('our Siegfried was doped by the Gibichungs').

As I have attempted to read from specific moments at which the lyrical voice falters, an impassable tension is maintained in all three collections of experimental verse between the need for detachment and the need for fulfilment. In *Intercessions*, the speaker vacillates unpredictably between a sense of resistance and attraction to the social world that it cannot easily overcome. Strict abstinence and baroque opulence figure as two accretive registers of this linguistic protest. In *Echo's Bones*, by contrast, the 'I' is split off entirely from the world in which it exists in order to produce a (deviant) poetic persona. In *Poems*, the speaker uses a sense of division from the social world to imply a change in the way that the national landscape is rooted – to 'Set free, set free without fear' as McGreevy translates from Jorge Guillén's poem, 'La salida'.[52]

Beckett's review of Devlin's *Intercessions*, which was published in the Parisian journal *transition* six months after McGreevy's review of the same collection, offers insight into the kind of artistic freedom demanded by the avant-garde:

> Art has always been this – pure interrogation, rhetorical question less the rhetoric – whatever else it may have been obliged by the 'social reality' to appear, but never more freely so than now, when social reality (*pace* ex-comrade Radek) has severed the connexion.[53]

Beckett refers to the international Communist leader, Karl Radek, who at the 1934 Soviet Writers Congress had dismissed James Joyce's *Ulysses* (1922) on account of its 'private language'.[54] The traditional Marxist explanation for the 'decadence' of *Ulysses* was that the truth of social life had become irreconcilable with the aesthetic quality of individual expression. Beckett's contention, in placing the 'social reality' in quotation marks, of art's diminishing obligation to appear as anything other than the irreducible complex in which we find ourselves foregrounds the impossible allegiance being made to such external standards. The freedom to present material irrespective of the demands of a particular public, tradition, or social structure is bound up with his understanding of art's capacity to inquire, remake, and even emancipate the expressive act from ideological pressures ('whatever else it may have been obliged by the "social reality" to appear'). In the context of Irish censorship, Beckett's defence of a pure interrogative art bears comparison with Erich Heller's thesis in *The Disinherited Mind* that the modern artist had been left outside of his / her immediate environment due to a peculiar contraction in the circumference of the real.[55] Here 'social reality' can provide no ulterior motive for art to adhere to, explain, or dissect (as Beckett is only too happy to admit in response to Radek). Rather what is being advanced in this passage is an idea of creative expression that cannot be absorbed by rational use or justification, either as a conscious aim of the poet (who may be unaware of what she or he is communicating) or as an explanation for what his / her 'art' might mean once it has been completed.

NOTES

1. Over the past three decades, scholars and students of modernism have been asked to cover ever more territory both geographically and historically through the rise of international associations that promote Modernist Studies. However, as this essay will show, the permeation of modernism in Irish culture is highly uneven and largely refuted by an empirical overview of its cultural climate during the 1920s and 30s. As a movement of international influence across all of the creative arts during the early twentieth century, 'modernism' indicates a close exploration of the workings of individual consciousness, a distrust of transcendental values and essences, and the abandonment of ornamental features.

2. My thanks to Emma Cheshire, Svetlana Shadrina and Linda Nicol for permission to quote from the Faber & Faber and Cambridge University Press editions of Samuel Beckett's collected poems and letters, which are reproduced here by the kind permission of the Estate of Samuel Beckett c/o Rosica Colin Limited, London. I am especially grateful to Robert Ryan and Margaret Farrington, co-executors of the Estate of Thomas McGreevy, for permission to quote from Thomas McGreevy's *Poems* (1934) and letters. Neither the Irish Writers Centre nor the Irish Copyright Licensing Agency have been able to provide me with any information about the copyright situation concerning the Estate of Denis Devlin, and I have been advised to forge ahead having shown due diligence on the recommendation of James Mays (the editor of *Collected Poems by Denis Devlin* (Dublin: Dedalus Press, 1989), hereafter referred to as *CPDD*). On his return to Ireland in 1941, McGreevy changed his surname to 'MacGreevy', inserting the Gaelic prefix 'Mac' before his anglicised surname (as Ernie O'Malley had added the 'O' in front of 'Malley'). This essay adopts the earlier spelling of his name for consistency. 'McGreevy' is the name used officially for purposes of registration, the name under which *Poems* (1934) was first published, and the name of address used by his European contemporaries.

3. See James MacFarlane and Malcolm Bradbury's *Modernism: A Guide to European Literature, 1890–1930* (London: Penguin, 1978) and Michael Levenson's *The Cambridge Companion to Modernism* (Cambridge: Cambridge University Press: 2011).

4. See Christopher Butler's *Modernism: A Very Short Introduction* (Oxford: Oxford University Press, 2010).

5. See Terence Brown's 'Ireland, Modernism and the 1930s', in *The Literature of Ireland: Culture and Criticism* (Cambridge: Cambridge University Press, 2010), pp.88–103.

6. Brown, p.91.

7. Brown, p.93.

8. Brown, p.92. McGreevy's Catholic reading of T.S. Eliot is arguably more complicated than Brown suggests. He was in fact critical of the devotional turn that Eliot's later work had taken after *The Waste Land* (1922) and disliked 'The Hollow Men' (1925) because of its over-literal use of prayer. See McGreevy, *T.S. Eliot: A Study* (London: Chatto & Windus, 1931), p.59.

9. Seamus Deane charted this proposition in a series of four lectures entitled 'Religion, Liberalism and Modernism in Europe and Ireland, 1830–1970', which were given at the Notre-Dame Institute (O'Connell House) during June–July 2011.

10. Deane, ibid.

11. See S. Bhreathneach-Lynch, 'The Academy of Christian Art (1929–1946): An Aspect of Catholic Cultural Life in Newly Independent Ireland', *Éire-Ireland* (Autumn-Winter 1996), pp.3–4.

12. S.B. Kennedy, *Irish Art and Modernism: 1880–1950* (Belfast: Queens University, 1991), p.209.

13. See the August and March 1929 editions of *The Dial* (79.2, and 86.3, respectively), which feature Ó'Faoláin's 'The Wild Goat's Kid' (137–143) and O'Connor's 'The Song of Liadain' (189–190).

14. Brown, 'Ireland, Modernism and the 1930s', p.99.

15. Despite the Abbey Theatre's preoccupation with peasant themes, genuine exceptions to the national drama were developed on rival stages. The Dublin Drama League (1919–29), directed by Lennox Robinson and chaired by W.B. Yeats, remained very much a place apart from the official taste of Irish culture during this period, promoting a number of European plays that exhibited surrealist, expressionist, and modernist influences. Though its activities stopped after the 1929 season, the League was temporarily revived by Robinson, George Yeats, and Olive Craig during the 1930s to produce 'uncommercial' plays on Sundays. So unsuited, however, did the organisation prove to Dublin's reactionary climate that its creators found themselves actively opposing plays that they had, in effect, promoted: first in the case of Sean O'Casey's *The Silver Tassie* (1928) and then four months later with Denis Johnston's *The Old Lady Says No!* (1928). See W.B. Yeats's letter of rejection to O'Casey: 20/04/1928; *The Collected Letters of W.B. Yeats, Electronic edition, Unpublished Letters (1905–1939)* http://www.nlx.com/collections/130; and Johnston's second (and finally rejected) typescript draft of *Shadowdance*, later called *The Old Lady Says No!*, with holograph corrections by W.B. Yeats and others, in the Denis Johnston archive at the University of Victoria Libraries Special Collections.

16. Beckett to McGreevy: 05/10/1930; *The Letters of Samuel Beckett: Vol 1, 1929–1940*, ed. by Martha Dow Fehsenfeld and Lois More Overbeck (Cambridge: Cambridge University Press, 2009), p.50. Hereafter referred to as *TLSB*.

17. See R.F. Foster, *Words Alone: Yeats and his Inheritances* (Oxford: Oxford University Press, 2011), p.143. A 'Great Irish Revival Number' had been featured in the January 1886 edition of the *Irish Fireside*, a popular Irish weekly edited by Rose Kavanagh.

18. For further exposition of the same argument, see Emer Nolan's 'Modernism and the Irish Revival', in *The Cambridge Companion to Modern Irish Culture*, ed. by Joe Cleary and Claire Connolly (Cambridge: Cambridge University Press, 2005), pp.157–172; and Lionel Pilkington's 'Cumann nGaedal and the Abbey Theatre, 1922–1932', in *Theatre and the State in Twentieth-Century Ireland* (London: Routledge 2001), pp.86–111.

19. J.C.C. Mays, 'Introduction', *CPDD*, p.24.

20. Brendan Behan to Sindbad Vail, *Points* 15 (Autumn 1952), p.71.

21. See 'Michael Smith Asks Mervyn Wall Some Questions About the Thirties', in *The Lace Curtain*, 4 (Summer 1971), pp.77–86, for a personal account of Irish public opinion and discourse at this time. For book-length studies on the topic, see Michael Adams, *Censorship: The Irish Experience* (Dublin: Scepter Books, 1968), and Julia Carlson, ed., *Banned in Ireland: Censorship and the Irish Writer* (London: Routledge, 1990). For a revisionist account that inverts rather than reassesses dominant stereotypes about Ireland's cultural isolationism at this time, see Brian Fallon's *An Age of Innocence: Irish Culture 1930–1960* (Dublin: Gill & Macmillan, 1998). Though Fallon does not dispute the existence of restricting forces, he argues that other cultural factors, such as the failure to revive the Irish language, exceeded the negative impact of censorship.

22. See Lauren Arrington, '"We have no gift to set a statesman right": Representation, Reform, Subsidy, and Censorship', *W.B. Yeats, the Abbey Theatre, Censorship, and the Irish State: Adding the Half-pence to the Pence* (Oxford: Oxford University Press, 2010), pp.1–14.

23. Francis Hackett, 'A Muzzle Made in Ireland', *Dublin Magazine* (new series) 11.4 (October-December 1936), p.16. The experiences that Hackett's Danish wife recounts in her *Irish Diaries* reveal much about the extent of Vatican control over Irish affairs. Her journal was published posthumously in Dublin in 1994. See Signe Toksvig's *Irish Diaries* (Dublin: The Lilliput Press, 1994).

24. See Jochen Schulte-Sasse, 'Foreword: Theory of Modernism versus Theory of the Avant-Garde', in Peter Bürger, *Theory of the Avant-Garde* (Minneapolis: University of Minnesota Press, 1984; first published 1974), pp.vii-lv (p.xv).

25. A similar distinction to that being made here has been used by Alex Davis in *A Broken Line: Denis Devlin and Irish Poetic Modernism* (Cork: Cork University Press, 2000), *passim*, to indicate a tangential relationship between 1930s Irish poets and various avant-garde movements across continental Europe. Tim Armstrong also employs the concept of an 'avant-garde', specifically in relation to Thomas McGreevy, but also with regards to Denis Devlin and Brian Coffey, in 'Muting the Klaxon: Poetry, History and Irish Modernism' (see Alex Davis and Patricia Coughlan, eds, *Modernism and Ireland: The Poetry of the 1930s* (Cork: Cork University Press, 1995), pp.43–74). No social or technical connection is being suggested here between these 1930s poets and the existing Irish avant-garde – which includes David Lloyd, Maurice Scully, Randolph Healy, and Catherine Walsh – though their importance to contemporary Irish poetry has often been discussed retrospectively in such terms.

26. *CPDD*, p.104.

27. *CPDD*, p.65.

28. Devlin acted as a foreign diplomat in Paris before he was made the Irish Ambassador to Italy.

29. Devlin to McGreevy: 15/02/1937; TCD MS 8112/12.

30. *CPDD*, p.62.

31. *CPDD*, p.62.

32. Like the oncoming train in 'Daphne Stillorgan', the deconstruction of pastoral is vital to the disruptive homecoming of Beckett's 'Sanies I' in which the poet-cyclist loops about the coastal towns and villages north of Dublin leaving a trail of mud in its wake: 'a Wild Woodbine / cinched to death in a filthy slicker'. However, once again, the expected disturbance of a calm pastoral scene fails to remove these animal spirits from the lyric: 'distraught half-crooked courting the sneers of these fauns these / smart nymphs / clipped like a pederast as to one trouser-end'. *The Collected Poems of Samuel Beckett*, ed. by Sean Lawlor and John Pilling (London: Faber & Faber, 2012), p.13. Hereafter referred to as *CPSB*.

33. Johann Wolfgang von Goethe, *Poems of Goethe*, trans. Edwin H. Zeydel (Chapel Hill, NC: University of North Carolina Press, 1957), p.33. For Beckett's engagement with

Goethe, especially his transcriptions from Goethe's autobiography and *Faust*, see Mark Nixon, *The German Diaries, 1936–37* (London: Continuum, 2011), pp.65–74.

34. *CPSB*, p.5.
35. *CPSB*, p.5.
36. 'Offal' may be a pun on Offaly, a county located in the very centre of Ireland.
37. McGreevy, 'New Dublin Poetry', *Ireland To-Day* (October 1937), 81–82 (p.81).
38. *CPSB*, p.10.
39. *CPSB*, p.10.
40. Beckett to McGreevy: 26/04/1935; TCD MS 10402: 'the *Dublin Magazine* is out, but my poem not in'. The June 1936 number of *transition* opens with a section entitled 'Vertigral', which places three of the poems that had appeared earlier in *Echo's Bones* ('Dortmunder', 'Malacoda' and 'Enueg II') after James Agee's 'Lyric' and 'A Song'. See *transition 24: a quarterly review* (June 1936), 7–38. All of the poems that feature in this section experiment with dawn and evening settings.
41. *CPSB*, pp.10, 22.
42. *'then dawn came* and I had to waken' [translation mine; italics added].
43. *CPSB*, p.22.
44. 'Serena II', Enc. Beckett to McGreevy: 03/11/1932; TCD MS 10402/35.
45. 'Serena III', Enc. Beckett to McGreevy: 09/10/1933; TCD MS 10402/55.
46. *CPSB*, p.14.
47. *CPSB*, p.15.
48. The Custom House was burnt down by the IRA on 25 May 1921 during the Anglo-Irish War of Independence.
49. *Collected Poems of Thomas MacGreevy: An Annotated Edition*, ed. by Susan Schreibman (Dublin: Anna Livia, 1991), pp.19–20. Hereafter referred to as *CPTM*.
50. See Beckett's 'Humanistic Quietism', *Dublin Magazine* (July-September 1934), pp.79–80. While Beckett was right to centre his review on the importance of this speculative moment, the manner in which he did so has slanted the reception of McGreevy's *Poems*. His selective treatment of McGreevy's asceticism denies the social and political force of his poetry and the very real conceptual obstacles with which it grapples. Beckett makes no attempt to select from a broad range of poetic material, but extracts textual samples from four of the most personal religious passages in McGreevy's writing (the quotations from 'Gloria de Carlos V' and 'Seventh Gift of the Holy Ghost' being particularly apposite for his purposes). There is little evidence to support the view that other writers fell in line with the scope of Beckett's analysis, or even proceeded from the same assumptions.
51. *CPTM*, p.17.
52. *CPTM*, p.80.
53. Beckett, 'Commentaries: Denis Devlin', *transition 27* (April-May 1938), 289–294 (p.289). Denis Devlin had originally asked Beckett to review his collection of poems for *Ireland To-Day*, but it was McGreevy who wrote the review. See Beckett to McGreevy (04/09/1937): 'I would much rather you did the Intercessions for Ireland To-day than I did' *TLSB*, p.530. McGreevy had previously commented on the typescript of *Intercessions*, which Devlin had presented to him for advice on revisions. See Devlin to McGreevy: 22/01/1937 TCD MS 8112/11 and 15/02/1937 TCD MS 8112/2.
54. See Karl Radek, 'James Joyce or Socialist Realism?' (August 1934), delivered to the Soviet Writers Congress, *Contemporary World Literature and the Tasks of Proletarian Art*, pp.151–154. Together with the Bolshevik, Dmitriy Manuilsky, Radek had attempted to stage a second German revolution in October 1923 before Lenin died.
55. Erich Heller, *The Disinherited Mind: Essays in Modern German Literature and Thought* (Cambridge: Bowes & Bowes, 1952).

Geoffrey Squires

Modernism, Empiricism, and Rationalism

The term 'modernism' was originally applied to the radically new departures in the arts in the first three decades of the twentieth century. Here I am concerned with the changes in literature, but there were parallel developments in the visual arts and architecture, and in music and the performing arts such as ballet. The rationale for all these innovations was the sense that the modern age was so different that it required something quite new in the arts, that they should register a clean break with what had gone before.

That 'break' was partly a matter of the climactic events that marked the beginning of the new century – the First World War, the Russian revolution, and the turmoil that followed these – but also the more general throwing off of the social and ideological norms that had prevailed during the later nineteenth century. Technology, in the form of electricity, the internal combustion engine, and the increasing use of concrete, also played its part. Life had become decisively urban. Rimbaud's *'il faut être absolument moderne'* acted as the slogan for the new generation.[1] The suffix 'ism' spread not only across politics but the arts too (Vorticism, Futurism, etc) implying that these too were open to abstract theorizing or rational analysis (the Greek suffix *ismos* denotes a system of thought or practice). Everything had to be re-thought, re-formulated. One stimulus for this was negative: the burial of the optimistic nineteenth-century notion of 'progress' in the trenches of the Great War. The role and status of women also began to change, partly as a result of that war, and the political and social status quo was challenged not only in the heartlands of Europe but in the 'peripheral' countries of Iberia, Scandinavia, and of course Ireland. Revolution is not too big a word for what was happening.

There remained, of course, many continuities and sometimes the artistic break was not so clean either, involving a paradoxical re-discovery of much earlier themes and forms: the medieval (including Pre-Raphaelite), mythic (including Celtic), or even primitive, as in Stravinsky's *Rite of Spring*. Yeats's work is a curious

Irish University Review 46.1 (2016): 38–47
DOI: 10.3366/iur.2016.0199
© Edinburgh University Press
www.euppublishing.com/journal/iur

combination of the backward-looking and forward-looking, allowing one to see him as both traditionalist and modernist, and making him a particularly difficult figure to place historically and artistically. Whatever one's judgement, there is no question but that his mental apparatus – what he brought cognitively to the world, in terms of an interest in theosophy, Celtic myth, or Noh theatre – had a profound influence on what he wrote at various stages in his career. For others, including Joyce, the situation pointed towards a cyclic or at least non-linear view of history, of things coming round again, and the search for forms that would embody this. In general, however, the abruptness of the linear break was evidenced by the reaction of the majority of the public to these artistic innovations: bewilderment, rage, incomprehension, and rejection.

With hindsight, we can see the rationale more clearly than many at the time could. The world changed and was changed in profound and far-reaching ways. So the agenda of modernism now seems broadly justified, which is not to say that over time it did not produce its own counter-reaction that appealed to tradition. However, the problem with the term comes with the passage of time. It seems strange that now, over a century later, we are still using it as a contemporary concept to describe certain kinds of writing and writers. Modernism is, on the face of it, an old, even dated idea, so how can we still employ it as a useful and viable label? One response has been to modify it to reflect those changes over time, so we have 'late' modernism and 'post' modernism, labels which acknowledge that things did not stay still over the subsequent decades. The difficulty with these is that they still refer to the original concept as a baseline. The problem, to my mind, is the deeper one of using a chronological, historical marker in the first place and in this short piece I would like to explore a quite different way of thinking about it. This employs two basic philosophical ideas which are often contrasted or opposed, namely empiricism and rationalism.

In simple terms, empiricism holds that the world comes to us through our senses: *nihil in intellectu nisi prius in sensu*: nothing in the mind that is not first in the senses (a dictum that Beckett characteristically truncates at 'intellectu').[2] 'Naïve' empiricism treats this sensory data as the incoming raw material which our minds process and build on; more complex versions allow the mind an earlier role in selective perception. Both, however, see our thinking as grounded in 'experience' and this word more than any other signals the empirical stance, most often associated with the eighteenth-century philosophers Locke and Hume. In England in particular that view is often reinforced by the pervasive notion of 'common sense'.

The term 'rational' is trickier. In ordinary language use it means reasonable: the opposite of emotional, instinctive, or intuitive. However, philosophical rationalism has a more precise sense, referring to what we bring to our encounter with the world: the mental or cognitive structures, schema, frameworks, and ideas which allow us to make sense of what is going on. If the empiricist focuses on 'experience' the rationalist focuses on 'consciousness': Descartes' *cogito* or Kant's 'categories'.

Each of these terms generates its own cluster of related concepts. 'Experience' connotes events or incidents and the situations and settings in which these take place. Such experiences may in turn lead to reflection or trigger the imagination. 'Consciousness' typically assumes interpretation or decoding and implicates language itself in the process. Rather than the empiricist's 'reflection' it involves 'reflexivity' i.e. thinking about thinking. Like most simple oppositions this one has long since been refined and qualified to the point where the initial contrast becomes lost in a haze of nuance. However, this basic list of terms does suggest a different way of looking at modernism. To put it crudely, it suggests the intrusion of rationalism into empiricism. In other words, what people saw previously and unproblematically as experience is now overlaid or penetrated by layers of analysis, to the point where the very notion of experience comes to seem somehow old-fashioned or even innocent.

If we accept, for the moment, this hypothesis, the obvious question is: why? Why did writers and others become more concerned with consciousness, language, and reflexivity in the early decades of the twentieth century? The answer I think lies not in the arts themselves but in the growth of organized knowledge, what the French call *science* and the Germans *Wissenschaft*, both of which involve the idea of 'knowing'. The late nineteenth and early twentieth centuries saw major developments in the natural sciences, first chemistry and biology and then physics. These developments in the natural sciences were in turn applied in various forms of technology, such as machines, gases, electricity, and medicines. Mathematics influenced the visual arts and would later impact on literature. And although economics initially emerged as a distinct discipline back in the eighteenth century, the other social sciences – anthropology, sociology, psychology, and linguistics – really took off in the early twentieth. Where in the past the humanities – philosophy, history, and literature – had dominated higher education, now they became just one faculty among others.

There is certainly some distance to travel from the fundamental notions of Cartesian or Kantian rationalism to the cognitive schema or frameworks represented by such disciplines, and it would require a careful account of the evolution of the modern concept of consciousness to map out that journey properly, an account which might itself need to draw in areas of psychology and linguistics as well. It might be useful to distinguish between basic philosophical rationalism and the wider sense in which it is being used here. Nevertheless we are concerned in both cases with what we bring to our encounter with the world, indeed how that world is constituted or constructed, as against simply perceived or experienced.

The impact of these developments on literature can be seen in two ways. First, and most obviously, in the incorporation of terms, references, and forms of discourse from such disciplines. The language of the natural and social sciences began to enter writing and the other arts in a way that it had not previously, although we have to look mainly outside Ireland to see this. Secondly, and more subtly, in a shift of awareness, involving new facets or levels of consciousness. People began to realize that the self was the 'self', that language was 'language', that myth was 'myth', nature was 'nature', culture 'culture', history 'history', art 'art', and so on. The addition of these quotation marks signals a kind of distancing, a standing back. No longer could these things simply be taken for granted as natural, normal, self-evident, given, or true. One effect was a subtle displacement of the authorial 'I' which hitherto had stood at the centre of things as the unchallenged manager of the text.

However, modernism itself was not a single, unified phenomenon but rather a cluster of related movements, and before going any further we need to consider how two of these – Imagism and Surrealism – look in terms of the underlying distinction posited here. In philosophy, imagism was originally associated with empiricism where it referred to the idea that we form images of percepts from which we can then build concepts, a kind of intermediate stage in the process of cognition. Later empiricists dismissed this stage as unnecessary. In poetry, imagism refers to the short-lived but influential movement in the second decade of the twentieth century which advocated the direct presentation and juxtaposition of images unmediated, explained, or linked in any way.

In terms of the analysis here, this constitutes a form of extreme empiricism – a total reliance on the input of the senses without any recourse to the intellect. While the Imagist movement was itself very brief, the centrality of imagery to poetry became a major tenet of much twentieth-century poetry and nowhere more so than in Ireland, where examples of such condensed imagism in early Irish poetry were sometimes allied to an interest in European Imagism or Chinese and Japanese verse among a number of poets including Heaney and Mahon.[3] This arguably drew Irish poetry in precisely the opposite direction to rationalism and if anything reinforced its empiricist leanings.

As far as I am aware, surrealism has had very little influence on Irish poetry. However it was an important movement in continental Europe and as such needs to be addressed. At first sight it would seem to be a kind of anti-rationalism, challenging any kind of organized cognitive structures. It may be useful here to draw a distinction between surrealism, which claims to transcend rationality, and 'sousrealisme', i.e. under-realism, which subverts such rationality through liberating the unconscious, a notion which draws on psychoanalytic theory. However, they both also arguably challenge the notion of experience, as the normal everyday process of engaging and transacting with our world. Significantly, such work in literature and the visual arts often seems to invoke dreams rather than our waking, lived experience.

To return to the main argument: it would require a much longer essay than this to show how the empiricist/rationalist distinction works out in actual poets or poems, but a few pointers can be given here, using the most recent anthology of Irish poetry, edited by Patrick Crotty with a preface by the late Seamus Heaney.[4] Section VII (The Sea of Disappointment: 1922–70) and Section VIII (Transformations: 1971–2009) cover most of the period when modernism might have been an issue and thus act as a useful baseline for the discussion here. It must be said right away that the vast bulk of the material in these two sections lies squarely in the empiricist tradition, a fact that no doubt reflects the realities of twentieth-century Irish poetry but also the predilections of the anthologist.

The empirical emphasis is signaled first and foremost by the presence, often explicit, of the 'lyric I', 'lyric' to be understood here not always as sweet or beautiful but as personal or autobiographical, the lived I. The term is perhaps justified by the fact that even where the experiences are painful, as they often are, the poem transforms them into something that is worthy of song. In other cases, the 'lyric I' turns into the 'narrative I'. The distinction is not clear-cut, but where the former often captures a particular situation or even moment, the latter has more of a dynamic, evolving, story-telling quality. The narrative may of course be concerned with the lives of others, and a good deal of Irish poetry in the mid-twentieth century documented the often depressing social realities of the time: one thinks in particular of the work of Austin Clarke. In other cases again, the lyric I becomes the 'implicit' I of observation, where the presence of the poet is indicated by the description. Many poems in the anthology fall into this category, to the point where the 'I' disappears into a kind of selfless subjectivity. This triangle of the lyric, narrative, and implicit is precisely that, a common space defined by three points, and many poets and poems move freely within it. The book includes some of the finest examples of the genre. Indeed it goes a long way towards defining what is sometimes described as the 'mainstream' of Irish poetry, what is regarded as the norm, indeed what some editors look for or require.

All of these kinds of poem arguably still lie within the empirical tradition, so the question arises as to whether there are any in the collection which in some ways lie outside or beyond it. The most obvious, Brian Coffey's *Third Person*, is simply omitted,[5] as is (unaccountably) the rest of his work. Coffey's very title signals a shift away from the centrality of the 'I'. A different kind of shift is evident in the work of Maurice Scully which is represented in the anthology. Scully's work often comprises mini-narratives, accounts of incidents or situations in a domestic or social setting, but what makes it different is that the 'I' itself is put in question. Scully's introspection leads to the realization that the single, unified 'I' is often a fiction or at least construction, as if we had a 'reflexive-I' perching on the poet's shoulder, commenting on his normal, engaged, situated self. Scully's poetry can be seen as an example of the stream-of-consciousness writing which is more familiar to us in prose.

The 'I' is challenged in a quite different way in the work of Randolph Healy, whose work is not represented in the anthology. 'Not everything is flat like a board' begins one poem,[6] and Healy's poetry moves between the objective and subjective in a way that I find unique in modern Irish writing. The sense of other forms of knowledge – mathematics and the sciences – is present in many of his poems, giving the 'I' a provisional status, just one reality among others. To cite these three particular poets as ones who question the received 'I' of Irish poetry should not be construed as ruling out others; the issues are simply too complex to be addressed in this brief essay.

Language is a second litmus test of the empiricist/rationalist distinction. In one sense all poets are 'language poets' in that they are intimately concerned with the use of words. However, modernism implies a concern with language as such, and in some poets this awareness accompanies and problematizes what is being said. In Catherine Walsh's work (not represented in the anthology) there is often an autobiographical element, but the authorial voice comes and goes, the latter sometimes in a total preoccupation with the object of description, but at other times in the engagement with language itself. The very means of expression becomes the subject of expression, a phenomenon embodied in the broken and scattered layout of the text on the page. Another poet whose awareness of language as language permeates much of his work is Paul Muldoon, where sometimes the content of the poem is itself subject to linguistic play. The difference between formal and colloquial registers is also an issue in some cases; Paul Durcan exploits the latter well. In a quite different way, language is also a reflexive question for those whose knowledge of Irish means that English is not simply taken for granted as the means of expression.

An appreciation of and feel for the natural world is surely one of the great constants and strengths of Irish poetry, but the rationalist will want to ask what kind of concept or construct of nature is involved. The question is a particularly piquant one, because nature seems like one of the most 'natural' or directly experienced topics for poetry and therefore unproblematic. However, the concept of nature can vary greatly. Some have argued that early Irish 'nature' poetry was in fact a literary invention or convention. Indeed it seems that the language then had no equivalent for our modern term, the natural world being regarded as part of God's wider 'creation'.[7] Nature was a central theme in European romanticism but there were differences between the vaguely pantheistic view of Wordsworth, the French *la nature*, and the German *Natur*. Heaney's first volume was entitled significantly *Death of a Naturalist*. The shift from a rural to a largely urban population changes our perspective, with the countryside coming to seem like a refuge, a place we visit to re-charge our batteries. More recently the environmental movement has affected our perceptions of the natural world. And if we alter the topic from nature to farming the view also changes, from Virgil to Kavanagh or Heaney. There is simply not room here to explore the various perceptions and treatments of 'nature' in modern Irish poetry, but paradoxically this apparently simple and obvious theme may yield some of the most interesting evidence of implicit rational frameworks or constructs.

The term 'culture' can be used either in the broad sociological/anthropological sense of the way of life of a group or the more restricted artistic or literary sense of the arts. Sometimes these coalesce. In the early twentieth century the apparent disintegration of Western culture and society was sometimes expressed in literature and the visual arts by the use of collage, most famously perhaps in Eliot's *The Waste Land*. What is striking, despite Yeats's oft-quoted 'things fall apart', is how little collage has been used in modern Irish poetry, and this raises questions about the historical, social, and cultural constructs that have informed or shaped Irish writing. The subject is so broad and complex that one hesitates even to broach it but one point can be hazarded. If Irish poets were not preoccupied with social and cultural 'disintegration' it may be because their more immediate experience was of conflict: a war of independence, followed by a civil war, followed by either latent or actual conflicts up to and including the most recent 'Troubles'. Irish poetry is thus often concerned with conflict and identity: the national identity of a newly established state, and the challenges to that from both within the island (John Hewitt asserted a distinct Northern Protestant identity) and from external, cosmopolitan, or global culture. It is thus difficult to arrive at a reading of modern Irish poetry without a careful analysis of the contemporary politics. This bears out the need to excavate the (sometimes implicit) rational schema and concepts which affected such writing and the ways in which personal experience was permeated by the wider political scene. Irish poets are typically, though not universally, concerned with Irishness in a way that their European counterparts are not concerned with Frenchness, Dutchness, Swedishness, or whatever. This emphasis is reinforced at a national political level: Ireland is a small country but with a good deal of 'soft power'.

However, this wider political reading should not obscure other lesser themes. For example, one sees the development of a distinctively urban, as against rural, poetry in the work of Thomas Kinsella, Michael Smith (not included), or Ciaran Carson among others. Louis MacNeice strikes me as a very 'modern' poet in his themes and styles, without necessarily being a modernist. The preoccupation with Irishness is challenged by a much more cosmopolitan awareness in Paul Muldoon's work, and some of the younger poets in particular evidence a much broader, relativised, European consciousness.[8] Trevor Joyce's later work shows a range of historical and cultural awareness which goes well beyond the conventional bounds of 'Irishness'. And if Ireland is moving into a post-conflict phase, one might expect poetic themes and forms to reflect that shift in some way.

The past is ever-present in Irish culture even today and this raises the further question of how modernism affects the perception of history. Historical narrative, as imagined or reconstructed experience, forms a natural part of the empiricist tradition, and not a few Irish poems refer back in this way.[9] Equally, however, it can be seen as providing a structure for the interpretation of the present, exemplifying a rationalist approach, most famously in Pound's *Cantos*. In general, one would expect modernism to challenge the notion of history as a given and to explore it as a construct: as 'history'. Revisionism has been a significant feature of modern historical studies in Ireland but I am not aware of any obvious impact of this on modernist poetry, and the question must be left open. Likewise the relationship between modernism and other aspects of the culture, such as religious belief or political ideology, would require much more detailed analysis than is possible in this essay.

However, modernism as I have construed it here surely leads to a radical questioning of the very category of 'art'. This has been perhaps most obvious in the visual arts where new forms challenged the traditional, conventional notions of representation from the early twentieth century on, leading to the now familiar objection: is this art? Few of the inclusions in Crotty's anthology would seem to challenge traditional ideas of what a poem is, although one may note the strikingly free verse of some of Thomas Kinsella's work or the unusual form of David Wheatley's *Sonnet*. For more radical examples of innovative or experimental poetic forms one has to look beyond the book to the work of Catherine Walsh, Trevor Joyce, and younger more 'experimental' writers. One aspect of such work is the creation of relatively open sequences or poetic 'fields', sometimes combining prose and verse, rather than the discrete, self-contained poem that one tends to find in anthologies. However, it is difficult to think of Irish poets who have challenged the notion of a poem in the radical way that Joyce did the novel or Beckett the play.

This brief *tour d'horizon* runs the risk of making only passing comments on writers who deserve much fuller treatment, and should be read in that light. However, I think it demonstrates that a purely 'empirical' reading of such work, in terms of personal experience, an assumed 'I' and an unproblematic view of language, nature, or culture is simply inadequate. We need to ask how the poets filtered, ordered, and interpreted their experience in terms of existing presuppositions, knowledge, cognitive frameworks, and concepts, in other words what they brought to their worlds: the rationalist question.

To sum up: for the modernist, the problem lies, surprisingly perhaps, in knowledge. We know too much: too much to continue writing purely and simply out of experience. As twentieth or twenty-first century beings, knowledge is both our birthright and our burden. It can even lead to a kind of paralysis, an inability to say anything; one thinks of Beckett's struggles. And nowadays knowledge comes to us not simply through the organized disciplines of study but through the ever-present and ubiquitous sources of the media and the internet which flood our consciousness. However, even this brief analysis will have shown that the ways in which such knowledge may shape or penetrate personal experience are exceedingly complex and subtle – there is no such thing as 'pure' experience – and that it is probably better to see the empiricist/rationalist distinction as a spectrum, and a multi-dimensional one at that.

I would like to end with two comments, one historical, one personal. If we want to find an earlier example of this kind of radical shift I suggest we look back, as Eliot did, at the Renaissance, which saw a similar explosion of new knowledge and ideas and in particular at the

Metaphysical poets, who attempted to reflect this in their writing: *'and new philosophy calls all in doubt...'* (Donne).[10] The fact that their work in due course gave way to quite different forms and styles should make us cautious about trying to project all this forward in our own time.

The second and final reflection is personal. In recent years, several books of my poetry have been translated into French.[11] At the launch reading of one of these, I was asked the inevitable question about how my work had changed over the years. I replied that there had always been a tension in it between the empirical and the rational but that I thought there had been a shift towards the latter over time. People nodded and we moved on. Afterwards I wondered if an Irish or English audience would have taken this on board quite so easily, given the deep empirical bias of those two cultures, a bias which underpins the notion of the 'mainstream'. So there may be an additional, cultural slant in what I have presented here as a general argument. Perhaps I should emigrate.

NOTES

1. From *Une Saison en Enfer* (A Season in Hell), 1873. The date is surprisingly early; Rimbaud was ahead of his time in this as much else.
2. Although the statement is usually attributed to the Peripatetics I have never yet found it in Aristotle. It seems to have entered the mainstream of European philosophy via Aquinas. Leibnitz's further qualification (*nisi intellectus ipse*: unless the intellect itself) is credited with opening the door to rationalism. As regards Beckett, the parrot in *Malone Dies* finds it impossible to complete the celebrated statement, thus articulating a form of nihilism.
3. Irene De Angelis, *The Japanese Effect in Contemporary Irish Poetry* (London: Palgrave Macmillan, 2012).
4. Patrick Crotty, ed., *The Penguin Book of Irish Poetry* (London: Penguin, 2010).
5. For a discussion see Donal Moriarty, *The Art of Brian Coffey* (Dublin: University College Dublin Press, 2000). See also Benjamin Keatinge and Aengus Woods, eds, *Other Edens: the Life and Work of Brian Coffey* (Dublin: Irish Academic Press, 2010).
6. Randolph Healy, *Green 532: selected poems 1983–2000* (Cambridge: Salt, 2002), p.34.
7. For a discussion of the issue see Geoffrey Squires, *My News for You: Irish Poetry 600–1200* (Bristol: Shearsman, 2015).
8. This can be seen as a curious reprise of the 'nativist/non-nativist' controversy in the interpretation of early Irish poetry. See James Carney, *Studies in Irish Literature and History* (Dublin: Dublin Institute for Advanced Studies, 1979).
9. For a longer example see Thomas McCarthy, *Merchant Prince* (London: Anvil, 2005).
10. From John Donne, *An Anatomy of the World* (1611).
11. *Sans Titre* (Untitled), 2013; *Paysages et Silences* (Landscapes and Silences), 2014; *Pierres Noyées* (Drowned Stones), 2015; all translated by Francois Heusbourg and published in bilingual editions by Editions Unes, Nice. A further volume is planned for 2016.

J.C.C. Mays

The Third Walker

Billy Mills's *Imaginary Gardens* was published by hardPressed poetry in 2012.[1] The text comprises one hundred untitled poems of varying length, in predominantly short lines, separately presented on every unnumbered page. The book-title echoes a famous phrase from Marianne Moore's poem *Poetry*, 'imaginary gardens with real toads in them', and the front cover contains a photograph of an unidentified stone-mullioned window, the inserted glass reflecting blue sky and cloud (part of Adare Castle, I am told.) The opening poem places you in the picture:

> these trees
> this grove
> this garden
>
> lost
> in morning
>
> the very edge
> of day
>
> an order
> sun imposes
> random
>
> these shrubs
> these beds
> this pathway
>
> stand & wonder
> why these walls
> these trees
> that very foxglove

Irish University Review 46.1 (2016): 48–62
DOI: 10.3366/iur.2016.0200
© Edinburgh University Press
www.euppublishing.com/journal/iur

wait now
spring
will come
again (p.1).

    The process of description is eidetic. Three groups of lines deliver vivid images of a garden at dawn and are followed by a fourth group that pivots, or hovers, between 'order' and 'random': perhaps a contradiction or paradox, or perhaps denoting the sun's impartiality or indifference, shining on everything without distinction. The description then begins over again, and again gives pause. What at first sight might read as third-person verbs resolve themselves as imperatives addressed to us, as readers, leaving the shrubs, beds, pathway simply noted and listed. We begin to wonder, perhaps, at their random particularity: why 'these' and not others? The final set of lines beginning 'wait now' reinforces the conundrum. Are they also addressed to us as an imperative or is 'wait' to be understood as a third-person verb, its subject being the various components of the garden? This time, both options appear to be open: the garden may be waiting, perhaps for interpretation, the imposition of meaning; or, we are being told to wait, for meaning to emerge or not, as the case may be. You read back over, puzzled and with greater attention to what may seem like obfuscation. The different emphasis imparted by the carefully positioned articles and demonstratives ('these, this, the, that') is certainly deliberate, as is the repetition of 'very' and the echoing and counterpointing of vowels and consonants ('these trees', 'the very edge | of day'). There could be a pun on 'mourning' or an allusion to Lorine Niedecker's 'very veery | on the fence', but where do these things lead? And why draw attention to a foxglove that flowers in June–July in order to introduce and close with thoughts of the return of spring – thoughts more usually associated with autumn than to 'the very edge' of summer (*vide* Shelley's 'Ode to the West Wind')?

    If such features catch your attention, you will become involved in what is happening. No page of text in this book will be entirely complete and the hundred pages overall enact a process like a film slowed down to its separate frames: even as they connect while they advance, each one retains a sense of separate omnidirectional possibilities at the time it is encountered. A complete story contained in one frame of a poem or a faster projection would provide different kinds of satisfaction but both would override the point. The poem on the second page adds details to the previous poem and further qualifies what we might usually take for granted; we get a statue and blue forget-me-nots but we learn that such things placed around us get buried under modern developments. The syntax is again ambivalent so that the words either celebrate what was nearing perfection or record only its loss; and, in such a state between light and darkness, a repeated 'as if' balances hope against the possibility that hope is unfounded. There will be change, but whether for good or ill is beyond our ken. The word 'utterly' describes the garden either buried under a geological process of drift even more completely than under a housing estate or preserved by the utterance that helped make nature appear paradisal in the first place. The statement of this truth in twenty-two short lines is alive with words and phrases that shift their meaning and function before our eyes. The alternate ways in which they can be read draw closer together as we ponder them and supply a hovering rhythm of forward motion. We are thereby more prepared when the third poem recuperates the previous elements, to present us with a question that is no less challenging, because we are not absolutely sure what 'it' is. The answer is an image:

> snail trail
> on the path
>
> a snail itself
> on the path
>
> curve
> in the sand (p.3).

Is the snail's curve in the sand of the drift that washes over the grass, or does sand make up the surface of the path? Does the curve the snail makes or embodies mirror a primordial truth about the way things happen, pursuing their own course rather than a linear development?

Such is the way a patient reader is encouraged to wind into Mills's poem as the pages turn, and this is evidently not a book for gentle skimmers. The situation clarifies as the details condense; 'the process needs | rhythm | needs time' (p.14), 'out of death | we grow | that which grows' (p.19). Earlier questions are answered in a way that leads to further, deeper questioning: for example, the dawn that might disorder what it illuminates in the opening poem is described at greater length in poem 27, but in a way that causes other meanings to expand and shift. Nouns and actions hanging weightless in participle constructions gradually discover a subject, at first the impersonal 'one' and 'we' and 'you' until this eventually becomes 'I' (p.33) and the pronouns become individual. By such means the shadow of a plot develops, and the reader is carried from Limerick to Dublin in the memory of the speaker where previous themes are mirrored, that is, enlarged and clarified. The return modulates into a conclusion of a poematic sort that brings the book to a close but leaves its subject open. This is not a Romantic construct that resolves a dialectic between reality and dream, present and past, in order to confront a transformed past in the future. It is a poem that insists upon presentness in the way Gertrude Stein does in her lecture on *Composition as Explanation*:

> Composition is the thing seen by every one living in the living they are doing, they are that composing of the composition that at the time they are living is the composition of the time in which they are living. It is that that makes living a thing they are doing. Nothing else is different, of that almost any one can be certain.[2]

If one reads the poem to wrap it up, to make sense of it, one could delude oneself by thinking one has reached a conclusion in poem 93:

> come near
> this glimpse
> of all we need
>
> nothing here
> stand in the garden
> say life is so
>
> & mean it strange
> to be here again
> awake in beauty.

But the poem hasn't gone a long way round just to deliver this: the end is as indeterminate as the beginning. The two poles are matched by opposites within the poem like images of man and nature, water and land, straight and curved, day and night; and their 'certain symmetry' (p.3) is the mainspring of the poem's trembling energy. Each separate poem opens new connections and fresh incongruities. If they ever came wholly together, the world of the poem would implode.

The corollary of Stein's claim – that only the present will unlock our proper relation to past and future – is that the life of Mills's book lies in patient attention to what meets our eyes on every succeeding page. 'Words flow out | & down | the page' as the page and the world flows (p.30); 'earth water fire & air || but mostly water' (p.99), from which human life emerged. Lines of text sometimes fall in thin columns, they are sometimes interrupted and become a dribble or are renewed with greater force, they sometimes divide or even disperse into mist, they sometimes become a downpour or freeze on windscreens. The flow or pace is controlled by single or double spaces between groups of lines, accentuated occasionally by single or multiple asterisks; and within lines by more devices, such as lines positioned above or below spaces, colons, brackets, a single word in quotes, a question mark (and not a single comma or full stop anywhere). The pace is equally controlled by meaning and grammar: how a line does or does not connect with a previous line. Puns sometimes set up collateral conjunctions and reverberations: just as frequently they wait to be discovered. As we read we might remember the images of lines 'curved resilient & worn' (p.78), following the snail's track and the sun's course. The method is so subtle that one notices the one unambiguous run-over – 'in-| effable' (p.56) – as one notices the question mark (p.100). At the heart of this process is the relation between words and music: the placement of words as determined by their grammatical meaning and the different relation established by their sounds. The relationship can emphasise, destabilize, and co-exist in a multitude of ways that make up snatches of harmony 'heard beyond | the ear's range' (p.90). One might therefore suppose the only conclusion can be pen-ultimate:

> it makes no sense a future
> walk beyond the bounds
> & see the things you wanted
> drifting who was & was not
> sleeping under pressure
> intense snatches heard the ear's
> range displayed silent &
> sweet as night enclosed these
> trees feel it makes no matter
> along this line weaving
> something unfinished yet (p.91).

* * *

Catherine Walsh's *Astonished Birds/Cara, Jane, Bob and James* was published simultaneously with *Imaginary Gardens* by hardPressed poetry. It likewise comprises a hundred unnumbered pages of text, but the page-size is larger and in a square format. Walsh took the photographs on both covers, and the view of a tended garden with mature trees below a picturesque hill might seem as well suited to *Imaginary Gardens*. The hill is easily recognizable as The Diamond in Letterfrack, at the edge of Connemara National Park; and the garden lies above the industrial school, notorious for the brutal neglect and sexual abuse of its pupils, that was closed amidst public outcry in 1974.

This is another garden with real toads in it. They are of a kind that warrants more urgent treatment, which in turn produces a very different poem. A cursory glance at the text communicates something before we even begin to read: the typeface is Arial, one that pushes out more boldly from its background than Mills's Times New Roman that lies wreathed among residual serifs. This is a book that is going to be more confrontational or, better say, more dramatic. Glancing more closely, the first two pages of text line up equally on the left-hand margins, but on the pages that follow the text moves in a three-phase progression towards the centre, beginning at different levels before returning to the margins again; indeed, at the turn on pages 4–5, the matching alignment takes the facing pages as an enlarged single area on which to work. It thereby mirrors the double title and anticipates the most obvious structural feature of the book: it is a diptych, a text folded over itself. My text-references number the parts continuously and the arithmetical asymmetry of the parts is deliberately unimportant: this is not that kind of poem. (And I might add the hundred pages of Mills's poem might easily have been 99 or 101: their concern is with millennia, not centuries.) Meanwhile, to take these preliminaries no further, a reader familiar with *Imaginary Gardens* will notice at once that, while the second book uses many of the same typographic means to communicate how to read the lines, these are fewer and simpler: the striking exploitation of the relation between sound and sense is replaced by other measures, to different effect. Fittingly, even the use made of the blurbs on the back covers is different. *Imaginary Gardens* quotes Carol Rumens's succinct review of Mills's *Lares/Manes: Collected Poems*, and both her review and the earlier book provide a background to the intense rumination worked through in the present instance. Walsh chooses to quote two shorter comments that emphasize what she engages with and attacks, and the second of them slyly prepares for the element of parody in the second half of her present poem.

The outline structure of *Astonished Birds* is clearly signalled and needs to be so because it is imposed on a rush of feeling that could easily become inchoate. Pages 1–7 form a kind of prologue that takes off from a supply-and-demand situation spiralling madly out of control: birds and fish feed on each other like critics feeding on poets and vice versa and are emblematic of a destructive way of life. Pages 8–15 continue with facing slabs of long lines (with a choric hiccup on 9) to be summarised at the head of 16 in two lines: '[to be sure I had not wasted my time here] | (end of OPTIC VERVE A COMMENTARY)'. The pages forcefully challenge what they oppose, almost as if it was alive and might at any moment speak back; they make clearer what is not than what is, and the point about this poem is that the unspoken, controlling forces are at the edge, squeezed out, skewed. Page 16 is as direct and in your face as plain statement can manage, and so *Astonished Birds* begins again, the title in caps, on page 17. As the pages advance, the text becomes more personal with references to work and children, the speaker acquires a gender and refers to Irish predecessors, and, as she becomes more contextualized, calms down. In subsequent facing pages (pp.22–23) the form even gains lyrical shape as she indulges in memories of other times and places. It is no surprise that page 24 begins again with the words 'Astonished birds' but from here the tone and subject settle and broaden further, with little or no distraction from disruptive forces that turn imagining on its head. Constraints relax and there is even room for a knockabout, happy fairy tale about fish free from birds (pp.27–29). Earlier complaint becomes elegant plaint, running smoothly down the pages, once a double stream and later wiggling, turning words about ('oh yeah?' p.39), having fun:

> intransigent
> aeratesia
> yr woes
> belittle you
>
> slightly
> bright (p.41).

From hereabouts on, with insouciance at first, she comes into her own and takes over the issue of control. The satire broadens to face down money, power and manipulation on equal terms. The last page of *Astonished Birds* begins 'we are not there yet' but ends with

> what feeds me can feed another honest paradox of my cloak;
> ní leath do bhrat ach mar is feidir leat an chontu. Nodding back at
> Brehon law; don't spread your cloak farther than you can fold it.
> (p.45)

The story of *Cara, Jane, Bob and James* begins after a gap on page 46 and is told mainly through the eyes of the four characters with frequent interjections concerning them and the course of their tale. They are wending their way back to their car at the end of a day out in Connemara, along a shoreline not unlike that around Letterfrack or perhaps further north. The narrator is only partly in control; the characters have a life of their own, sometimes going their own way, sometimes 'helped' to go differently. She tries out explanations and suitable descriptions (e.g. pp.52–53); she could be wrong or over-interpreting; jokes arise adding uncertain details, she tries on words for fit and there is genuine humour in her wild surmise. The narrative voice is more detached than in *Astonished Birds* but also more generous. The characters are trapped in their thoughts and to that extent victims – 'travelling by in | the slipstream' (p.73) – but the teller of their tale has a broader understanding of the constraints we all live under. They reach their car and begin the second phase of the journey home. In the largely unspoken action in the growing dark, Cara comes up in the estimation of Bob, who has emerged as the leader (driver); James too mounts in importance and is given the last words; Jane, so dominant at the beginning, ends up by feeling carsick and alienated (p.86). When they reach home, the story of their day out has only confirmed the ineptitude of their relationships (p.91); they are all 'just biding time' (94) while 'hardly wanting | to know' (p.100):

> extemporising on
> that notion of being
> state futures
> luminosities
> taste friendship
> realism life
> and other
> obstacles (p.100).

Nothing is easy about this book as a whole. I don't mean the way it is written: it says what it means precisely in every phrase and line. It is difficult because it is so exactly poised that we don't know, because the author seems not to know, the answer to the questions she poses: she can only show us how things might balance out in a poem. The anger in *Astonished Birds* is palpable, and the author does not hide the way it disturbs her. She is alienated by the exploitation of what should preserve and enhance life's opportunities. 'Life in the haze of doing' (p.10) sums it up. There are comforts in the past but they are only that, not solutions: behind the visitor's view of an East Sussex landscape lies the constraining world in which it was formed and is remembered: eighteenth-century enclosures and the shadow of Mrs Thatcher's government. The first part of the book traces a personal recovery and the second part acts on it with hardly a backward look; indeed, the aggressors in the main are seen as victims, exploited in their turn, and not just as pathetic but as genuinely funny. Irish poetry has always hidden its sharpest criticism under the mask of comedy – in our time, we have Aidan Carl Mathews and more extravagantly Paul Durcan – and the present instance is distinguished by its genuine sympathy for a sick society. The four characters involved are pathetic, but also simply a hoot. If you weren't laughing, you'd want to cry. That's a rare thing when it's part of a larger argument about poetry as a model of consumption in a market economy that is fast consuming what it feeds.

* * *

Mills's and Walsh's books, despite their merits, are sometimes resisted as the work of difficult poets writing for a narrow audience. The put-down is inappropriate – remember Pound's admonition in *Homage to Sextus Propertius* XII: 'A flat field for rushes, grapes grow on the slope' – but it is worth trying to understand the grounds of reluctance to accept. It could be simply a matter of product recognition. Poets of an experimental kind have been inclined to spend more time on their writing than on advertising, and larger bookshops are reluctant to stock books in non-standard sizes that don't tick all the boxes for computerised stock-handling, re-ordering, and payment. Book-length poems don't fit classroom-timetables either, and compromises made to accommodate the full range of student ability necessarily narrow the range of what can be assigned. Additionally, writers of this kind publish mainly in little magazines and small presses founded by themselves, and when they appear together it has most prominently been in anthologies bearing words in their titles like 'Other' and 'Alternative'. Such labels can suggest something secondary: second choice or *salon des refusés*; work by poets pushed out of the mainstream by their lesser ability, or shy of it, or because of a better-than-thou disposition. One can only respond that Irish poets appearing under such labels were never a group and, if they sometimes appear to be one, it is largely by default. They went separate ways from their beginnings, many of them only meeting personally at a conference in New Hampshire as late as 1996.[3] The connections established there have been friendly but loose and their books continue to be unpretentious and cheap. Their common project is the opposite of vanity publishing, the respect of others involved in making the same kind of poetry being always more important than fame and fortune.

The literary-history explanation boils down to the same thing and ends by putting the same poets on one shelf and keeping them off another. The establishment of New Writers Press in 1967 is an agreed-upon turning point. It was a time when the Irish economy was recovering and the country as a whole was beginning to look outward towards Europe. The publishing venture inspired a number of young writers with a sense of purpose they were glad to assume brought them close to James Joyce and Beckett, and such earlier overlooked writers as MacGreevy and Coffey were recovered. The New Writers' project continued actively in Dublin through the 1970s and subsequently evolved into the annual SoundEye Festival in Cork which looks to establish connections with like-minded writers in North America and the UK. The success of these two enterprises has certainly gained public recognition, and the work of Trevor Joyce, who played a central role in both of them, and Maurice Scully, who did something similar in publishing and organizing during the same period, has been recognized by their election to Aosdána, along with Michael Smith, co-founder of New Writers' Press. If this story is less happy than one might have hoped, it is because it hasn't changed anything else. Election to an august body by one's peers does honour to the cause one espouses, but the subventions that make lives easier for a few individuals come from a tax-paying public who are no wiser about the cause they subsidize. The exchequer pays out for the good reason that travelling poets spread good will round the world in a way that offends nobody: it is a happy and economical arrangement that smooths the way of understanding and commerce so that, in the end, we taxpayers benefit too. There can be no complaint about this and the side effect to be deplored is a cultural one. The image projected is necessarily the one that travels best and is most quickly recognized. Because the package is so convenient, even efficacious, it becomes the official shorthand history and best intentions have killed the thing they love. We can prevaricate and speculate whether the theorists are correct. Is the avant-garde by definition an urban event, inimical to a culture that has forever been and still is residually rural? Haven't all these experimental writers come from Dublin, or the suburbs of Dublin? And if this argument offends, don't other authorities tell us that setting up cultural barricades against repressive authority has lost all credibility in an age of 'liquid modernity' (Zygmunt Bauman)? In short, in a post-historical world of future trading where monetary value is subject to 'quantitative easing', poetry that hoped to change the world by new means is just deluding itself – as *passé* as 1960s sideburns and writing cheques.

The answer appears to me that poets who engage with their task as poeïsis occupy a position in society similar to people who run small hotels or make organic cheese. Such persons measure success not simply by numbers (footfall, output) but in doing a job in a way that is constantly under threat in a consumer society where the majority assumes low cost and convenience are the prime criteria. In 1987, the industrial school at Letterfrack whose haunted garden appears on the cover of *Astonished Birds* was reborn as a furniture-design and manufacturing college, and it kept up with the times to evolve into a college for line-managers trained to oversee quantity production in often distant locations able to draw on cheap or unskilled labour. The fortunes of literary culture on this island follow the same pattern, which is one that political commentators have also remarked. Following the outward-looking stirrings of open democratic politics in the North during the later 1960s, further progress was made at the cost of an inward-turn towards more rigid sectarian positions that consolidated during the 1990s. In the Republic, concern with national identity has certainly not lessened as we have come to think of ourselves vis-á-vis the global economy and, ironically, wider horizons are confronted with a backward turn to cultural roots. At the same time, we rejoice to discover that James Joyce the writer attracts more paying guests when he becomes a popular street festival; and we hope the diaspora – now an avant-society under post-conditions – will self-colonize during the year of 'The Gathering' (a tourism-led initiative to boost the economy: I write in the year 2013). The loop neatly secures the 'interstitial mode of production' (Hamid Naficy) in which Ireland strives to succeed, and it is for precisely this reason that alternatives are now most needed. The non-affiliation of those outside the process of commodification makes them not hobbyists but the most effective critics of that process, and their distance from the establishment opens a space for blunt truths to be spoken. A good example is Walsh's blistering attack on a well-known feminist poet who turned herself into the very thing she boasts of being liberated from:

> Formulaic creed, won't happen either; as with a surfeit of
> dinner or the set rota of limited menus. This fascination,
> predilection for discovery, discussion of, the room, or lack
> of it. The notion of time to oneself. After these years
> for that to still be a recurrent theme, hemmed in by so much
> industry. Of necessity, there will be more
> ... so quintessentially of its class/time/era. (p.10)

Nothing could be plainer. Culture as a medium of exchange is devalued by misapplication. Convenience food for the mind offers poor nourishment, and a prolonged diet of the same leads to overdependence and macular degeneration. We are not there yet: we should look up, take stock of where we are, and check where we should be.

* * *

A writer to put alongside the alternatives I have set out is Harry Clifton. His work is so widely circulated and well-known that there is no need to supply detailed commentary on either of his last two collections, *Secular Eden: Paris Notebooks 1994–2004* (2007) and *The Winter Sleep of Captain Lemass* (2012). They have been appreciatively reviewed on both sides of the Atlantic and have won prestigious prizes, while Clifton's appearances during the past three years as Ireland Professor of Poetry have been highly successful. He has been lauded by poets across the range of the Irish curriculum (Durcan, Heaney, Longley, Mahon, *et al.*) and welcomed as an addition to their company. At the same time, he ticks many of the boxes that make him look like an 'other' Irish poet. Widely travelled, he is on record as saying that he writes as 'a citizen of the English language who happens to have been born in Ireland' and 'a poet is a citizen of language rather than a place'. He publically resisted a suggestion that poetry should be used to promote Brand Ireland at the time of his appointment to the Ireland chair, and later described his hope for what he would have achieved at the end of his tenure as: 'To have said a few words on behalf of that side of Irish poetry that faces outwards, not inwards, that inhabits an open not a closed endlessly self-consolidating introversion.' The position had been bravely stated by poems like 'God in France' in *Secular Eden*, and the *Winter Sleep* volume, returning to home ground, explores and confirms its personal depth and historical resonance. Clifton's priorities – outward-looking and concerned with poetry as making – would indeed appear close to many writers in that movement in Irish writing that began in the 1960s. The cover of *Secular Eden* even happens to use the same illustration – André Kertész's *Chez Mondrian* – as Cork University Press's *Modernism and Ireland: The Poetry of the 1930s* (1995). This puts a spin on Fintan O'Toole's claim in *The Irish Times* that *Winter Sleep* is 'arguably the first great work of Irish poetic post-modernism' by accidentally suggesting Clifton's book completes a process which intervening writers did not. This is not the case: two different kinds of poetry are involved and the relation between what one can call traditional poetry and experimental poetry can be misunderstood. After all, Kavanagh visited Pound in Washington and Montague hung out with Spicer in San Francisco. Clifton's voice is notably independent and he has won respect from both sides. One can detect particular affiliations – Mahon is most often mentioned, sometimes MacNeice – but any connection is more a similarity shared with all writers of modern well-made poems. What distinguishes Clifton's writing from that of the 'others' is not his call for Irish poetry to be true to its deeper self – to put poetry before Irishness – but the way he understands poetry, which is, essentially, traditional.

There is nothing wrong with tradition: *au contraire*. Handing on skills ensures they are not lost and does not preclude returning to first principles to cope with new demands. However, it sometimes gets stuck in sentiment or suspicion – old ways are preferred because new ways are unfamiliar – and a good thing becomes an obstruction. The methods of Irish poetry are predominantly traditional and, while Clifton has been articulate about the need for an enlarged and independent world-view, he has been relatively silent over the way this should be expressed. Perhaps one could say there is a mismatch between the ideas, the attitudes, the perspective, and the continued use of the conventional short poem. In the same way, verses do not have to advance with an eye on set metres and patterned rhyme-schemes, and books of poems do not have to be made up from separate lyrics. Traditional means in poetry can be used with great skill and individuality, and Clifton has established a place in recent Irish poetry like that of James Fenton in the UK, which I intend as the highest compliment. But however intelligently and pleasingly the job is done, it seems to me not completely consonant with the general position he takes; or maybe it is all of a piece, in a quietist kind of way. Mills, Walsh and the like instead want out of the rut altogether because books made up of finished separate poems, however carefully balanced to make up a larger whole, can package and diminish experience. Alternative poets want to write poems in which no part is itself complete and where the means immerse us in a continuous present. The notion is not new: Browning's *The Ring and the Book* (1868–69) works on a similar principle, as does the film *Rashamon* (1950), but Ezra Pound attempted head-on to exorcise the cult of durable form in *Hugh Selwyn Mauberley* (1920) and succeeding poets like Charles Olson and Robert Duncan renewed the attempt in the 1940s. I repeat, open-form poems are not inherently superior to collections made of separate poems – see Shakespeare's *Sonnets*, or *Discrete Series* and *Primitive* by George Oppen (a poet discreetly acknowledged in *Imaginary Gardens* 69, 78) – but they make manifest the business of beginning over and over, acknowledging that the task of shaping cannot be final. Such a patient aesthetic has produced long works like Scully's *livelihood* (2004). By definition it distorts and excludes less of what it tries to embrace. The content of the writing stays alive to the exact extent that it is not consumable.

Imaginary Gardens is a good example of this alternative. Few pages are particularly quotable or memorable; they speak to the inner ear and very likely offer less immediate satisfaction than writing in more regular metres or stanza forms. Words are simple and repeated, but the recycling style is well suited to a planet moving towards catastrophe at a rate that can no longer be ignored. If one reckons, as some of us do, that language is in meltdown as English flattens to accommodate the pressures on it, the alternative is not to search for further resources to exploit but to use them more carefully, to turn the process of change back on itself. It would be foolish to deny that Ireland has nurtured more than its share of conventional good poets, many of whom are alive and writing today. The most prominent representatives write poems that give pleasure and familial reassurance at home and abroad. But a conservative or timid tradition is not preserving the past: it is getting lost in it, like First World War generals fighting tanks with horses, as Stein said,[4] or townspeople holding onto country things that were disappearing in their childhood. There is at the same time a way of putting the alternative argument that is worthy of attention. Making poems out of special moments is like putting animals in a zoo – successful to the extent that it makes nature extra-ordinary, a Saturday treat – but it is possible to write of things as they are without commodifying the result. It doesn't make you rich or famous unless by accident, as happened to Beckett after *Godot*. It abjures conventional falsehoods that make life seem easier, so it is realistic; but it is also idealistic and consequently abandoned to a minority. *Pace* Prime Minister Thatcher (aka TINA), There is an Alternative.

The other kind of poetry is not so rare in the world at large, and there is more of it in America than in conservative Britain, but, while the Irish contingent is relatively small, it makes a good showing. Its prolonged beginnings might have made it more durable and the lack of interest more sceptical: for example, set the work of Trevor Joyce alongside that of Charles Bernstein, or of Walsh alongside that of Lyn Hejinian (such comparisons have been made by others). Comparable Irish writing takes less for granted and communicates the reasons it is written the way that it is, which makes it more human. The same could be said of comparisons with English examples. Irish poets are rightly sceptical of the production-line poetry rebels who have emerged from Cambridge and London. These Irish poets have used opportunities, not been carried away by slogans, and there is a sobriety and humanity – and excitement – that imparts singular distinction. I do not know another poet who – working out of Olson and using what he has learned from French phenomenological writers and an intimate knowledge of classical Persian texts – explores ways of living in the present as Geoffrey Squires does. Nor do I know of another poet who has worked out her frustrations with Irish society, including literary society, as deftly as Walsh in *Astonished Birds*, and then shown such deep sympathy with its victims as in *Cara, Jane, Bob and James*, with such hilarious results. The processes of Mills's involving style are matched in Scully's, whose engaging manner takes a somewhat different direction, and of course several other names could be drawn into the discussion. These writers are distinguished by a commitment to address large topics in a way that keeps alive their relevance and importance. The *way* writers write – poets in particular because of what Edward Thomas called the 'instinct for finality' that bears more heavily on verse than on prose – is what they ultimately communicate. There are different ways. The less popular need not be dismissed because it is idealistic. Dostoevsky's Grand Inquisitor held that such 'other' is contrary to history, and that is exactly my point.

NOTES

1. Billy Mills, *Imaginary Gardens* (n.p.: hardPressed Poetry, 2012). All references below are given in parentheses.
2. *Gertrude Stein: Writings 1903–1932* (New York: The Library of America, 1999), p.523 (pp.521–29). The essay by R.M. Berry cited in endnote 4 below (pp.37–41 esp.) glosses the point made by Stein.
3. Recorded in *Assembling Alternatives: Reading Postmodern Poetries Transnationally* ed. by Romana Huk (Middletown, CN: Wesleyan University Press, 2003), where Trevor Joyce contributes a piece on 'Irish Terrain: Alternate Planes of Cleavage' on pp.156–68. Joyce was one of several Irish writers who were completely unknown to Huk when final arrangements for the conference were made in December 1995. (Only Mills, Scully, Walsh – and Paul Muldoon! – were on the list of Irish invitees at that time.)
4. Cited by R.M. Berry in a cogent discussion of the relation between formally experimental writing and its subaltern position in history: 'The Avant-Garde and the Question of Literature', in *Avant-post: The Avant-Garde under 'Post-' Conditions* ed. by Louis Armand (Prague: Litteraria Pragensia, 2006), pp.35–56.

Alex Davis

Paper & Place: The Poetry of Billy Mills

Among the 'previously uncollected work' gathered at the end of his *Lares/Manes: Collected Poems* (2009), the 'Proem' to 'Paper Places' reprises a key preoccupation of Billy Mills's poetry, and quietly broods on the antinomy that, to this point, it had appeared to present:

> for the past 35 years
> or so
> (you know)
> I've been thinking about
> how places are written
> how poems are found
> . . . .
> & first I thought
> they both exist
> (you know)
> close the book
> & the poem's still there
> humming with energy
> waiting impatiently
> turn your back:
> the room's still there
> the river's flowing
> the rocks erode[1]

The seeming disjunction of 'paper' and 'place', the incompatibility of poem (or language in general) and the extra-linguistic reality of rooms, rivers, and rocks, threads its way throughout Mills's previous collections, which constitute an extensive attempt (in Mills's words on the poetry of Maurice Scully) to 'explor[e] the process by which poetry might map a complex world'.[2] In 'Of Isostasy: Eastbourne', from *Properties of Stone* (1996), the isostatic equilibrium

Irish University Review 46.1 (2016): 63–74
DOI: 10.3366/iur.2016.0201
© Edinburgh University Press
www.euppublishing.com/journal/iur

or balance between the earth's crust and the mantle on which the former rests becomes an ambivalent image of art's relation to the world:

> gathering specimens
> of isostasy: Eastbourne
> by moonlight the artist
> contrives these effects

But such a pleasurable condition of 'rest' – as the verb 'contrives' implies – can encourage artistic quietude, 'a position comprising / complacency seen in / the absence of rhythm'. It ignores the fluidity that the geological concept of isostasy identifies – that everything flows, contrary to the quite human 'feeling' that

> the properties of stone

> are silence & stillness
> promoting the objects
> rigidity tending
> to stasis

The properties of language, no less than those of stone, have to be grasped as somehow corresponding to the processual nature of the world, as 'a stream of articulate / movements   language / a question of service' to that complex world.[3] The 'service' that poetry might render the world has the faint echo of that which Martin Heidegger famously found in the work of Friedrich Hölderlin, the latter holding that 'the formative and artistic need is a true service men render to nature'. However, the poetic dwelling Heidegger extrapolates from the German poet – in which, as Michael E. Zimmerman summarises, 'nature … first grants the "open" in which the mortal poet can bring forth the "saying" to ground the world needed for … the self-disclosure of the earth'[4] – is distinct from the kind of poetic 'mapping' Mills attributes to Scully's work and which arguably characterizes his own. While a great deal of Mills's poetic output could be assigned to the genre of ecopoetry, it is not governed by Heidegger's late belief that poetry's relationship to the environment is, in the words of Jonathan Bate, 'a presencing not a representation, a form of being not of mapping'.[5] While the first term of the title to Mills's collected poems, *Lares/Manes*, recalls Rainer Maria Rilke's interest in the Roman household gods (from as early as his 1897 collection *Offerings to the Lares*), Mills does not belong among the poets whom Bate, following Heidegger's reading of Rilke, invokes towards the close of his impassioned work of ecocriticism, *The Song of the Earth*:

> As the solidity of things is replaced by the evanescence of commodities, so the poets must stand in for the ancient Roman *lares*, those everyday gods who guarded hearth and home. On another level, as the realm of nature – the wilderness, the forest, that which is untouched by the human, the Being that is not set upon – has diminished almost to vanishing-point with the march of modernity, of technology and consumerism, so a refuge for nature, for the letting-be of Being, must be found in poetry.[6]

Both the notions of 'hearth and home' and 'the realm of nature' figure significantly in Mills's work, from his first collection, *Genesis and Home* (1985), to *Imaginary Gardens* (2012), and the Dublin and Connemara peregrinations of *Loop Walks* (2013). However, Bate's Heideggerian vocabulary, I believe, would invite from Mills the accusation of 'pseudo-religiosity' he levels at the work of Gary Snyder and Ted Hughes in his online essay 'Sustainable Poetry'. Here, Mills praises the 'phenomenological poetry' of Geoffrey Squires – in whose poetic sequences such as *Landscapes and Silences* (1996), *Littoral* (1999), and *Pastoral* (1999) the influence of Maurice Merleau-Ponty is clearly discernible – for its balanced exploration of the mutually enriching interaction of mind and world. But his judgement on Ric Caddel's 'Fantasia in the English Choral Tradition', from *Uncertain Time* (1990), is truer to the ecological thrust of his own poetry. Caddel's 'ecocentric poetry' shows humanity 'placed in the weave of things' – a comment Mills develops elsewhere in this same piece:

> If the role of philosophy is to inspire action, the role of poetry is to be in the world. Like the laws of physics, like mathematics, this poetry is descriptive, not proscriptive. It also accepts the sceptical view that full knowledge of the world cannot be attained through the medium of the senses. However, it sees this as a failure of the senses, not as an argument for the idealist position, and works towards the clearest possible approximation. Rather than saying that nothing is unless it is held in the mind of a human observer, it asserts that many things are that have never been perceived, and that for most things that are perceived, the perception is imperfect. This is a necessary part of the humility called for earlier. We are part of the weave of things, and our view inevitably depends on where we sit in that weave. That's all. Everything goes somewhere.[7]

The humble, even laconic, recognition that one exists within 'the weave of things' prompts, as its inevitable corollary, the belief that the function of poetry is to describe – however approximately or provisionally – our embeddedness in the material world. Hence, in this same essay, Mills's abjuration of the pathetic fallacy as a form of self-aggrandising domination of nature by means of the poetic troping of the environment in human terms. Yeats provides a memorable example of this kind of anthropomorphism in his proleptic 'elegy' for Lady Gregory, 'Coole and Ballylee, 1931', in which, standing forlornly in a 'copse of beeches' beneath a 'wintry sun' at Coole Park, the speaker declares: 'Nature's pulled her tragic buskin on / And all the rant's a mirror of my mood'.[8] Contrast this with the third of Mills's tributes to the late Caddel in *Three for Ric – from the Old Irish, roughly* (2004):

> news for you
> stag tongues
> winter snows
> summer's gone
>
> cold gale
> low sun
> short course
> tide's run
>
> cold's caught
> bird's wing
> ice time
> that's my song[9]

The poem frames the natural world with the human, the (dead) addressee of the first line balanced by the appearance of the speaker in the last. The intervening ten lines would appear to develop a conventional enough poetic fallacy – in which human grief at human mortality finds a chime in the wintry environment – that is broadly comparable to the manner in which in Yeats's poem an abject 'Nature' provides the 'mirror' to the persona's 'mood'. However, the demonstrative pronoun in the final line – '*that's* my song' – asks us to read the poem itself as enmeshed within the natural phenomena described, not as finding its reflection *in* them. The 'winter snows', the 'cold gale', the 'ice time' – these are not figures for the speaker's sorrow, but part of the 'weave' of literal 'things' among which the inferred event of the addressee's death and the poet's 'song' occur or 'sit', to employ Mills's term. The poem's minimalism does not preclude pathos, of course; but it is not achieved through stripping back to its bare essentials pastoral elegy's conjoining of nature's mourning to that of the poet's (as in the *Lament for Bion* or Milton's *Lycidas*), a convention that still hovers in the wings of Yeats's staging of 'Nature's buskin' in 'Coole and Ballylee, 1931'. Rather, the poem is indicative of Mills's resistance to a tendency he views as characterising much contemporary poetry, in which, in the words of 'Sustainable Poetry', 'the world exists to serve as a stage set for the enactment of human dramas, ... reflect[ing] the moods of ... the poet'. In such works, the world 'exists only when written'.

Mills's mistrust of the pathetic fallacy and, by extension, pastoral poetry because of its purported subjugation of objective nature by the human subject relates to his interest in the Irish tradition of *dinnshenchas*, a genre in which topography is intimately bound to, and explicable by, the stories or 'lore' associated with particular places. Mills is alluding to the verses of the medieval *Dinnshenchas Érenn* in his claim that a poem from Catherine Walsh's *Making Tents* 'links back to an old Irish idea of poetry as a *literal* mapping of the landscape'.[10] For Mills, 'landscape' is always prior to such poetic 'mapping'; in the words of a poem from *Tiny Pieces*:

> first
> the world
>
> next
> the word
>
> imperfect
> charting[11]

Tiny Pieces was originally issued as a chapbook by Randolph Healy's Wild Honey Press, and subsequently included as a section of *What is a Mountain?*, published under Mills and Walsh's hardPressed Poetry imprint in 2000. The version of *What is a Mountain?* collected in *Lares/ Manes* differs significantly from the original, in that it omits three combative prose sections, 'marginalia', 'the nature of nature', and 'sour notes', that, among other concerns, usefully expand on the 'imperfect / charting' explored in many of the poems in this volume and elsewhere in Mills's work. In 'the nature of nature', Mills refers to the 'early Irish nature poetry ... to be found in the *Metrical Dindshenchus*, or Lore of Places', contrasting Walsh's *Making Tents* with 'Pastoral: the landscape as possession'. The latter is a 'poetry of empire', which, drawing on an essay of David Lloyd, Mills identifies not only in the work of the planter-poet Edmund Spenser, but also in Patrick Kavanagh's and Seamus Heaney's pastoralism, 'the intellectual product of land-hungry descendants of the dispossessed peasant classes'.[12] By way of contrast, Mills advocates 'Poetry as map: not of boundaries or holdings, but of the lived landscape', which, in his view, Walsh's *Making Tents* provides in the literalism of its cataloguing of place-names:

> The river
> The field at the school
> The 2 acres
> Martin's
> Jordans'
> Dan's field[13]

In *What is a Mountain?* Mills, having quoted these lines, revisits his pugnacious comment that Walsh's is 'a Seamus Heaney poem with all the crap removed', inviting us to contrast Walsh's use of the *dinnshenchas* tradition with that of, for example, 'Anahorish', 'Toome', and 'Broagh' in Heaney's *Wintering Out* (one might also compare Mills on Spenser with Heaney's treatment of the English poet in 'Bog Oak', from the same collection).[14] For Mills, Walsh's poetry is a kind of 'periplum', his choice of term a conscious echo of Ezra Pound's employment of the Phoenician sailors' *periploi* – 'not as land looks on a map / but as sea bord seen by men sailing' (Canto LIX) – as an 'image', in Hugh Kenner's gloss, 'of successive discoveries breaking upon the consciousness'.[15] Mills's own poems are *periploi*, approximate 'chartings' by a consciousness that is always situated, never omniscient to the 'weave of things' in which it is braided. Thus, in the prose of 'marginalia', while Mills is conscious of '[t]he materiality of language', he is wary of the abandonment of 'lyric as an exploratory mode' as exemplified in Language writing, in which he perceives an abrogation of the 'authority' of the 'user' of a language in favour of a spurious celebration of its 'autonomy'.

In *Logical Fallacies* (2002/2004) 'place is / out there', and thus its description is always relative to the self that experiences it: 'place the word / here stripped /not there'.[16] In contrast to *The Cantos*, Mills's oeuvre often embraces, as in these lines, a pared-back minimalism that recalls that of Lorine Niedecker more than that of Pound's epic periplum. The titles to a number of Mills's publications flag the brevity of some, although by no means all, of their contents: *Tiny Pieces* (1998), *A Small Book of Songs* (1998), *A Small Book of Birds* (2004). Hence the aptness of the epigraph to *Properties of Stone*, from the Presocratic philosopher, Anaxagoras, whose surviving fragments present the view that the apparent heterogeneity of the universe as it currently exists should not blind us to the fact that, in its origins, it was basically homogenous; hence, his claim that: 'all other things have a portion of everything', bar the Mind). As a consequence, the tiniest conceivable particle is never simple, but always complex, always divisible; in the words of the fragment of Anaxagoras that Mills cites: 'Neither is there a smallest part of what is small, but there is always a smaller (for it is impossible that what is should cease to be).'[17] While one would do well to bear in mind Mills's wry self-disparagement in 'Paper Places' that, while he had set out to 'educate [him]self' with the 'usual stuff', including philosophy, 'recently / . . . / I've tried to keep it simple', Anaxagoras' emphasis on the complexity of the 'small' is reiterated in Mills's recurrent preoccupation with the careful observation of the 'tiny'; as, for example, in the injunction to both author and reader in *A Small Book of Birds*: 'swallows / (count them) / on the wires'.[18]

This imperative is indirectly obeyed in 'Reading Lorine Niedecker', from *Five Easy Pieces* (1997), which concludes with a quotation from a postscript to a letter of Charles Darwin to Asa Gray: '"I have been making / some little trifling observations / which have interested / and perplexed me / much."'[19] Darwin's self-deprecating words are as applicable to Mills's poetic 'observations' as to they are to Niedecker's; both possess an 'exploratory integrity', in Michael Palmer's judicious judgement on the American's work;[20] and 'integrity' is precisely the quality Mills has identified in the Irish poet to whom he is most deeply indebted, Brian Coffey.[21] For Mills this entails the acknowledgement of poetry's provisional quality, even, indeed, its relative unimportance – witness his allusion in this poem to Niedecker's citation, in her poem 'Darwin', of a passage from *On the Origin of Species*: 'Species are not / . . . / immutable',[22] which, in Mills's text, reads: 'the poem / (let us confess it) / is not immutable'. This belief also, one presumes, underlies Mills's admiration for another poet in the Objectivist nexus, George Oppen, who 'remind[s] us that there is a life outside, and more vital than, poetry', and whose thirty-year repudiation of poetic composition, consequent on his joining the Communist Party in the 1930s, Mills compares to Coffey's contemporaneous poetic hiatus in the decades prior to the publication of *Missouri Sequence* in 1962.[23]

In *What is a Mountain?* Mills attributes Coffey's poetic silence to domestic issues, such as those movingly documented in *Missouri Sequence*: 'children's lives / that fill my cares'. Yet Coffey's poem is itself proof that the homely has the capacity to 'turn' the poet 'to sudden starting words';[24] and, as noted above, throughout his

career Mills too draws inspiration from the *lares*, although he is
mindful too of the spirits of the dead, the *manes*, as in his reflections on
the genocide advocated in Spenser's *A View of the Present State
of Ireland* in *What is a Mountain?* and the bombing of Hiroshima in
Genesis and Home. *Imaginary Gardens* takes its title from Marianne
Moore's famous claim, in 'Poetry', that poets must be '"literalists
of the imagination"', and 'present / / for inspection, "imaginary
gardens with real toads in them"'.[25] Moore – herself, like Mills, a
poet with a penchant for the small and complex – is not just
demanding a poetry that engages with reality; she is equally
displaying, in Bonnie Costello's words, 'humility about the
imaginative appropriation of the object, and indicat[ing] a world
that language cannot capture'.[26] The meditation on the poetic
representation of the object-world in *Imaginary Gardens* is informed,
in the words of 'the nature of nature', by a similar 'humility in the face
of a world which *is*':

> out of nothing
> almost air perhaps
> these words come
> from mind
> an imperfect garden
>
> mud on the walls
> & our feet
> & in our hair
>
> to find
> elaborate
> sing[27]

The 'imperfect garden' of the poem, the product of a mind, conceived
(as in Anaxagoras, perhaps) as 'elaborat[ing]' or ordering the world,
recognises the object's stubborn alterity (Moore's toad) in the facticity
of that all-pervasive 'mud'. But such recognition is not an abrogation
of poetry, even if the poet shares Moore's belief that 'there are things
that are important beyond all this fiddle'.[28] The subtitle of Mills's most
recent volume, *Loop Walks*, is *Words for Voices*, the eight poems
constituting a powerful attempt to map words to landscape through
matching spoken poetic rhythm to that of the walks themselves (the
book includes detailed performance notes, a score by David Bremner,
and a recording of the entire work). As a piece of performance art,
Loop Walks is a sustained – and engrossing – *articulation* of the

reflection in 'Paper Places' that poem and locality are interconnected 'systems':

> each part in place
> to make the poem
> the place
> & they are
> what they are
> (you know)
> remove one part:
> everything changes[29]

Mills's print and online essays frequently return to the issues of rhythm and prosody in others' poetry. In conclusion, I wish to consider this aspect of poetic form in Mills's own work through a brief analysis of his practice as a translator.

In *5 Horace Traductions* Mills gives versions of five odes by the Roman poet. One meaning of 'traduction' offered in the *OED* is the act of traducing or defaming another – and one of these five traductions was first published in an anthology mischievously entitled, after Byron's *Childe Harold*, *Horace Whom I Hated So*.[30] Other more germane meanings of the word include to hand down from one generation to another, to convey from one place to another, and to translate (from Latin *tradere*: to pass over, to bequeath, to entrust). Mills conveys or transmits some of the sound of Horace's original opening to *Odes* 1.9 by choosing (in the spirit of a number of Pound's translations, including his version of *Odes* 3.30) English words close or identical in sound to the Latin, as in his rendering of

> *Vides ut alta stet niue candidum*
> *Soracte nec iam sustineant onus*
> *siluae laborantes, geluque*
> *flumina constiterint acuto?*

as:

> d'ya see how Soracte stands banked up
> with stiff shining snow nor the labouring
> trees sustain the onus
> the streams acutely frozen[31]

Mills's boldly colloquial opening even catches what one commentator describes as 'the lively and conversational' tone in the ode's initial lines.[32] But the real strength of Mills's translation is exhibited at its close, in his striking endeavour to approximate the extreme hyperbaton of the original. In an exuberant moment in 'What I Owe the Ancients', Nietzsche says of his 'delight' in Horace's odes: 'In certain languages what is achieved here cannot even be *desired*. The mosaic of words, in which every word radiates its strength as sound, as place, as concept, to the right and to the left and over the whole, this minimum in the range and number of its signs, the maximum which this attains in the energy of the signs – all this is Roman and, if I am to be believed, *noble par excellence.*'[33] Whatever the validity of Nietzsche's final clause, the 'mosaic of words' at the end of *Odes* 1.9 bears out the truth of the remainder of his remark:

> *nunc et latentis proditor intimo*
> *gratus puellae risus ab angulo*
>   *pignusque dereptum lacertis*
>   *aut digito male pertinaci*

A literal English translation gives us something like the following: 'Now the pleasing laughter of the girl in hiding comes from the secret corner, and a token is snatched from an arm or a coyly resisting finger.' Yet entirely missing in this rendition is the syntactical unveiling of the Latin, as, in David West's commentary, '[t]he three words *latentis proditor intimo* establish a triple mystery which is resolved in the next line', as the girl, betrayed by her laughter, is revealed, hidden in the corner.[34] Mills's characteristic minimalism and the nonlinear movement of his syntax manages to catch something of the movement of the Latin:

> & pleasing   revealing   laughter
> from corner show willing
>   a token resistance game
>   of hide & go seek

In *What is a Mountain?* Mills draws attention to Joseph P. Clancy's description, in *The Earliest Welsh Poetry*, of the '"radial" structure' of 'the nonlinear modes' of medieval Welsh poetry, adding: 'He could equally have been discussing the works of Maurice Scully, Catherine Walsh or Geoffrey Squires' – or, for that matter, the poetry of Mills himself.[35]

NOTES

1. Billy Mills, *Lares/Manes: Collected Poems* (Exeter: Shearsman, 2009), pp.304–5. A selection of the poems in this sequence of nineteen poems (excluding the 'Proem') was first published in *Seven Paper Places* (Green River: Longhouse, 2006).

2. Billy Mills, 'Other Places: 4 Irish Poets', in Harry Gilonis, ed., *For the Birds: Proceedings of the First Cork Conference on New and Experimental Irish Poetry* (Sutton: Mainstream Poetry/Dublin: hardPressed Poetry, 1998), p.27.

3. Mills, *Lares/Manes*, pp.138, 137, 139.

4. Michael E. Zimmerman, *Heidegger's Confrontation with Modernity: Technology, Politics, and Art* (Bloomington: Indiana University Press, 1990), p.125; Zimmerman quotes Hölderlin's letter of 4 June 1799 at ibid. See also the essays collected in Martin Heidegger, *Poetry, Language, Thought*, tr. Albert Hofstadter (New York: Harper and Row, 1971).

5. Jonathan Bate, *The Song of the Earth* (Cambridge, MA: Harvard University Press, 2000), p.262; Bate quotes the Zimmerman passage on p.258.

6. Bate, p.264.

7. Billy Mills, 'Sustainable Poetry', Elliptical Movements (4 Mar. 2013), https://ellipticalmovements.wordpress.com/2013/03/04/sustainable-poetry/, accessed 15 Aug. 2015. Bate – the author of a recent biography of Hughes – discusses Hughes at *Song of the Earth*, pp.27–9. For further discussion of Squires's phenomenological poetics, see my *A Broken Line: Denis Devlin and Irish Poetic Modernism* (Dublin: University College Dublin Press, 2000), pp.148–58.

8. W.B. Yeats, *The Poems*, ed. by Richard J. Finneran (2nd edn, New York: Scribner, 1997), p.248. Gregory survived Yeats's tribute until the following year.

9. Billy Mills, *Three For Ric* (n.p.: hardPressed Poetry, 2004), n. pag.

10. Mills, 'Other Places', p.34; emphasis mine.

11. Mills, *Lares/Manes*, p.221.

12. Billy Mills, *What is a Mountain?* (Monaleen: hardPressed Poetry, 2000), n. pag. The essay by Lloyd to which Mills refers is '"Pap for the Dispossessed": Seamus Heaney and the Poetics of Identity', in *Anomalous States: Irish Writing and the Post-Colonial Moment* (Dublin: Lilliput, 1993), pp.13–40; I discuss the relevance of this essay to Lloyd's own poetry – which is discussed by Mills in 'Other Places', pp.32–3 – in 'Modernist Topoi and Late-Modernist Practice: *With Special Reference to the Work of David Lloyd*', in Paige Reynolds, ed., *Modernist Afterlives in Irish Literature and Culture* (London: Anthem, forthcoming, 2016).

13. Catherine Walsh, *'idir eatortha' and 'making tents'* (London: Invisible Books, 1996), p.76; *Making Tents* was originally published by hardPressed Poetry in 1987.

14. See Mills, 'Other Places', p.34; cf. Heaney's reflections on the pastoral tradition in 'In the Country of Convention: English Pastoral Verse', in *Preoccupations: Selected Prose 1968–1978* (London: Faber, 1980), pp.173–80.

15. *The Cantos of Ezra Pound* (13th imp., New York: New Directions, 1995), p.324; Hugh Kenner, *The Poetry of Ezra Pound* (Norfolk, CT: New Directions, 1951), p.103.

16. Mills, *Lares/Manes*, p.282.

17. Such infinite regress resembles that of Zeno's Paradox, as the commentary to the edition from which Mills cites observes: see G. S. Kirk and J. E. Raven, *The Presocratic Philosophers: A Critical History with a Selection of Texts* (Cambridge: Cambridge University Press, 1957), p.378. The quotations above are from fragments 12 and 3, respectively.

18. *Lares/Manes*, pp.304, 302.

19. Ibid., p.95; cf. C. R. Darwin to Asa Gray, 8 June [1860], *Darwin Correspondence Project*, http://www.darwinproject.ac.uk/letter/entry-2825, accessed 15 Aug. 2015.

20. Quoted in Peter Quartermain, *Disjunctive Poetics: From Gertrude Stein and Louis Zukofsky to Susan Howe* (Cambridge: Cambridge University Press, 1992), p.2. The 'artisanal' nature of some of Mills's collections, such as the 'holograph' first edition of *Logical Fallacies* (2002) and the handwritten cover to *What is a Mountain?*, is

reminiscent of Niedecker's holograph collections, her 'homemade' and 'handmade' poems.

21. Billy Mills, 'Coffey/Dante/Pound: A Personal Encounter', in Benjamin Keatinge and Aengus Woods, eds, *Other Edens: The Life and Work of Brian Coffey* (Dublin: Irish Academic Press, 2010), p.164; see also Billy Mills, *Behind all Archetypes: On Brian Coffey* (London: Form Books, 1995).

22. Lorine Niedecker, *Collected Works*, ed. by Jenny Penberthy (Berkeley: University of California Press, 2002), p.295.

23. Mills, 'marginalia', in *What is a Mountain?*, n. pag.

24. Brian Coffey, *Selected Poems* (Dublin: New Writers' Press, 1971), p.33.

25. Marianne Moore, *Complete Poems* (rev. edn, 1981; London: Faber, 1984), p.267.

26. Bonnie Costello, *Shifting Ground: Reinventing Landscape in Modern American Poetry* (Cambridge, MA: Harvard University Press, 2003), p.87.

27. Billy Mills, *Imaginary Gardens* (n.p.: hardPressed Poetry, 2012), n. pag.

28. Moore, *Complete Poems*, p.266.

29. Mills, *Lares/Manes*, p.305.

30. See Harry Gilonis, ed., *Horace Whom I Hated So* (London: Five Eyes of Wiwaxia, 1992).

31. Billy Mills, *5 Horace Traductions* (London: Levraut de Poche, 1997), n. pag.

32. *Horace: Odes Book I*, ed. Roland Mayer (Cambridge: Cambridge University Press, 2012), p.109.

33. Friedrich Nietzsche, *Twilight of the Idols*, transl. by Duncan Large (Oxford: Oxford University Press, 1998), p.76. For a modern appraisal, see R.G.M. Nisbet, 'The Word Order in Horace's *Odes*', in Michèle Lowrie, ed., *Horace: 'Odes' and 'Epodes'* (Oxford: Oxford University Press, 2009), pp.378–400.

34. *Horace Odes I: Carpe Diem: Text, Translation, and Commentary*, ed. by David West (Oxford: Oxford University Press, 1995), p.45.

35. Mills, 'the nature of nature', in *What is a Mountain?*, n. pag.

Claire Bracken

Nomadic Ethics: Gender and Class in Catherine Walsh's *City West*

A section of Catherine Walsh's long poem *Optic Verve* features a wandering character, searching through the bins of a Tallaght housing estate in Dublin:

> he is looking
> for food examining rubbish
> with delicate sniffing discarding
> trekking many roads / similar junctions[1]

The subject here is a body on the move, 'looking', finding, 'sniffing', and 'discarding', searching for survival in his 'trekking' of 'many roads'.[2] While the absence of commas or grammatical markings enable a fluidity that matches the subject's own movement, at the same time the use of the line break mark between 'roads' and 'similar junctions' highlights a break or pause, a stopping of his tracks in a homogenous terrain ('similar') of seeming choices that are, inevitably, all the same. The wandering character – searching for food and without shelter – functions as an embodiment of the abject poverties of the post-Tiger era (and, indeed, of the inequities of the Tiger period itself), marginally placed as he is within this late capitalist milieu of 'similar junctions', a 'world' where 'terribly intact box-like parameters exist', and of 'quick commodification arrogance attempting dominance'.[3]

Indeed, one of the main targets of *Optic Verve* is the narrative of neo-liberal progress so central to Ireland's twenty-first century political economies, evident for example in the collection's critique of the Fatima Mansions regeneration project. This project, which ran from 2003 to 2010 – thus spanning the Celtic and early post-Tiger years – saw the demolishing of an economically and socially disadvantaged inner city Dublin housing complex, followed by its redevelopment. In an extended prose section of *Optic Verve*, a speaker questions the motivations guiding the regeneration project, noting: 'If there were no Luas line nearing completion (or bankruptcy) would anyone with

Irish University Review 46.1 (2016): 75–88
DOI: 10.3366/iur.2016.0202
© Edinburgh University Press
www.euppublishing.com/journal/iur

access to power give a damn?'.[4] There is also a personal note embedded in the voice throughout, as Walsh herself grew up in Rialto, close to the Fatima Mansions. The piece concludes with a (mournful) meditation on loss, as the figure of a wanderer once again appears:

> Winter. About a year ago, the junk-addicted son of a widowed flat-holder in Fatima died twisted up, wrapped in an overcoat, huddled on the doorstep of his recently deceased mother's home. Dublin City Corporation (that same one that so publicly bestows titles and accolades on the strategically needed deserving) did not recognize him as a tenant so he was locked out. Alliances. He had been living there all his life. Home.[5]

Unlike the homeless figure 'trekking the roads', this man is frozen in situ, 'locked out' of his 'Home', dying tragically on its doorstep. Indeed, if the movement of the subject in the first example is partly signalled through an absence of grammatical boundaries, this character is inflected with containment through the technicalities of the prose style. A similar moving subject – he cannot access the resting place of home, and is moved into the extreme stasis of death itself.

What these examples from *Optic Verve* powerfully enact is an exposure of the hypocrisies of Ireland's neo-liberal politics, with its aggressive exclusions of persons and communities from conceptualizations of what constitutes the nation/home. In both, the idea of movement is figured in quite complicated terms. These figures are moving bodies that are intensely managed and restrained, as enforced movement functions simultaneously as containment: a restricted form of nomadism, an affixed journeying. It is this form of affixed journeying that I will explore in this essay, looking specifically at the way nomadism is engaged in *City West* (first published in 2000), Walsh's collection previous to *Optic Verve*. If the later collection takes critical stock of some of the effects and residues of Celtic Tiger excess and their continuation into the post-Tiger era, *City West* traces an immediacy of living in Tiger postmodernity, harnessing a nomadic paradigm as an ethical navigational model through the environs of late capitalism.[6] Traced across Walsh's oeuvre are nomadic images, with journeying a key aspect of her writing, a restless poetics that does not stay still. As I have argued elsewhere, in analyses of *Idir Eathortha and Making Tents* and *Pitch* respectively, Walsh's poetry's restlessness, its being on the move – physical, psychic, virtual, textual – enables major interventions into the paradigmatic structures of both Irish Studies and Irish feminist criticism.[7] This essay will focus on a different type of intervention, specifically analyzing the critiques of late capitalist Celtic Tiger Ireland in the collection *City West*, a book that engages the concept of movement itself in all its complex possibilities and restrictions, freedoms, and limitations, developing a nomadic ethics that treats seriously the intersecting relations of gender and class in twenty-first century Irish culture.[8]

City West is invested in movement through embedded locations, travelling swiftly through space(s), harnessing the energy and speed indicative of the Tiger period. Throughout, the collection figures a nomadic self that also takes time for moments of rest. An analysis of the potentialities of affixed movement constitutes the first section of this essay, which analyzes the text's experimental engagement with configurations of visceral embodied experiences, fragmented and dispersed forms of self, and temporally creative disjunctions and non-linearities. The argument is that in this drawing of emplaced nomadism, *City West* engages theoretical possibilities for living through and with postmodernity, with the text establishing the potentialities of swift and creative movements that are co-joined with forms of stasis. Thus, while nomadic movement is figured as providing creative navigations, immobility is shown to convey comforting solace and much needed rest to speakers caught up in the disorientating whirlwind speeds of late capitalist change and modern 'progress', 'these disassembled and dissembling times'.[9]

However, this is not to suggest the text presents a utopian imagining of an emplaced nomadic position. As the opening examples from *Optic Verve* demonstrate, being moved and stopped are integral experiences of the restrictive containments and managements of late capitalism. In the second part of this essay, I explore representations of working-class spaces in *City West*. The book engenders what Eric Falci has termed 'pointed critiques of capitalism in Ireland' (p.197),[10] calling into question neo-liberal ideologies of progression, in particular the placing of working-class communities on the rhetorical margins of Tiger self-congratulatory discourses concerning economic success. The ways in which working-class communities, and working-class mothers in particular, are constructed and othered as 'threat' and 'hindrance', as well as rendered invisible and inconsequential in the late capitalist eye, are subtly highlighted throughout. *City West* figures such ideological markings in terms of mobilities that disorient, forcibly move, and exhaust in Tiger Ireland, in addition to functioning as oppressive containments of certain bodies and lives. Enmeshed in the sexual and class politics of the time period, stasis is a feature of these classed spaces and bodies, as intensely managed and contained sites.

While Walsh's nomadic journeying selves reveal the ways in which bodies are both *moved* and *contained* within and by such discourses, as they move and are moved through the terrain of Celtic Tiger Ireland, at the very same time *City West* also harnesses the liveable potentialities of emplaced nomadism (as explored in the first section of this essay). Infusing the body's fixities and moving emplacements with a mobility of becoming, of potential, the work provides some creative negotiation to the management of classed and gendered subjectivities in late capitalism. Constructions of selfhood are marked by both restrictive containment *and* a creative non-linear mobility that eschew progressive forward movement with a nomadic journeying that encompasses road-blocks, resting sites, and cyclical passages. In this way, the book enables serious critical reflection on the problematic ideologies that shape and govern the material realities of working class women's lives, as well as opening up moments of possibility from such restrictive conditionings.

Walsh's collection thus articulates a complex and nuanced configuration of affixed nomadism, with the dynamics of mobility and immobility both playing a part, integral components of affective selves, moving in, around, with, and through embodied forms of emplacement. Representing the restrictions and creative possibilities of living in Irish postmodernity, evident here is a configurative investment in bodies living (and moving) with, through, and in their socio-cultural environment. In this respect, the collection demonstrates what critic John Goodby terms (referring to the work of Geoffrey Squires) a 'poetics of perception', with a 'self immersed in its environment',[11] signalling the ability of experimental poetry to be deeply and ethically embedded in its socio-cultural times. The question of ethics and experimental poetry has been addressed by Matthew G. Jenkins in his book *Poetic Obligation*, where he counters ideas in the 'poetry world' that experimental poetry has 'nothing to say about how human beings might live better together', making the case for the 'centrality of experimental poetic form to new ways of thinking about ethics'.[12] What I am suggesting here is a specific exploration of such a claim, arguing that Catherine Walsh's *City West* configures an ethics that generates a complex nomadic navigational paradigm for thinking about gender and class in late capitalist Ireland. As Rosi Braidotti notes: 'What nomadic ethics stands for ... is a regrounding of the subject in a materially embedded sense of responsibility and ethical accountability for the environments s/he inhabits'.[13] Walsh's collection functions as just such an ethical nomadic subject, taking on accountability for the routes and avenues of its cultural milieu, staking critiques, as well as generating new pathways and lines of future journeying.

CATHERINE WALSH'S *CITY WEST*: NOMADIC FUTURES
AND NON-LINEAR PATHS

City West opens with a quotation from Doris Lessing's 1962 novel
The Golden Notebook:

> - the physical quality of life, that's
> living, and not the analysis
> afterwards or the moments of
> discord or premonition - (p.9)

In his excellent book *Continuity and Change in Irish Poetry*, Eric Falci
identifies Walsh's use of Lessing's lines as epigraph, noting the various
ways the collection reflects on life, subjective perception, and the social
environment.[14] The choice of quotation from *The Golden Notebook*
illustrates Walsh's interest in the immediacy of 'living', the 'physical
quality of life', substantiated by a criticism of the meditations of
before/after, which ultimately operate to separate and divide 'living'
into a linear arrangement. This critique is articulated in the structure of
the lines themselves, whereby 'afterwards' is placed on the previous
line to 'premonition', a separating out which is precisely 'not' the way
to live. *City West* provides its own poetic configuration of 'living' that
enables a fluidity of existence that resists progression and linear time
and functions as a social commentary and ethical critique of gender
and class in the Tiger era. In this respect, Doris Lessing's opening
quote becomes doubly apt, as *The Golden Notebook* effectively
interweaves feminist-socialist perspectives, thus marking both the
collection's interest in fluid modes of 'living' and the exploration of
lived social realities.

Michael S. Begnal notes, 'Walsh typically works in these large, open
forms instead of writing the self-contained lyric poem.'[15] In all of her
published books, she experimentally engages with this form of verse,
replacing self-standing poems with poetic fragments and
monologues.[16] Multiplicity and change characterize Walsh's writing,
as her poetry figures a continual variety of different speaking voices
and contextual locations, all the while favouring the opened use of the
entire poetic page to structured stanza form. Walsh's rejection of the
lyric form can be read as a rejection of the 'I', the subject and the one.
For Walsh, the poetic voice is multiple, never singular,[17] as the work
'endeavor[s] to record the vicissitudes and disjunctions of daily
experience, personal memory, and social life'.[18] *City West* is all about
life and living. Motifs of the breath pervade the collection:

> here now actually present
> doing seeing hearing sometimes
>   even understanding breathing days (p.21)

The present of actuality ('actually') in this text is multiply infused, rhizomatically and virtually directed in a variety of routes, as the reader is taken on a road-trip journey to a number of places and spaces, past and present: housing estates, gardens, circling motorways, and rural landscapes. Moreover, it articulates an insistent materiality, a force field of energy that enfolds within it an expansive array of life forms: human, animal, organic, technological, molecular: 'sigh light displacement of what / air humidity infinitesmal / minute particles mites' (p.71). In this respect, we can read *City West* as an instance of Braidotti's interpretation of *zoe*, a life force that exceeds and envelops the human in life's materialities: 'Zoe stands for the mindless vitality of Life carrying on independently, regardless of rational control'.[19]

Thus, *City West* moves away from a subject-based lyrical mode, and instead presents the self as an embodied nomad traversing its poetic spatial planes. Falci perceptively notes Walsh's use of the gerund in 'City', the first of the collection's three sections, as a way of 'encapsulating (at a tangent) experience'.[20] Indeed, throughout the first section of *City West* Walsh engages the present continuous tense to signal a body in motion:

> readying steadying giving taking
> loving making breaking coming in going out
> spending whiling listening playing
> tuning tiptoeing crossing   shh sleeping
>
> knowing they're knowing nothing
>
> enjoying this
> prolonged ride
> on the current   breezy day (p.17)

The image here is a moving self being blown by the 'current' of passing time in embodied and continuous connections of 'doing', a 'prolonged ride / on the current' of a 'breezy day', all the while 'loving', 'making', 'breaking', 'coming in', and 'going out'. The impersonal use of the continuous tense facilitates such a process, as it is not pinned down to a linguistic subject or a specific temporality, always instead being positioned in the impersonal terms of the event of becoming-with. The self passes through and within the territories of a deterritorialized landscape, all the while embedded in the materialities of life:

> walking home midnight through / over the
> Islandbridge gate
>   cycling Sandymount breezed (p.21)

Passing through is the nomadic, always on-the-move, condition figured in the 'City' section of *City West*. Drawing on the language of Deleuze, this can be located as a process of becoming,[21] as Walsh's bodies are in-between states: 'readying steadying giving taking' (p.17). The subject is dissolved in such a vitalist materialist analysis, and notions of individuality and structured coherence are consistently demobilized.

What then of the 'I'? Is there any space for selfhood in Walsh's collection? The second section of *City West*, 'Tangency', charts its very possibility through images of stop and rest. Throughout, movement is always inflected with immobility, as fluidities are tempered here, one example of which is the frequent usage of the words: 'point' and 'jot'. While Falci suggests that this section explores the volatile effects of the 'incessant movement' established in the first,[22] I would suggest that it, in fact, stabilizes ongoing movement. As noted in one poetic piece: 'why should stopping / not involve another part / of due process' (p.40). Nomads need their moments of rest and stop, these are part of the processes of journeying. The multiple territories or locations in the text function as 'resting places', as 'stop as pause' (p.40). It is not that there cannot be fixed points, but rather that these points are temporary, actualities which are always dynamically disassembled in the spirit of futuristic change. Thus, moments of becoming can encompass that of Being. The 'I', only used three times in the first section 'City' (two of which take the unstable question form -'am I?' (p.24), 'do I mean?' (p.22)) is increasingly used in 'Tangency' to signal the possibilities for self-definition in nomadic wandering. As one speaker notes: 'i i   more / ing' (p.50) – signalling an ability to voice the self. The use of the lowercase is important, as it highlights a mode of being that is a vital *part* of surrounding life – of *zoe* – never its overlord. This moving 'i' is then followed by 'more" 'ing', more processes of becoming and change: 'always / shifting moving on / going / over' (p.51).

It is in the final section of the work, 'Plane', that Walsh engages most incisively with the affective experience of nomadic wandering. Its title can be read spatially, the plane upon and through which such existence can occur. Falci identifies how 'though it putatively takes place in Dublin like previous sections', it also 'superimposes the west of Ireland onto its chartings of the capital'.[23] The text provides numerous fleeting glimpses of rural and urban landscapes – the modern City and the traditional West of its title[24] – operating by way of a motion of embodied peripheral vision as the nomadic self hurtles through space. Moreover, this space, this 'plane', encompasses not just geographical multiplicity, but non-linear temporality:

Robert Emmet hanged there
start   on the way to jeans shop (p.60)

The poetic fragment showcases the process of moving temporally through space ('on the way'). Robert Emmet's execution took place on Thomas Street in Dublin, and the speaker returns to this temporal location on her nomadic journey. The past functions here in non-linear terms, it is a resting place 'on the way to' another temporary stop: 'the jeans shop' of the present space. Moreover, throughout this section, the process of movement, the nomadic condition of journeying, is figured as a time that moves 'back and forth' (p.66), thus connecting it with Deleuze's description of the 'essence of a becoming to move in both directions at once'.[25] The effect of this is to place side by side the political imaginaries of the Irish past with the consumerist and commercialized economies of the late capitalist Tiger period, disrupting (neo-liberal) narratives of successive progression.

Thus, while the first section of the collection repeatedly draws on verbs of the continuous tense, the second displays an interest in 'rest' and 'pause', the final part is concerned with temporal configurations of the nomadic self. However, this does not imply linear development. All three elements pervade the three sections. The nomadic self, as articulated and configured in Walsh's *City West*, is a futuristic one, 'circulatory thought deemed consequential', and the many images of the circle (cycling, ring roads, roundabouts) scattered throughout *City West* operate to make clear its resistance to linearity. Nomadic wandering, or passing through, is concerned with the circle because it constitutes an eternal return. What returns, again and again, is the process of wandering, the becoming condition of change. To again engage again with a Deleuzean term (one which he reworks from Nietzsche), it is an eternal return of difference. Difference is what repeats in *City West*: 'missing / the point of missing the / point of missing / the point is not repetitive' (p.51). These lines bring together the two key elements of living for Walsh's nomadic self – with 'missing' we are once again in the continuous tense and a state of tantalizing and evasive becoming, while the 'point' infers the necessary moments of self-definition and rest. Both are repeated in different ways over the four lines, which conclude (crucially) with the phrase 'is not repetitive'. '[T]he point' 'is not repetitive' because we arrive at different points every time, the becoming nomadic process marking even the familiar unfamiliar, uncannily shrouded in 'déjà vu' (p.72).

ETHICAL EXPERIMENTS: GENDER AND CLASS IN *CITY WEST*
However, Walsh's collection does not simply allow for a wholesale positive embrace of the possibilities of this drawing of emplaced nomadism, with aspects of the paradigm itself shown to be an intricate part of the workings of Ireland's neo-liberal political economies. As Braidotti notes, 'advanced capitalism is the great nomad par excellence

in that it is propelled by the mobility of goods, data, and finances for the sake of profit and commodification'.[26] Ultimately, there is an ethical impulse to Walsh's configurations of this nomadic self that pulls in two directions simultaneously, with one concerned with how certain classed and gendered bodies are moved and restrictively emplaced and the other imagining liveability for these same bodies in a late capitalist Celtic Tiger Ireland, an epicentre of industry and wealth. Rather than look towards this centre, Walsh's poetry envisions its 'decentralized' (p.40) peripheries, Dublin housing estates on the outskirts of the city:

> wide sweeps housing on roads leading round
> housing cul de sacs closing encircling roads
> one or two towards motorway main
> roads roads bearing incessant
> weight (p.38)

The image here of the 'closing encircling roads' figures a stifling and suffocating space – cul de sacs with their closed endings and only 'one or two' allowing escape towards 'motorways'. Nomadic journeying here is revealed in its restrictiveness, as the circle functions as a movement going nowhere, an eternal return of restrictive containment. This implies a condition of moving entrapment that is reiterated at a number of different points in the collection:

> strangulating
>   tying avidly
> over   any citizen   (p.16)

The strangulation of the 'citizen' can be linked to motifs of breathing difficulties peppered throughout. At one point a speaker says: 'wheeze last / cough / wheeze today / activity' (p.13), while the suffocating nature of encircling is restated in panoptic terms:

> watching helicopters circling
> small estates sprawling
> Dublin flickering
>   (damaged
> not forgotten   (p.31)

These 'small estates' are not the celebrated spaces of Celtic Tiger Ireland, but places on the margins, moved along and controlled by the currents of neo-liberal control. But as Walsh thoughtfully reminds us, they are 'not forgotten' either, a phrase that can be read in two ways: on the one hand, as the collection's ethical attempt to figure snapshots and glimpses of these lived realities; while on the other referring to the more insidious ways in which underprivileged and working-class urban areas became increasingly constructed as sites of anxiety in the neo-liberal imaginary of the Tiger era (the gangs, the guns), spaces of supposed potential threat requiring ongoing containment and intense surveillance.

Walsh's social critique in *City West* is also directed towards gendered concerns. Figurations of motherhood are the most dominant and repeated image in the collection, specifically mothers in the marginalized housing estates of urban Dublin: 'baby in cot from nap in / morning / mother hearing sirens' (p.43). Embodied maternal subjectivity is figured in the text, with a number of fragments featuring pregnant women's voices: 'yes. for me. overdue. she says. / well. waiting. / getting' (p.15). Images of labour and pregnancy articulate the difficulties of liveability for some people in the Tiger era, with breathing difficulties again signified: 'one / day / long / tight / breath pushing' (p.14). Images of containment and restriction also continue to predominate:

> [over the road
> (she's saying she can't go
>   home sitting
>   radio
>
> (going   pram to shops
>
> (home
>
> [radio (p.17)

Line placement is crucial here. '[S]he can't go' signals an intense restriction of mobility, which the 'home sitting' figures all the more insistently. This is not a rejuvenating rest or pause, but a contained management, powerfully signalled in the negative use of the pronoun 'she', as her voice ('she is saying') becomes marked by inability ('she can't go'). Movement, when it occurs, is repetitive in its sameness – '(going pram to shops (home ' and the twice mention of the 'radio' reinstates the collection's interest in surveillance, control, and not being 'forgotten'.

Popular discourses about gender and class in the Tiger era focused insistently on the figure of the single mother. Like the gangs and the guns, this classed gendered body was marked with intense anxiety, as politicians wrangled over her welfare benefits. During the 1997

General Election, the leader of the Progressive Democrat party Mary Harney called for 'allowances for single mothers to be redirected to encourage them to stay at home with their own parents',[27] contributing to a conservative cultural and political discourse that questioned the 'generous' nature of social welfare benefits. Harney's position – essentially that single mother's benefits should be cut – generated significant media debate in the lead-up to the election, debates that took place over the bodies of some of the most disadvantaged women in early Tiger Irish society. Similarly, journalist Kevin Myers, in an infamous *Irish Times* column in 2005 generated a media furor and public debate when he wrote about 'MOBs' – 'Mothers of Bastards' (2005), a diatribe on single working-class mothers.[28] The media obsession over the single mother and her welfare benefits can be read into Walsh's repetitive use of the word 'radio' in the above piece. Infiltrating her home, her private space, the public discourses of the Tiger period position the classed mother as a contained figure, an intensely managed site. Walsh's formal use of the open-ended parenthesis in the section is significant in this respect, signifying the ongoing nature of containment.

However, parenthetical openness, in its refusal to finally close down and delimit, also establishes possibility, as Walsh's use of the blank page enables a configuration of an undetermined futurity in contained space. While *City West* highlights the way classed bodies are restrictively moved by neo-liberal forces of the Tiger period, one of its impulses is also to explore how emplaced forms of mobility can provide liveability for contained bodies in contemporary Irish postmodernity, particularly women's bodies marked as working class.

watching some one walking a
way down the road buggy pushing
along walking some one a
way down the road buggy pushing
along some one walking a way
down the road buggy pushing along
some one watching some one walking a
way down the road buggy pushing along
-with these problems in mind
this book was initiated-   (p.59)

Evident in this piece are the three elements of nomadic selfhood identified in the first section of this essay – movement (the 'ing' of the continuous tense), rest and self-definition (the 'some one'), and repetitive difference (each line repeats, but differently every time). The ethical possibilities of the nomadic configuration are also made evident here. 'Pram to shops / home' is invigorated with a process of 'buggy pushing' that is all about movement and change – the 'one' that is walking is in different syntactical arrangements in each line. Moreover, the panoptical gaze that attempts to fix the 'one' that is the buggy-pushing mother in the opening line is inscribed into the process of becoming itself, thus refused its supposed transcendental and governing power: 'some one watching some one walking a'. Thus, what is evident in this piece is a nomadic becoming space that provides the mother-figure with some release from the containments, curtailments, and anxieties of public discourse in the Tiger period. As the speaker so astutely notes, 'it was with these problems in mind / this book was initiated'. This is not a leap of utopian glee, but rather a mechanism that instills creative possibility within and alongside spaces of disorientation and restriction.

Walsh's experimental poetics deliberately dissolve coherent and fixed categories of the 'I', her work challenges identity politics in these terms. In an interview I conducted with her thirteen years ago in 2002, she expressed her concerns with feminist ideologies which seek to fix women's experiences and lives in predetermined categories, noting that this serves only to erase the complexities and varieties of female experience.[29] She particularly emphasizes this as a danger in terms of class difference. At the time Walsh was writing *City West*, when living in Tallaght, Dublin in the mid nineteen-nineties, women were attending university-directed writing classes, at least partially Arts Council funded. While the aim was female empowerment through creative endeavor and education, these women expressed their frustrations with those classes. Walsh saw this as a gap between the limits of pedagogical expectation, the understanding of the role of facilitators, and the women's own ability to access or deliver the material. There was a hiatus between the identity politics of the women's writing course and the lived realities and experiences of the women students attending, a hiatus based on an inability to properly register material differences existing between women.[30] In a more recent 2015 email conversation, Walsh crucially comments that 'there was no real top-down investment in ensuring quality outcomes or enabling other models', something which she saw as 'a series of missed opportunities and lack of expectations on the part of the various funders/organising bodies'.[31] The point that Walsh is making in these commentaries is not an unfamiliar one: the calling of liberal feminism to task for its class blindness, and the privileging of one particular standpoint as constitutive of the issues of gender politics. I bring it in here because it helps to shed light on the feminist-ethics of *City West*: the non-identity politics of the nomadic-becoming-self, and the ways in which this configuration can both reflect on and help circumvent the late capitalist control systems so prevalent in Celtic Tiger life.

Of particular interest in this essay has been the dynamics of emplaced movement integral to Walsh's harnessing of nomadic and non-linear forms of restricted and embedded movement. These can be read in ethical terms, as embodied feminist sites that register the complexities and contradictions of postmodernity, enabling critique, registering disorientation and restriction, as well as futuristic hope. Engaging non-linear, nomadic selfhood as a way of reflecting on late capitalist control systems that move and constrict classed bodies in restrictive ways, *City West* provides the mechanisms to creatively negotiate within such systems through the construction of intensely located mobile selves that enable critical reflection and critique at the level of ethical thought – *moving* that thought in vital and dynamic ways.

NOTES

This article is a revised version of material published in the monograph *Irish Feminist Futures* (Routledge, 2016). I gratefully acknowledge permission from Routledge to publish this material here.

1. Catherine Walsh, *Optic Verve* (Exeter: Shearsman, 2010), p.38.
2. Intriguingly, there are pronoun slippages between a number of subject positions in this poetic section, moving from child Niall, who is having his 'morning nap', to the homeless character referenced above and also to a horse. These slippages have the effect of dissolving some of the boundaries between separate embodied locations: between waking and sleeping, between child and adult, between human and animal.
3. Walsh, *Optic Verve*, p.39.
4. Walsh, *Optic Verve*, p.23.
5. Walsh, *Optic Verve*, p.24.
6. Indeed, the title refers spatially to a concept of decentralization, embodied by way of a play on the name of Ireland's 'National Digital Park' called 'Citywest' established during the Celtic Tiger era.
7. See Claire Bracken, 'The Love Affairs of the Irish Feminist Critic', *Facing the Other: Interdisciplinary Studies on Race, Gender and Social Justice in Ireland*, ed. Borbála Faragó and Moynagh Sullivan (Newcastle upon Tyne: Cambridge Scholars Publishing, 2008), pp.204–219; and '"Each nebulous atom inbetween" - Reading Liminality: Irish Studies, Postmodern Feminism and the Poetry of Catherine Walsh', *New Voices in Irish Criticism 5*, ed. by Ruth Connolly & Ann Coughlan (Dublin: Four Courts Press, 2005), pp.97–109.
8. *City West* was first issued by hardPressed Poetry, a press Catherine Walsh runs with the poet Billy Mills. It was subsequently republished by Shearsman Books in 2005. Catherine Walsh, *City West* (Exeter: Shearsman, 2005). All subsequent citations from the collection will be in parentheses.
9. Donna Haraway, *Simians, Cyborgs, and Women: The Reinvention of Nature* (London: Free Association Books, 1991), p.186.
10. Eric Falci, *Continuity and Change in Irish Poetry 1966–2010* (Cambridge: Cambridge University Press, 2012), p.197.
11. John Goodby, '"Repeat the Changes Change the Repeats": Irish Alternative Poetry', in *The Oxford Handbook of Modern Irish Poetry*, ed. by Fran Brearton and Alan Gillis (Oxford: Oxford University Press, 2012), p.614.

12. Matthew G. Jenkins, *Poetic Obligations: Ethics in Experimental American Poetry after 1945* (Iowa City: University of Iowa Press, 2008), pp.2–3, p.19. For an exploration of ethics and new directions in experimental poetry see also Catherine Wagner, 'US Experimental Poetry: A Social Turn', *Primerjalna Književnost* 37.1 (2014), 235–246.
13. Rosi Braidotti, *Nomadic Theory: The Portable Rosi Braidotti* (New York: Columbia University Press, 2011), p.122.
14. Falci, pp.196–197.
15. Michael S. Begnal, 'Anarchy of the Flesh,' *Poetry Ireland Review* 90 (2007), p.115.
16. Other works by Catherine Walsh include: *The Ca Pater Pillar Thing and More Besides* (Dublin: hardPressed Poetry, 1986); *Macula* (Dublin: Red Wheelbarrow Press, 1986); *Making Tents* (Dublin: hardPressed Poetry, 1987); *Short Stories* (Twickenham: North and South, 1989); *From Pitch* (London: Form Books, 1993); *Pitch* (Durham: Pig Press, 1994); *Pomepleat 1* (Limerick: hardPressed Poetry, 2002); *Idir Eatortha and Making Tents* (London: Invisible Books, 1996); *Astonished Birds: Cara, Jane, Bob and James* (Limerick: hardPressed Poetry, 2012).
17. This is also evident in an audio CD 'bodysounds' (2005), which is a recording of Walsh and Mills reading their work.
18. Falci, p.193.
19. Braidotti, p.99.
20. Falci, p.197.
21. See Gilles Deleuze, *The Logic of Sense* (London: Continuum, 2004), p.3.
22. Falci, p.198.
23. Falci, p.198.
24. Falci makes a similar point about the book's title in *Continuity and Change*.
25. Deleuze, *The Logic of Sense*, p.3.
26. Braidotti, p.17.
27. Alan Murdoch, 'Rainbow Coalition narrows gap', *The Independent London*, 27 May 1997.
28. Kevin Myers, 'An Irishman's Diary', *The Irish Times*, 8 February 2005.
29. See Chapter one in Claire Bracken, 'Nomadic Wanderings: Liminality and the Poetry of Catherine Walsh,' MA Thesis (University College Cork, 2002).
30. Bracken, 'Nomadic Wanderings', p.11.
31. Email conversation with author, June 2015.

Kit Fryatt

The Poetics of Elegy in Maurice Scully's *Humming*

Humming (2009) was Maurice Scully's first book-length publication since the completion of the eight-book 'set' *Things That Happen*, begun in 1987 with *Five Freedoms of Movement*, and finished in 2006 with *Tig*. The collective title of that extensive project alludes to Paul Celan's Bremen Prize acceptance speech: 'It passed through and gave back no words for that which happened [*was geschah*]; yet it passed through all this happening.'[1] Celan refers to the Holocaust, which in its enormity abolishes any language which might have been available to talk or write of it. Scully's deflected quotation is typical in its concern to register and record horrific experience without appropriating it. It is also characteristic in its interest in the unspoken and the unspeakable, which is maintained in *Humming*. The book is subtitled '[the words],' suggesting a libretto, 'as if to say,' as Meredith Quartermain notes in a review, 'here are the words to the music that you must already be *humming*'.[2] But that music is non-existent, or at least, idiosyncratic: it must be intuited by each reader from the words. And if we are to read *Humming* as the text of an imaginary song-cycle, then it is worth noting the implied accompaniment: not a musical instrument or ensemble, but a quintessentially unassertive hum. In interview with Marthine Satris, Scully remarks: 'The title could be taken to be anything from the background radiation of the universe to the babble of languages irradiating our planet, to the buzz of bees pollinating plants across the earth.'[3]

'Humming the words' is also an idiomatic phrase, and an oxymoronic one. Singers 'hum the words' when they have forgotten, or do not know them; in this sense, humming begins where verbal communication ends. 'Humming' may also imply temporization or equivocation, for which Scully's reserved, non-interventionist attitude to the world might be mistaken. These poems explore and document speech as it becomes meaningless through repetition and overuse or, conversely, points at which the previously unspoken

Irish University Review 46.1 (2016): 89–104
DOI: 10.3366/iur.2016.0203
© Edinburgh University Press
www.euppublishing.com/journal/iur

achieves articulation. But there is one unspeakable constant, and it is death. Not mortality or mourning, about which *Humming*, in its wry fashion, has a great deal to say, but extinction itself, of which by definition we cannot speak. The book is an elegy, dedicated to the memory of the poet's brother Brian, who died in 2004. It is in many ways a traditional one, working within and commenting upon the constraints of the genre, but especially compared with other modern Irish examples, it may strike the reader as unusual.

Humming has nine parts: two entitled 'Song', followed by a 'Ballad', a central 'Sonnet', another 'Ballad', two more 'Songs', and concluding with 'Jam' and 'Coda', which form a pendant to the symmetrical design of the first seven parts. Within these parts are poems with titles such as 'Sonnet Song', 'Ballad', and 'Song', as well as a majority of untitled pieces and two exceptions to the lyrical nomenclature, 'Snow' and 'For Seven Auditions'. The impression given is of a configuration at once nested — a 'Sonnet Song' or a 'Ballad' within a 'Song' — and exploded, since many of the poems so named are deconstructed versions of the common lyric forms. That simultaneous feeling of containment and dissemination is reflected in many of the book's master images: crystalline or cellular structures, honeycombs, pollination, ripples. *Humming*'s arrangement — the analogies with a musical score are irresistible, if in practice curiously imprecise — reflects the intricate patterning created by apparently random action in the natural world. The appeal to nature's cycles and systems, whether as a source of consolation or of horror, has been fundamental to the European elegiac tradition since Bion and Theocritus.

Peter Sacks, in *The English Elegy: Studies in the Genre from Spenser to Yeats*, begins his discussion of the conventions of the form by drawing attention to the linked figures of weaving and floral tribute, in which he sees the remnants of archaic vegetation ceremony. Funeral flowers, he writes, 'like the poetic language to which they are so often compared serve not only as offerings or gestures for respite, but also as demarcations separating the living from the dead'.[4] Scully's use of the motif takes this demarcative function beyond even the remote *human* past:

> A Neanderthal burial site found in the 1950s
> in a large cave near the village of Shanidar
> in the Zagros Mountains of Iraq contained the
> body of a man who had been laid to rest one
> early June day 60,000 years ago with bunches
> of carefully placed flowers: the first time
> flowers are known to have been used in a funeral
> ceremony.

> Analysis of the pollen deposits which of course
> are now all that remain of the plants shows that
> the tributes included cornflowers, hollyhock,
> ragwort, grape hyacinth, yarrow, St Barnaby's
> Thistle...[5]

This is the traditional, indeed, the original ('the first time') bier of pastoral elegy, with its catalogue of flowers. The separation of the dead subject from the elegist who weaves the textual framework is extreme even by the standards of a genre which uses the bier as a focus for anxiety, ironically submerging or allegorically subliming it at least as often as it is plainly evoked. It is a spatial separation, as indicated by the journalistic notation of place, and a temporal one, with linear time ('1950s', '60,000 years ago') implicitly contrasted to seasonal cycles which make possible pollen analysis and thus a determination of the time of year of burial. Perhaps most unsettlingly, however, the dead subject and the elegiac voice belong to different, if closely related, species. This distant predecessor symbolizes and in a sense substitutes the poet's brother, even as each of the very few individual details given about the latter mark differences between modern humans and their extinct 'ancestors':

> My brother is dead. I found him at the end of his bed.
> His brain weighs 1565g, his heart 465
> the document says & helps me know what a whiff
> of actuality feels like from those who know the facts of life.

> . . .

> My brother is dead. His wristwatch laid face up beside his bed.
> ('Ballad (Argument)', *Humming*, p.35)

Humanity is defined by both physical facts, here represented by heart and brain weight, and the technological capacity to measure them, while the wristwatch takes the place of pollen deposits as indicator of cyclical time. A later iteration of the motif makes the idea of time's mockery explicit: 'Take yr wristwatch off and lay it on the bed— / good—its three hands—*haa, ha-ha & ha-ha-ha* / circling circumstance under heaven.' (*Humming*, p.93) The bitterness of tone, in evidence in the bathetic internal rhyme of 'bed/dead' and the sarcastic admission that an autopsy report is a superior form of 'actuality' to the speaker's lived experience, only partially conceals an anxiety about the possibility of knowledge of the world, which is heavily circumscribed. The speaker does not 'know', he is 'help[ed] to know', not 'actuality', but what 'a whiff of what actuality *feels* like' [emphasis added], further mediated by those 'who know the facts of life.' Consciousness is alienation.

In *Poetry of Mourning: The Modern Elegy from Hardy to Heaney*, Jahan Ramazani identifies irony and deflection as crucial strategies in modern Western elegy: even the term itself is 'apparently oxymoronic', suggesting 'both the negation of received codes ("modern") and their perpetuation ("elegy")'.[6] Rejecting the compensations and comfort of mourning, modern elegy undoes not itself but other generic categories too: 'in becoming anti-elegaic, the modern elegy more radically violates generic norms than did earlier phases of elegy: it becomes anti-consolatory and anti-encomiastic, anti-Romantic and anti-Victorian, anti-conventional and sometimes even anti-literary.'[7] The modern elegy also grieves the disappearance of ritual surrounding the dead, the increasing social invisibility of death in the industrialized West; it mourns the 'dying of death' even in countries and cultures, such as Ireland, which have preserved a relatively large repertoire of traditional funerary practice. 'Ireland', Ramazani writes, 'is Western Europe's last national enclave for traditional mourning ritual, and Irish poets from Yeats to Patrick Kavanagh and Heaney mirror this social conservatism in their elegies [...] Yet even as they reflect the persistence of mourning ritual contemporary Irish poets like Heaney continue to lament its "attenuation".'[8] Impulses of denial and rejection — parody, satire, denunciation — are held in tension with a sort of self-reflexive nostalgia, in which elegy itself is mourned. A moment's reflection on 'Lycidas' or 'Adonaïs' will prompt the reader to question the novelty of this contradictory state; since my space is limited, perhaps it is sufficient to say that in modernity it has, under the influence of the great elegies of the past, become the default setting.

In *Humming*, the satiric and denunciatory function of elegy is directed at precisely the social conservatism that Ramazani identifies in the Irish product. In the first of the book's sections entitled 'Ballad', a lyrically-described rural scene devolves into a parody of a repetitive, lazy critical idiom:

> white gables, visibility for miles, an occasional
> car casually on route, spider cosy in one spot.
> Not much doing, a quiet day humming beauty
> permanence beauty permanence

packed tight with a
wealth of imagery
> *beauty permanence*
pervading nostalgia
> *beauty permanence*
remains on the level
of the deeply commun-
icative
> *beauty permanence*
rhythms delicately
balanced title poem
a gem
> *beauty permanence*
north of Ireland—
frighteningly accur-
ate—richness exuberance
> *beauty permanence*
Beauty Permanence plc—
('I was closing the machine when its edge', *Humming*, p.31)

Complacent commercialization of a Romantic ideal of immortal beauty is connected to the subject of much recent Irish elegiac effort, the political situation of the 'north of Ireland'. The lack of comment is itself significant: any reader familiar with the ways in which 'experimental' Irish poetry has been defined against a 'mainstream' preoccupied by 'family, nation and tradition', and as 'a "poetry of process" rather than "a poetry of product"',[9] will recognize the targets of Scully's satire. But it's also a curiously recursive and self-implicating attack: 'packed tight with a/wealth of imagery', insofar as it means anything at all, might well be applied to Scully's intense registering of visual detail, as might 'frighteningly accu-/rate'; his anger at the debasement of a once-radical aesthetic standard into critical cliché is inevitably pervaded by nostalgia; the ambiguous lineation of 'rhythms delicately/balanced title poem' is mischievously self-reflexive. Scully has all but enrolled himself into what he elsewhere calls 'the Gem School'.[10] The very meaninglessness of the consolatory mode makes it universally applicable and inescapable. What Ramazani, writing about Seamus Heaney, calls the 'elegist's harvesting of beauty from death' presents an ethical problem which is not to be solved by mere parody or denunciation.[11]

It is a particular problem for Scully, whose poetics are predicated upon an ethical stance of self-effacement: 'a poem is beautiful to the degree it records an apt humility in the face of complexity it sees but fails to transmit',[12] he wrote in a 1983 editorial for *The Beau* magazine; *5 Freedoms of Movement* (1987), the first book of what would eventually become *Things That Happen*, represents his initial attempts to put the theory into practice. But elegists are inevitably egoists: the death of another prompts reflection on, and usually anxiety about, achievement and ambition. Ramazani notes a tendency towards more explicit description and discussion of the elegized subject in the modern elegy, citing Yeats, Auden, and Ginsberg, but it is still a rare elegy that tells us more about the mourned person than the mourner.[13] Apart from the disquietingly intimate, yet clinical, details quoted above, we learn almost nothing about the poet's brother from *Humming*; he is actually named only in the dedication. Nor do we discover anything about his relationship with his brother. Not to name is a consciously anti-elegiac gesture: as Sacks notes, repetition of the name of the mourned subject 'takes on, by dint of repetition, a kind of substantiality, allowing it not only to refer to but almost to replace the dead.'[14] The withholding of a personal name signals the scope of Scully's project, as he suggests in interview: 'I've enlarged the frame and focus of the normal elegy to ... focus on life and living culture as well as on death and loss.'[15]

The book is conversely full of self-portraiture, variously ironized:

> Talents: one highly developed
> sense of victimhood
> an insomniac nature
> patchy concentration
> ditto education
> 2 ears, sensitive, eyes, ageing
> a bedrock inability to earn a living. ('Sonnet', *Humming*, p.26)

In a transition audacious enough to constitute parody of the convention whereby the death of a contemporary becomes an occasion to assess achievement and take stock of ambition, the poet turns directly from his brother's body to an evaluation of his poetic accomplishments, focusing specifically on lack of recognition by a literary establishment:

> I am 52. How old are you? I'm old enough to take a knife
> to any letter from the Arts Council for instance regretting et cetera
> because they know I think by now—now that I'm older than
> they are & longer on the job—I know perhaps a fact or two of life.

> But wait! It's the middle of the night & time to wake up
> I mean the middle of yr life & further along the ledge
> past the diggers & set foundations parent birds attack.
> You will discover starfish ingesting molluscs & ugly
> dishonesties between people. You will have been a poet. Why?
> ('Ballad (Argument)', *Humming*, p.35)

The autopsy 'document' becomes the Arts Council letter, the scalpel a letter opener. To 'take a knife to' the letter might mean simply to open it, or to shred it in frustration. The violence implied by the latter reading is echoed in the attacking birds and predatory starfish; in turn, predation in Scully's poetry is often connected to finance, which links back to the Arts Council's refusal. And this infernal complex of brutality, mortality, and money is the condition of 'hav[ing] been a poet': elegy turns inevitably and swiftly to self-elegy.

For a poet who aims at an 'apt humility' with regard to his surroundings, 'to interact with the world .... Not to meditate *on* the world, but to be *in* it',[16] elegy's attempts at control and mastery over nature and death, expressed as 'the pathetic fallacy of nature's lament',[17] must seem particularly uncongenial. *Things That Happen* might be understood as a prolonged wrangle with the idea of and necessity for order in art, with poetic *number* seen as at once 'something primal.... Symmetry'[18] and as an aspect of authoritarian power: 'Order—the giant / spinning in his / skin—'.[19] Though less prominent in *Humming*, such coercive forces still occasionally emerge:

> Two palace guards on watch—white gloves, red lanyards—under
>   big
> bearded naked hero-sculptures with clubs & spears about to do
> in the brains of their defeated under-gods among the hinges &
>   springs
> Stop. Tourists go passing in & out these gates in the sun—*lanyards*
> click-click *pedestal* click-click *rooftop chimneypot bird's flash* click
> *epitaph* click oh click click I was touring the lattice now that all the
> little cars were grey ah yes he said she said/hey they said I'm/
>   we've
> got a new book out have you seen it? they said
> ('Two palace guards on watch—white gloves', *Humming*, p.73)

It may be noted that the context again is votive, funerary ('defeated under-gods', 'epitaph') and productive of anxiety about literary success ('we've got a new book out'). In fact, Scully's discomfort with an understanding of the 'poet as imperious editor'[20] of his surroundings does not preclude the appearance of elegiac conventions in *Humming*: formalized or rhetorical questioning, repetition, multi-vocality, absorption of the individual death into a natural cycle. Indeed, the 'Song' that begins with the threatening presence of the 'two palace guards', the blandly consuming 'tourists', and self-important newly-published authors soon shifts to a pastoral scene of floral tribute:

> *Direct you to the flowers*
>
> *The evidence*
>
> *Printing their pollen-pictures forever on the world*
>
> *Direct you to the flowers*
>
> [...]
>
> *Come back then to the flowers*
>
> [...]
>
> *Down derry derry—*
>
> *Dance co-foragers to the flowers—*
>
> *Collect—deposit*
>
> *Find the flowers—*
> *work the flowers—*
> *farm the flowers—*
>
> *Collect—deposit*
>
> *Return—start again* ('Song', *Humming*, pp.74–5)

The ancient – and indeed, non-human – origin of the custom in the Neanderthal burial is recalled in *'pollen-pictures forever on the world'*, while *'Come back then to the flowers … Return—start again'* are archetypal examples of the verbal repetitions ('Yet once more') which (inadequately, and deliberately so) substitute for natural cycles.

In Sacks's psychoanalytic scheme, repetitive elegiac questions serve a tripartite purpose: to release affective energy, to deflect guilt by turning the elegist's focus 'outward to the world', and to approach, armoured in incantatory prophylaxis, the horror of mortality: 'Among the questions behind the ceremonious screen of questions, therefore, also lies the naked Why will no-one or nothing save us from death?'[21] Scully begins *Humming* with a series of apparent propositions which for the most part do not coalesce grammatically into questions:

> Look: if the coin had landed on its edge making the
> spaces to heads and tails the space of all probability
> patterns lit up to date stretched to an evanescent blur
> (one little thought experiment deserves another)
> then *you* this, *me* that, *plink*!
>
>   (knock)
>
> . . .
>
> If—rock of constancy, rubble of contingency—
> (pass the salt) giving the bracket its due, its
> space, its elastic content, bustle & itch
> (where's my sandwich?)
>
> . . .
>
> If you dedicate your little book to Mammy and get
> a prize—size matters—you know how it is—
> a million years of isolation and neglect. . .as if you
> deserve pampering *as by right*. Just write, right?
>
>   (knock)
>
> . . .
>
> If the Way of Art is a Hard, Hard Way
> as you heard some old Tin-Can say (dot)
> loud sing cuckoo—grows seed—blows mead
> and blossoms the wood now—
>
> If.
>
> If.

If...

Sing Cuckoo! ('Sonnet Song', *Humming*, pp.11–12)

The manner is modernist, parodic, and fragmented, but the matter is
profoundly traditional: the elegist turning attention from intimate
address ('*you* this, *me* that') to a world of 'probability', 'bustle & itch',
which despite perceptible 'patterns' seems indifferent to the mortal
fate of individuals. He is anxious about artistic labour and legacy,
derisive of a literary culture which rewards familial pieties (but where
does that leave a book dedicated to a brother?) and through a mixture
of neglect and 'pampering' encourages lassitude (resting on one's
laurels, perhaps). Literary inheritance is represented by Middle
English pastoral lyric and, by implication, the many parodies it has
attracted, the latter, whether by Ezra Pound or The Fugs, tending
to make crudely explicit the ever-present intimations of mortality
in the original. 'Just write, right?' meanwhile suggests a similar
modernization of the final line of the first sonnet of *Astrophil and Stella*,
whose author is the subject of an early example of the specifically
funereal pastoral elegy in English. Elizabeth Bishop's parenthetical
'(*Write* it!)' from that most comprehensive of modern elegies, 'One
Art', may also be a precursor.

'Sonnet Song' has a refrain of 'knock' and 'knock-knock', about
which the poet comments: 'The refrain is knock-knock (you know,
from those stupid knock-knock jokes). There are fourteen knocks —
that's it really.'[22] The echoic formula of the knock-knock joke forms a
trivial, puerile counterpart to the solemn ritual of elegy. Scully's
question is a projective *If*? rather than a despairing *Why*? but it
serves the same established purpose: to release contradictory feeling,
to focus attention upon the shifting patterns and cycles of the material
world, to approach death — awful, banal death — protected by
commonplaces which might fill the terrible silence that is returned to
our 'who's there?' Rarely content with plangency, and distrustful of
anything that might approach sentimentality, Scully adds this bathetic
(but still interrogative) pendant to 'Sonnet Song':

> Then a stray piece turned up called
> THE DOG.

THE DOG

> The dog is barking in the laneway again.
> Who owns that dog? Do you?
> Do you? ('Sonnet Song', *Humming*, p.13)

The first of *Humming*'s 'Ballads' offers another set of variations on elegiac questioning. It evokes traditional ballads in which a story is told in question-and-answer format, such as 'Lord Randall' (Child 12) or 'Edward' (Child 13), or in which questions play an important part in the narrative (such as Child 93, 'Lamkin,' or the many ballads in which riddles and paradoxes are proposed).[23] Such ballads frequently concern violent death, or a narrow escape from it, and situate it in a familial context. The ballad trope whereby successive family members present themselves to the protagonist (see for example Child 95, 'The Maid Freed from the Gallows') is also relevant here, as a form of the elegiac procession (which in the pastoral mode is composed of shepherds, nymphs and animals):

> I walked along and what did I see? Tomorrow's yr father's
>   anniversary.
>
> . . .
>
> Turn the room around and what do you see? Is it yr mother's
>   anniversary?
> Who died in a cave of darkness, who died in a cave of light.
>
> . . .
>
> Turn the beach upside-down what do you see? It must be yr
>   sister's
> anniversary? By forces too large for all of us she's drawn into the
>   cave.
> Greed tugs a string, the thing is done, it's over. In time and space.
> The plants inter-leave. I see. Revolve. Carry me home.
>
> *ha ha   ha ha*
>
> Sink yr desk in the dark. So much for study now. Later, magpies
>   in trees.
> It must be yr brother's anniversary. A drill cuts through wood, go
>   & do
> what you do in life and do it thoroughly, one circle, then another,
>   the
> bee's wings, the drill-bit spins, through steel, then rock, do go,
>   then
> slice, ice, down, dice, divine, die and die well. Good.
>
> *ha ha   ha ha* (*Humming*, p.25)

The first line establishes this in the tradition of *chanson d'aventure*, but the encounter is not with another person so much as his ritualized memory, 'yr father's anniversary', a memorial cycle that may either be a comforting return or a disruptive revolution, which turns things upside-down. The reversed room and beach suggest the landscape of dream, or dream vision, while the cave into which the female relatives go to die might carry some connotation of Orphic mystery. The final stanza acts as a compendium of the poem's motifs: circles, bees (by extension humming and honeycombs), wood (trees and flowers), ice (crystals and snow). The hum of the drill is a man-made counterpart to the hum of bees, the dust it generates to pollen. Rich in internal rhyme, often of quite a mechanical sort ('see/anniversary/activity/memory') the ballad devolves into echolalia, which looks like it may provide some sort of resolution: the eye-rhyme of 'do/go', the rhymes 'ice/slice/dice', the anagrammatic 'ice/dice/divine/die'. But 'die, & die well. Good.' is a shade too emphatic, too tritely consolatory, and immediately mocked by the refrain '*ha ha*'. There remains elegiac and emotional work to do.

Some of that work is done by the central section 'Sonnet', to which the poet offers a useful guide in interview:

> in the *Humming* book, there's a mirror section with some focus on mirrored reversals. The whole section — it's about ten pages — is called "Sonnet" (within which are embedded some actual fourteen-line *poemeens*, in the spirit of grubs in their cells in a hive). A dominating motif in this book is crystallization, honeycombing, replication, bees, pollen, and pollination, plus a little bit on bureaucracy. I used the mirror idea of splitting up, echoing but separating, taking the word "mirror" itself and seeing what I could get out of it, running a bit of it anagrammatically, putting it up to the mirror, as it were, so *rim* and then *door* and *slam*. A word like "rules" becomes "slur." I'm interested in the control that invisible rules can have. To highlight them and show them as tools of domination is something poetry can be deft at. And show that rules are not immutable.[24]

Such linguistic play suggests the eclogic and choral nature of elegy, in which the poet's voice is fractured in acts of self-suppression and self-dramatization, 'by which mourners not only lend ceremony to their rites but also intensify and indicate their own "work" as survivors'.[25] For Scully, these 'poemeens', which often have an echolalic dimension, are a source of liberation, drawing attention to 'domination' even as they elude it:

> *hear*
> *hearken*
> *hearse*
> *heart*
> *hearth*
> *heat*
> *heath*
> *heathen*
> *heather*
> *heave*
> *heave-ho*
> *ho-ho*
> *heaven*
> *ha-ha*
>
> ('Sonnet', *Humming*, p.48)

Here is the 'work' of elegy in aspirate, alliterative miniature, from a demand for auditors (hear, hearken), though sorrow (heart, hearse), the flower-strewn bier (hearse, heather), the ambiguously domestic situation of pastoral (hearth, heath, heathen), to overcoming, *throwing off* grief and promise of resurrection (heave, heave-ho, heaven), all mocked with 'ho-ho, ha-ha'. Derisive as this may seem of elegy's consolatory function, it might also be seen as the elegist's 'reluctant submission to language itself . . . the enforced accommodation between the mourning self on the one hand and the very words of grief and fictions of consolation on the other'.[26] Scully's submission to language is perhaps less 'reluctant' than most; indeed, as he notes above, its ludic properties are liberating, but nonetheless, the struggle takes place.

Sacks draws attention to another aspect of elegy's multi-vocality: its facilitation of alternate sympathy for and (self-)reproach of the mourner.[27] Scully frequently employs, in place of the lyric 'I', a semi-imperative generalized 'you' which serves a very similar purpose. This flexible voice offers interior monologue a level of apparent detachment, and can accommodate self-reflexive criticism of its own procedures:

> Trimming yr fingernails, each thin crescent, each
> time different, *you-you, you-you*, each the
> same, each repeating surprise. Follow
> the circle of yr wrist-

watch, one circuit, then one & a bit, then one &
another bit, at the very beginning beginning
beginning. Breathe. Three

four.

Can you be as tired as I am? Clap hands 5/5. Turn
the page, reverse the score. *You-you, you-you.*
Are you quite there yet? Is it alright?

Clap hands.

Insert a little translation here. Clap-clap. *The Precious
Mirror of the Four Elements* for instance.
How do you do. Touch it. Clap-clap.
('There is a pen on a notebook on a desk', *Humming*, p.67–8)

The Joycean author-god, paring his fingernails, has his self-absorption
ironically confirmed in the u-shape of the trimmings, but in the
questions – 'Can you be as tired as I am? ... Are you quite there
yet?' – the referent of 'you' changes from the self to the implied other.
When the poet returns to the imperative mode with 'Insert a little
translation here' the pronoun has been destabilized: is he instructing
someone else, or commenting wryly on his own impeccable High
Modernist affectation in incorporating a 14th-century Chinese
scientific treatise into his work? Self-indulgence blurs into self-
rebuke: defending the elegy (and in the process offering an early
definition of the genre as mood), Sir Philip Sidney claims it is 'to
be praised either for compassionate accompanying just causes
of lamentation or for rightly pointing out how weak be the passions
of woefulness'.[28] If modernity can add anything to this at all, it is
only an increased acceptance of self-contradiction: elegy has
always done both, but modern poets find less value in the art of
concealing it.

Second-person modes of address also facilitate consolatory closure,
to a rather greater degree than many commentators are prepared to
admit is desirable (or possible) in the modern (or modernist) elegy.
Humming ends with a utopian vision of artistic non-intervention in its
material, which is simply the world:

POEM

"This piece of paper you have just been handed is ...
Keep it. It advertises nothing, has no designs on you,

has come a long long way, to here, in silence, in the
   rain, free. As you are. You are. Now:
      breathe …" (*Humming*, p.94)

Like many such statements of resolution and recovery, this frames and depersonalizes what precedes it. 'This piece of paper' is both the book the reader has just finished, and a promise of ideal future achievement: the artwork that 'advertises nothing, has no designs on you' is perhaps impossible — it may be that the perfect work is a blank, something with no designs on' *itself* as well as the reader — but it remains a goal for which to strive. Or, 'It is hard/work whichever way/you look at it.' (*Humming*, p.56) Self-contained despite its scope, within Scully's oeuvre, *Humming* fulfils the traditional elegiac function of *transition*; announcing a definitive break between the epic achievement of *Things That Happen* and the light fantastic of 2014's *Several Dances*.

NOTES

1. Paul Celan, *Selected Poems and Prose of Paul Celan*, transl. by John Felsteiner (New York: W.W. Norton, 2002), p.395.
2. Meredith Quatermain, 'Bees: Maurice Scully, *Humming*', *Golden Handcuffs Review* 1:14 (Winter/Spring, 2011), 233–7, p.233.
3. Marthine Satris, 'An Interview with Maurice Scully', *Contemporary Literature* 53:1 (Spring 2012), 1–30, p.30.
4. Peter Sacks, *The English Elegy: Studies in the Genre from Spenser to Yeats* (Baltimore and London: Johns Hopkins University Press, 1985), p.19.
5. Maurice Scully, 'A Neanderthal burial site found in the 1950s', *Humming* (Exeter: Shearsman, 2009), p.28. Subsequent references to *Humming* in parentheses.
6. Jahan Ramazani, *Poetry of Mourning: The Modern Elegy from Hardy to Heaney*, (Chicago: Chicago UP, 1994), p.1.
7. Ramazani, p.2.
8. Ramazani, p.23.
9. John Goodby, *Irish Poetry Since 1950: From Stillness into History* (Manchester: Manchester University Press, 2000), pp.301–2.
10. Maurice Scully, *Livelihood* (Bray: Wild Honey Press, 2004), p.18.
11. Ramazani, p.343.
12. Maurice Scully, 'As I Like it', *The Beau* (1983), p.10.
13. Ramazani, p.6.
14. Sacks, p.26.
15. Satris, p.30.
16. Maurice Scully, 'Interview', *Metre* 17 (Spring 2005), 134–43, p.143.
17. Sacks, p.21.
18. Satris, p.23.
19. Scully, *Livelihood*, pp.140–141.
20. Metre, p.142.
21. Sacks, p.22.
22. Satris, p.21.
23. Francis James Child, ed., *The English And Scottish Popular Ballads* (Boston and New York: Houghton, Mifflin and Company, 1882–98).
24. Satris, p.26.

25. Sacks, p.25.
26. Sacks, p.2.
27. Sacks pp.35–6.
28. Sir Philip Sidney, 'A Defence of Poetry', *Selected Writings*, ed. by Richard Dutton, (London: Routledge, 2002), p.123.

Romana Huk

'Out Past / Self-Dramatization': Maurice Scully's *Several Dances*

Introducing her interview with Maurice Scully in *Contemporary Literature* in 2012, Marthine Satris describes him as having 'turned away from the lyric', given its association with 'the official history' of mainstream twentieth-century Irish poetry.[1] Instead of adopting 'the form of the personal lyric dwelling on the complex dynamics of identity on a postcolonial island', she argues, Scully 'insisted on cutting a new path for his poetry, creating Irish writing in which the nation as a concept rarely figures and avant-garde work that reminds us always of the material circumstances from which the words emerge'.[2] However apt these statements are, at heart, their binary, either/or logic – delimiting turns *against* both lyric and collective concepts like nations; advocating turns *toward* materiality from which words somehow 'emerge' – invites reductive reading, and is unsupported by the easygoing inclusiveness of Scully's attentions in his new volume, *Several Dances* (2014), which one reader calls a 'retrospective', the poet's *reculer pour mieux sauter*.[3] Indeed, Scully's particular sort of inclusiveness, meaning his willingness to both 'orbit' and move on from structures for making sense of '[e]verything',[4] does articulate a philosophy of both identity and collectivity – even nation – in this work, however lightly it may be offered. Lightness on one's feet is itself offered here as both an ethical 'state' and an ontology of sorts, and 'Lyric: Bal/ancing' – as the third poem's title has it – is, very importantly, its method and study. That this title's provocative split calls up for me Wordsworth's manifesto, *Lyrical Ballads*, may be just my problem; but starting-points in ballads, sonnets, and other 'lyric' as well, of course, as dance structures *do* abound in this book, so no reader should – for the sake of focusing *just* on 'material circumstances', narrowly defined – ignore their cooperative artifice and (sometimes troubling)[5] collective memory, their 'ghost of "architectural" form invoked',[6] since their author clearly does not.

What has lyric to do with any radical phenomenology's choreography? This volume asks that question, as Scully has for

Irish University Review 46.1 (2016): 105–118
DOI: 10.3366/iur.2016.0204
© Edinburgh University Press
www.euppublishing.com/journal/iur

years now, alongside other poets of Ireland's avant-garde whose 'distinguishing (not inhibiting) feature', as Sarah Bennett writes (acknowledging the work of Alex Davis and Eric Falci before her) is that in it 'the lyric subject persists' – in tandem with, I would argue, what she names 'an interest in perception ... [which] is perhaps the most compelling commonality in these poets' work'.[7] Yet what distinguishes Scully's from, say, the lyric phenomenology of American poets from William Carlos Williams (invoked throughout the volume) to George Oppen (also invoked) is that Scully – again, I believe, like other Irish avant-gardists – queries existentialism's 'singular' approach to phenomena, achieved as Heidegger thought through the phenomenological reduction (*epoché*) or 'bracketing' of an individual's preconceptions from the perception of things. As he puts it in *Several Dances'* first poem, in 'severally'-restarted-approach to a 'calm autumn morning', it *as it is* 'outside [the community of] our / perceptions' (p.14) is elusive – his 'brackets' *adding back in*, with the warm word 'community', what Heidegger's *epoché* would most pointedly expel on its way toward what solipsists, in the old phrase, claim doesn't exist: that which is 'outside our perceptions'. Instead, Scully's speaker in attempted elaboration slows, shifts, and wonders: 'in which outside / ... which ...' – given the inseparability of each to each in community and all of us over time. His very wondering – like his noting earlier of 'ripple of leaf-shadow / over those books there' (p.13), its 'restless surges and retreats' that 'burn care- / fully across representations' – becomes part of the work in this poem, 'On a Light Ground: Eye Dance', to both 'think (dab) / a fossil horizon' that dates itself – a lyric precipitate in time, his particular 'eye dance' that morning – while writing in loosely-formed lyric quatrains and tercets that acknowledge, too, the 'light ground' of the 'community of' perceptions informing his own.

This poem also begins to weave in the volume's epigraph from Frank Samperi, with which Scully qualifies Williams' infamous Objectivist credo 'No ideas but in things': 'Sunlight is / on things' (p.9). As the volume's seventh poem, 'Sunlight', further unfolds it, 'sunlight on a mountain village re-divides solidity' (p.23). In other words, Scully's understanding of perception is *severally* that it is indeed *of* things ('That they are there!' – which for Oppen constituted his Heideggerian 'theology'),[8] *and* of how changes in material circumstances shift perception of them – sunlight, say, rippling over phenomena, or the ubiquitous pebble dropped in a pool in this volume, causing (like, perhaps, a word learned or repositioned) 'a single shiver on the surface [that] changes everything' – *as well as* of how changes in embodied perception's 'dances' toward apprehending things shift them too. If Yeats's dancer and dance yoked the particular to the eternal, fact to (neo-Platonic) form, Scully's post-Heideggerian, post-Merleau-Pontian, post-(even)-Lakoff-and-Johnsonian dances embrace their participation in evolutionary change instead: each one humbly adds to accumulating 'orbits' of formal possibilities – imagined literally as such (in outer space) near the volume's end, even as this one begins with us 'in the circle of the mind'. (That the first word of the volume, 'Dapple', is also the last of his Coda in 'Orbit', further suggests an update on 'enlightenment' I'll return to later.) Scully's is, it seems, an improbably 'both/and', *inclusive* phenomenology, one that unfolds in step with the immediately perceived even as it remains attentive to its own artful motions redanced in the light of previous possibilities and offered up as 'additions to the world / not representations of it' (p.15).

Thus this volume engages 'art' (broadly defined) as an inescapable part, *already*, of any 'material circumstances' that give rise to perception or poetry – indeed made *in order to* experience materiality, like the 'fossil horizon' painted in this first poem which the poet will 'live' in 'for a bit': a to-be-left-behind architecture that nonetheless 'ghosts' subsequent ones. It sets the stage for the back-and-forth 'stepping' or dancing that, particularly since his volume *Steps* (1998), with its Irish epigraph '. . . *agus a haon, dó, trí*' (explained as '*& one, two three* a phrase commonly used to count out the steps in Irish dancing lessons' (p.70)), combines bodily perception with communal-cum-individual artifice in the task of perceiving 'what is' and *dasein*, or being in the world.[9] Hence all the theatrical 'directions' in the volume, beginning with the one that follows the book's title on its second title-page: '[for voice]' (p.7). Readers perform, or inhabit/animate, the structures/moves the poet makes in order to get at the world he in turn tries to 'capture'. Therefore, too, the book's opening and repeated recourse to metaphorical webs, like spider webs, woven and 'wet' (p.13), even 'glistening' (p.49, with Irish prefix *glé*), yet always poised to be broken up or 'smack[ed]', as the book's last word performs it (p.137).[10]

The delicacy of these 'dances' we're invited to join produces the volume's extraordinary lightness of touch (the word 'light' operating multivalently in my phrase), and yet its phenomenological investigations result in anything but 'light reading'. Cosmic – even theological – speculation enters in as the poet moves out past both self-centred lyric *and* twentieth-century cancellations of its preconceptions in the 'limit-thinking' and *being-toward-death* that Heidegger proposed for seeing past the self. Scully's particular form of divine comedy (as we might call it, if we see this work making its additions, too, to Samperi's to Dante's) *does* take up the theme of mortality, if 'lightly', as it simultaneously sings 'the Huuuman /

Limit-at-tation Blues' (p.118) and, more vertiginously, considers both the undelimitability and the fragility of us.[11]

*

Yet to follow up on Satris's insight, it is certainly true that the poems in *Several Dances* are often exceedingly direct and tactile. The first is a good example of this, though it seems significant that the natural actor we encounter and accompany – a mother-spider – weaves her means of perception from out of her own body as well as between bits of existing artifice: the hedge and the trellis,[12] which support the first web encountered in the volume:

> Dapple of mother-spider
> at the centre of its wet
> web between a hedge & a
> trellis. After work, the
>
> wait. Place your foot
> there. Then place it
> there. Pitch a rock
> in the pond: hear that
>
> difference over there.
> I-me-myself are moving
> forward
>
>   forward
>
> to that left behind, through
> air, to that placed shimmer
> ahead. Forward. Carry your
> spinning circle, a drop
>
> lands, little by / connects
> [pendant speck] reverberant. (p.13)

This mother-spider's dance-steps into listening are mirrored by those of the recalled boy who will, ten pages later, in 'Tango', 'sway' attentively in air, having come '[t]o know every branch of those trees / beside that house' by finding that 'if we step here, then there,

> ...Thumb, middle finger, the little & ring acting as light
> supports to the wrist moving in its bony balance holding
> the stem & point inking across to thought & eye in a world
> placed bright way through. (p.22)

Instead of the world perceived *'right* way through', as one expects in conventional lyric whose 'eye' is deemed capable of penetrating 'universality', this boy's' is 'placed *bright* way through', mirroring the mother-spider's tentatively 'placed shimmer' at the limit of what she can connect with. The boy's spider-like line is achieved in reverse, in a sense, by 'point inking across to thought & eye', so that 'a world' is posited – in revision of Wordsworth's 'mighty world / of eye, and ear, – both what they half-create / and what perceive' – through incoming perception being met by outgoing and only provisional *writing*, an 'inking' that succeeds preparatory 'inching' along tree limbs, a bodily ('bony') 'lyric bal/ancing'. 'Point' as incremental destination merges with its other definition as intended 'meaning' in Scully's poetry; it therefore radically updates even Brian Coffey's epic-revision of epiphanics in *Advent* (1975)[13] which most famously reminds itself that '[w]e are always in human circumstances / no angels and prone to forget / we can work only from point to point' (p.41). Whereas Coffey's epic mightily attempts to resolve its chronological study of an increasingly benighted world by imagining time's still-point in a triptych of 'ikons three' whose pivot, the crucifixion, provides a way to look out *across* it, Scully's last poem before his Coda offers a very different notion of what an ikon might do, as I'll explain in closing below. He prepares us for it, in these first poems, by assenting to 'live here for a bit' in each fossil horizon/orbit he inks – 'not *across* no but along' (p.14, my emphasis).

So what comes by the tenth line above to dance 'along' in sympathetic movement with the mother-spider (instead of continuing to represent her) is our lyric subject, though its doing so forces up its rethinking as such in order to proceed 'out past / self-dramatization' (p.51), or twentieth-century New Critical lyric subjectivity presented as unified 'character' rather than responsive presence.[14] Scully's 'I-me-myself' conglomerate thus splays into parts as the latter two – used customarily to make oneself the 'object' of a clause or place extra emphasis on oneself – shift from consolidation and self-centralization to, instead, 'moving / forward // forward' over line-ends in a redefinition of movement that involves back-and-forth dance-steps between the 'left behind' and the 'shimmer[ing]' ahead: i.e., a kind of immediate yet reflective speaking-in-transit. This speech is in many ways far *more* personal than the 'personal lyric' which, Scully says in interview, he wrote at the start, before 'develop[ing] in another direction'.[15] Its lines are temporally, even privately, sited, issuing/inking from the poet's moment-by-moment perceptual experience met by remade memory, like the web out of the spider. But rather than offering a pre-fab dramatic subject for our identification it *takes us with it*, most intimately; this is paradoxical autography open to company, for readers to voice/dance *with*, given what its very titles – from 'Jig' and 'Tango' to 'Tap Dance', 'Ballad' to 'Sonnet' – acknowledge: that many of our choreographies are shared at relatively recent cultural root. But remembering one's own particular perceptions is crucial, as we'll see, so Scully's work remains 'personal' or other to its reader, too – we're not allowed to subsume it: 'I draw the line / you do too' ('Lyric: Bal/ancing', p.18).

Important to my reading of these lines is that the sound of troubling 'challenge' in them – 'I draw the line' – is not avoided, but channeled instead into the dynamic of 'alongness' emphasized since the opening poem, whose provocative last words finish out the line quoted above with 'not across no but along. One. / Border. Forever'. Connected to the drawing of poetic lines themselves, borders seem not only unavoidable but necessary, paradoxically, for *not* 'crossing' another, and for traveling *with*. Indeed, they might be said to replace Heidegger's vision of limits as productive *memento-mori* with *being-alongside*, the border with otherness becoming an insight-producing position in time – and language. As readers see by way of a pun in 'Ground', 'knock[ing] *against* /another boarder' at school is, on the other hand, rather more painfully transformative, causing the boy's tin whistle he was piping to 'jab sharply into his upper palate', 'mark[ing] him out for / / language at an early age' (p.48). Collision here *wounds* into change of tune, and concomitant awareness of one's own (solipsistic?) 'line' (or language), whereas elsewhere in the book language is encountered and remade more positively as simply another, larger architecture that like a trellis supports growing/ changing human energies. And though '[m]ost populations hardly notice the alphabets they live through' (p.87), as he puts it in 'To Balance' (yet another title whose echo of precedents, like 'Lyric: Bal/ ancing', signals ongoing 'living through' of provisional structures), Scully is keen to investigate 'things that happen' on the way to language. As he pictures it via a meeting of astronomical and biological imagery in 'Imprint Studio', '[h]igh speed collisions of tiny ideas' in a child's galaxy of a brain taking in adult gossip and other kinds of encountered language – '*gabble-gabble-gabble* as it / grows around its pergola' – are made into livable if changing structures by one's own lyric 'idiosyncrasies' in perception:

> Droplets of connective gel you
> take in as a child, personal ornamentation,
> quietly unique idiosyncrasies—minúte,
> unrecorded, disappearing—keep their
> place in their fluidly mapped geometry,
> an abstract system made tangible through

> language's spiralling ribboning as you
> lived it ... (p.27)

Such evolutionary images of language's 'spiralling[s]' – reminiscent, too, of Celtic and other ancient as well as modern life-images that recur in the book, like the DNA that will appear on its final pages – suggest an all-but cosmic symbiosis between language and its learner. Yet the anecdote of the boy's encounter with it in 'Ground' seems violent, *un*natural. It takes place at the 'ELIGP', an acronym explicated by Scully as 'Eternal Learning Institute of the Gaelic Phantasm' (p.125) – another kind of architectural ghost, it would seem, though one 'institutionalized' and reified in a way so unlike the 'abstract system[s]' being 'made tangible' above. This anecdote transforms what Scully recalls in interview as a 'wholly positive' autobiographical experience of being sent to an 'all-Irish-speaking' boarding school when he was ten[16] – the same age as the boy in this poem painfully 'marked out for language', which is proclaimed 'the *right* age / in fact: 10 years, 3 months, 3 days' (p.48). The ridiculousness of this statement – its surgical precision about 'right' timing for what the volume's other poems view as a 'fluidly' occurring process – suggests the potential violence of inorganic *imposition* of artifice rather than evolving use of it (and Scully's response, perhaps, to the 'vehement nationalism' he later encountered in Dublin at another all-Irish-speaking school).[17]

But this seemingly negative comment on retrievals of Gaelic is significantly qualified, too, in the volume, not only by Scully's frequent use of Irish language – its often pivotal work beside English effecting yet another practice of 'alongness' – but also, more complexly, by the book's recollective imperatives (another of its updates on Wordsworth). Moving 'forward' means '*back* and forth', as we've seen; the consequences of moving solely in '*then-then-then*' fashion—as 'Lyric: Bal/ancing' parodies it by beginning oxymoronically with 'It's resolved. / This is what you need', implying a too-simple update on Olsonian projective poetics—are grave if linguistic histories are forgotten. As Scully says in interview, immersion in Irish, and its prompt to think furthermore of 'the difference between the English spoken on the farm and the English of Dublin', 'were the seed of the attraction to language' for him.[18] Yet 'balance' is key; in 'Ground', there is faltering after being 'marked out' by the 'Words and Music' of an acquired native tongue: 'Deciding always to have your private mind / in ... in fact losing the skill to impart your / full-mind' (p.48; Scully's ellipsis). From the purview of Scully's inclusive practice of recalling *and* moving on from structures, full-on return to one seems potentially threatening to, even substitutive of, the 'private mind'; the gravity of its authentic/authorized/capitalized 'Words and Music' would seem to pull back into its orbit the 'personal ornamentation' that 'unique idiosyncrasies' allow in 'Imprint Studio' above. Like a native language lost, these too seem to need safeguarding from politicized *impositions* of structures – here, by recollection of one's own 'geometr[ies]' language helped make 'tangible' above, as well as earlier-learned choreographies as alternatives to larger and perhaps unsavory political and cultural moves. Scully suggests that the latter evolve uncontested if the child's 'folding land-ridge' (or language), as 'Sunlight' had it, isn't preserved as *comparable* artifice – or as another language, producing what this volume values most: choice or 'chance' against the otherwise sunlight-occluding economic and self-serving power structures that pretend some 'natural' right in our Dantean dark wood:

> The wolf in the plot has a forest made for it,
> then it fits, a glove, a cloak, fur, politics.
> Curved lines of light dissolving into leaf-tip over leaf-tip.
> Terms, conditions, fog at the mouth of the tunnel.
> ' S an t-airgead?
> In the child's language—long ago & far away—'dance.'
> Then that stone, put that stone in yr hand beside this one
> here on the table, its sound ready, its space already occupied,
> for this boy, here, preoccupied, small, to stand back,
> to think. Stand back, melt. Stand back, invent. Back-to-back.
>   Meant. Stand.
> *I dteanga an ghasúir—rince.*
> In the child's folding land-ridge—long ago & far away—echoes
> echo everywhere. Everywhere. So.
> Solid. Blend. Sink. Breathe. Chance.
>
> ('Sunlight', p.23)

Like a 'small' David up against Goliath, the boy here pits his wits *and* his Irish dancing lessons against wolves in sheep's clothing who invert natural processes, tailoring a forest for the cloaking of their work. 'Fog' adds to the bewilderment of a culture that wonders – perhaps especially after the *Tíogar Ceilteach*, masquerading in Irish – 'And the money?' (line 5 above; 'Notes', p.125). Intentional be-'wilderness'-ment is clearly the opposite of what sunlight's beams do in this volume – illuminate and 're-divide solidity' – in that it obscures and *absorbs* (money *and* light; 'light dissolving into leaf-tip over leaf-tip'), instead of presenting new possibilities for what seems unchangeable and objectively 'real'.

The poem recalls an alternative to the wolf's 'plot' in the overall cultural (and increasingly 'global' or corporate) narrative: another, younger language, its David-like stone put by the one already there on the table, trusting 'an aural shiver between two things present' to 'change everything'. It involves, like sunlight, 'melt[ing]' seeming solidities and inventing new ones, 'standing *back*' to think past them, dancing between to echoes – '[e]verywhere' – of once-learned strategies for perceptual foothold less likely to succumb to abstraction's foggy lines, its '[t]erms, conditions'. 'Whose life is this?' the speaker wonders in seeming readiness for full upheaval; the question that follows – 'Where's the dog?' – not only delivers comic relief from the enormity of it (the next question being: '[Where's] [e]verything'), but suggests the proximity of the accepted/mundane and the potentially life-changing. What makes this poem bearable given its asking of what Heidegger would call 'ultimate questions' (though he bracketed the political/economic, as Scully never would), is that its last word summons up the poet's greatest hope: 'Chance', used potentially as both a noun and a verbal directive. Putting things beside other things *changes* things as perceived – though here, the 'echoes' are also things 'So. / Solid' that must be 're-divided', too, in new light. 'Blend[ing]' and melting is what our lyric *subject* must do, in *addition* to preserving his idiosyncrasies; as for this book itself, which the poet sends off not *quite* as Chaucer did ('Goe litel boke', he tells it, but rather than be preserved wholly intact his must 'reade the rocks'), movement into the future for both person and poetry is as a 'prety fascicle' that must 'flee/floor, dive, bricks – swim' (p.48). Fascicle means not only an installment of a book (as this volume might be seen as yet another installment in Scully's long-running work, *Things That Happen*) but also, in biological terms, close to what he calls 'a mesh of energies': a bundle of *structures* such as nerve- or muscle-fibres (or, indeed, conducting vessels in plants) that support life's growth – i.e., the 'trellis' of artifice-plus-energies we simultaneously are, inherit, and make. Such structures are inherently neither good nor bad, as the poem before 'Ground', 'Ballad', concludes: 'Grid. Bad. Grid. Good'. But crucial to their usefulness and their longevity is, paradoxically, their breaking up, as at the beginning of 'Ground' (whose title echoes the first poem's 'Light Ground' of community perceptions/forms):

> Then pieces break off the first and hit
> upper layers of a subsequent that tilt into
> a previous half-established abandoned. (p.47)

Breaking forward to recall the near-lost; orbits added and continuing; circles of the mind; a community's future tilting for structural support into memory in 'the neighborhood / where all's in place / moving apart' ('Lyric: Bal/ancing', p.18). In sync, we might say, the boy is asked to 'Stand back', 'Blend. Sink', *as well as* 'flee ... dive, bricks – swim' – if, instead of receding into 'Rigid grid' (p.46), he's to open up his own 'solidities' of thinking and 'Breathe. Chance'.

So too – and again as with the spider's web – the poet's poem requires stopping upon it, 'waiting' (another recurring word in the volume), and listening; as 'Lyric: Bal/ancing' has it, the poet's 'hearing' is, like the spider's, '[p]ressed to the paper / ink wet softest at / the apical bud', listening for what 'lands' and is 'reverberant' on his page (pp.18, 13). The perceived includes not only what his produced structure allows him in his immediate environment – though he continually asks us to keep *that* in earshot too, recommending, for example, that we 'stop / now & listen to / the bough-top' (p.55) like the boy encountered earlier in 'Tango' – but also 'echoes', as 'Sunlight' located them, 'everywhere'. The latter constitute key 'materials' in the book, issuing both from deep time – or 'what is called the past' (p.49), which he suggests is but a name – and from his own history, from his previous poems and from others' lyrics/ architectures for perceiving and for 'tapping out messages' (p.130).[19] The book's frontispiece concretizes the metaphor with a drawing of an ear intercepting what looks like a page covered with 'glyphs from the rongorongo tablets, undeciphered' ('Notes', p.125), some of which exceed the margins – a jokey play, perhaps, on the poet's as a hypertextually expanding '*web*-page', too (particularly if one needed to google 'rongorongo'). Scully describes his work as a 'threaded web, connecting roots over long distances', which is – clearly increasingly, given our evolution through (*pace* Heidegger) technology – 'part of the way we all experience the world, I think' (p.14). (The glyphs' life beyond the page also suggests their having shaped our daily moves/ eye-dances in ways we've yet to apprehend; more on this below.)

Therefore, for example, Williams' 'This is Just to Say' appears frequently in various echoing musics, recalling his influential phenomenological credo delivered through its unsatisfying 'message' whose sensuality *and* sweet sorrow both depend on the 'things' – plums – no longer present, but still giving rise to his 'ideas'. In Scully's volume, Williams' poem becomes – ironically – less a poetic statement about things than a refrain, a music or dance for moving/ thinking (like Williams' 'Poem (As the Cat)', which echoes more subtly in the volume). And one that he keeps hearing and remaking – in, for example, 'Just to Say', whose title is of course an echo of Williams'. But 'threads / snap' to its precursor as, amid digressions, the poet near mid-poem re-attempts its objective 'stamp' of a start: 'I have eaten / the plums / that were in / the icebox', etc. Scully re-begins: 'I have / I might / I will' but then allows in more of 'life's odd angles' (p.25) on the other solidities present – some additional cereal, mice in the kitchen – as well as only-seemingly unrelated sensual echoes the plums inspire, however uncertainly and from 'the what 19th century // sexual entanglements / politics envy'. His perceptual idiosyncrasies – Williams rarely admitted to influences from the nineteenth-century, certainly – allow Scully to focus not so exclusively on objects, things, or 'plums' like Williams, but also on his work to

> *plumb* the shadowy
> dailiness sliced side-
> ways into the career-
> ing shiver of the actual
>   (my emphasis, p.93)

– which is to say to 'light' the otherwise 'shadowy' in dailiness, *'the that in which'* objects appear, as the next line has it (via a near-quote of Oppen, his 1965 volume *This in Which*), a task that in Scully's view (unlike Oppen's) requires a very long plumb line indeed. Listening to Williams in this poem brings up much more in the way of 'unbidden fruit' (p.94; the play on 'forbidden' fruit underlining the inclusive poetics at work here) – like George Gascoigne, who wrote the first essay on versification in English, as well as, on the other hand, Mallarmé's 'dice' thrown against the solidities of verse forms. Thus its title, 'This is to Say: Sonnet', reflects not the form of the work so much as the poet's back and forth movement between available musics on the way to his own, his moving things out from and into sonnet-like boxes and a pot (like the one Williams' cat steps into), and his thereby 'turn[ing] into English / what I thought I could' while also 'pop[ping]' *à la* Mallarmé 'Paradigm[s] of the Obvious' (like Asch's in his 1950s 'conformity experiments' with community pressure on individuals). All of which illuminates 'just say[ing]'s' unruly and pleasurable ('tingly') mesh of intimacies/energies in the intersection between shadowy thought's hearing and the 'shiver of the actual', a job that, as one line-end above suggests, sheds new light on 'ways into the career', too – that constant *other* imperative of this volume, which never forgets that the poet must 'make / some money to live' (p.17). '[Y]ou will not get all of me, no' he asserted earlier, in 'On a Dark Ground: Work Dance', targeting art-arbiters asked bluntly to 'give [him] some money' (p.17). Not in the old style, certainly, of audience-pleasing lyric exposure – but this later poem suggests a strategy through which something rather more, at least, of the generatively 'private' *is* 'impart[ed]' in the work – and thus some reversal of 'losing the skill to impart your / full-mind' might evolve.

Yet what a 'full-mind' *is*, exactly – or even a life – is a recurrent, 'ultimate' question in the volume. In the late poem 'Echo' Scully asks, 'When exactly / are you born / when exactly / do you fade away'; only illusorily, he suggests, do 'left-hand / margins ... make a / blade' to separate one 'full-mind' from others' thoughts before it, and only foolishly might one want to 'end yr story / with a shiny ribbon / tight about its / awkward bulk amen' (p.112). He offers instead a recurring experience of being 'in a gliding dhow / in sunlight' (having lived in Lesotho, near where such graceful boats do indeed glide). 'Dhow' is also, of course, a homonym of Tao, which views life as ungraspable via concepts but intuited in one's everyday being as it partakes of shared 'is-ness'; its interswimming yin and yang might be seen to augment the volume's orbiting images of interconnectedness inspired by Celtic mythology. Yet Scully's more complex, evolving perception of 'is-ness' produces in *Several Dances* a kind of 'wave-theory' of identity that brings ancient 'fossil horizons' through to poststructuralist ones to contemplate the undelimitability of 'the person', given its growth up through language and other helpful 'trellises' that (if by breaking) shape its living on through 'additions' to them. The enormity *and* comedy of this vision plays out through the dhow image in the book's final pages, which ask (in fading print): 'how far exactly a life across the ocean wave could go / when or how fast or however otherwise by water could it / be so made for a s/lavish little copycat like you' (p.136). Admission to having slavishly 'copied' others' moves is simultaneously the poet's 'lavish' gift to us, a gift of continuing/ communal life (rather than Heidegger's arresting thoughts of singular death). And it may be Scully's version of Coffey's 'greatest gift' one friend can give another, with which he ends *Advent* in hope – meaning the capacity to sacrifice self, as Christ did, rather than the planet and ourselves to greed. But Scully's 'threads everywhere // story ( ) this story' will neither be tied up with a 'shiny ribbon', making it *his* alone to give, nor *ended* in 'amen', as is Coffey's epic, its last words, 'so be it', translating *amen* from the Aramaic (p.42). Indeed, if we read the second line-end above backwards, he's reversed Coffey's amen to move forward in query instead: 'could it / *be so* made'. Certainly he asks us to reverse his letters in (by its title's direction) 'Backing Vocals' – a poem that comes *after* the Coda *and* the book's 'Notes' in this volume that refuses to end where it ought to. Here Scully perhaps qualifies Joyce's 'riverrun[ning]' 'recirculation' of energies which start up *Finnegans Wake* by asking us to read the note he (again like Williams) leaves us, but do it *backwards forwards*, as I've been suggesting – '*reverof* DNA / *yawa* DNA' (p.129) thus becoming 'AND forever / AND away'. 'AND' is indeed the key word in this volume, its lyric, 'private' additions operating *along* with collectively-determining materials, DNA. Movement forward is thus Abrahamic and not Odyssean; there is no going back, but, by accumulative logic, what's back *is* us, and full of dancing lessons.

Therefore Scully listens back and forth but not panoramically *across* like Coffey; for him, the vision of language's changing – 'all those small vowels' carried on by 'chipped & gnarled' consonants', getting stuck in 'pools of isolation' *and* 'flow[ing] on' to 'strange locations' (p.118) – is what reveals spiritual dimensions: 'This is an ikon. / This is the way that / it shimmers' (p.188), like the 'shimmer ahead' of 'dapple of mother spider' at the start of the volume. This vision of movement and change itself as divine – 'the spiritual creative energy that / permeates all life (yes) and stimulates growth' (p.46) – updates Gerard Manley Hopkins's radical vision in 'Pied Beauty' (which famously begins: 'Glory be to God for [*not* pure but] dappled things') by ending 'Orbit', with its image of discarded astronaut urine frozen in space, unexpectedly beautiful, 'crystalline', on the word 'Dapple' (p.120). The opening but not closing parenthesis suggests another orbit begun, as this book was with this word. So inclusive is Scully's ontological study, his appreciation of even what we would put behind us (though it doesn't, as in this case, disperse as we expect), that human limitation itself emerges paradoxically as opening, chance, plumb-line and intimation of immortality. This he perceives through his ikon's 'split blisters'

> a little as it were
> canyon seen from above—
> far—human limitation
>
> (limitation limitation) (p.118)

– the latter becoming itself an echo, with 'bits that stick' to defy limits in this 'delight[ful]' 'process' of delving/listening. Which is itself a movement backwards/forwards that illuminates this book's opening, most enduring and only seemingly simple directive:

> *I dteanga an ghasúir - rince.*
> [In the boy's language - dance.]

NOTES

1. Marthine Satris, 'An Interview with Maurice Scully', *Contemporary Literature* 53.1 (2012), p.2.
2. Satris, pp.2–3.
3. See note ten below. Satris's approach to Scully's work is an example of what Sarah Bennett argues is "the deracinated criticism" that the avant-garde Irish poets "tend to attract" (see note seven below).

4. Maurice Scully, *Several Dances* (Exeter: Shearsman Books, 2014), p.23. Subsequent references in parenthesis.
5. See, for example, 'Ballad [Irish]' in *Several Dances* (p.80).
6. Satris, p.14.
7. Sarah Bennett, 'Love, Sorrow and Joy: Aubade for the Irish Poetry Avant-Garde', *Wave Composition* 5 (August 8, 2012), np.
8. See L.S. Dembo, 'Interview with George Oppen', *Contemporary Literature* 10:2 (Spring 1969), 159–77, 163.
9. *Dasein* means 'being there'. Invented by Heidegger to bring his teacher Husserl's 'egological' idealism back down to earth, it nonetheless relegates perception of 'what is' to the eye of the (single) beholder.
10. Augustus Young, in review of Scully's long-running project, 'Things That Happen', briefly notes this image in earlier volumes as figuring the poet's work in 'making intricate patterns endlessly, and easily brushed away'. (I especially like Young's Scully-like play with sonic coincidences that matter: 'He's a serious writer, or spider.') http://www.goldenhandcuffsreview.com/gh9content/14.php
11. My last four words here are from Anglo-Welsh poet David Jones's *In Parenthesis* (London: Faber & Faber, 1937, p.183). Jones's accumulative, palimpsestic, 'postcolonial' writing (as I read it), illuminating previous structures that accompany/bedevil present perception, looks forward to Scully's project.
12. The latter rhymes with the titular image of Scully's last book, *A Tour of the Lattice* (2011; a reworking of 'Things That Happen', 1981–2006).
13. Brian Coffey, 'Advent', *Irish University Review* 5.1 (Spring 1975), 33–70.
14. See Jonathan Culler on the narrativization of lyric, 'Why Lyric?', *PMLA* 123:1 (2008), 201–206.
15. Satris, p.7.
16. Satris, pp.10–11.
17. Satris, p.11.
18. Satris, p.11.
19. Many may hear here the great W.S. Graham's poem 'Clusters Travelling Out', wherein he 'tap[s]' to his reader 'along the plumbing of the world'.

Niamh O'Mahony

'Releasing the Chaos of Energies': Communicating the Concurrences in Trevor Joyce's Appropriative Poems

In a 1934 review of Herbert Read's book, *Art Now*, Roger Fry criticizes Max Ernst's collages as failing to manifest the 'unconscious urge which governs a genuine artistic sensibility' (245).[1] Close attention to Ernst's art reveals his practice as a process of 'deliberate and conscious invention or adaptation', Fry says. This 'deliberate[ness] and conscious[ness]' stands in opposition to the psychoanalytic unconscious and 'intuitive unreason' which are said to characterize art and criticism in the Surrealist tradition. The Surrealist affirmation of collage and other appropriative forms as abstruse and abstracted proved problematic for critics such as Fry, and yet these parameters still delimit our contemporary definitions of collage, even as contemporary poets put these practices to different uses. This essay addresses Trevor Joyce's appropriative practice and his capacity to gather text together and produce poems which are distinctly expressive and meaningful.

Joyce's appropriative practice demonstrates the importance of developing the contemporary definition of appropriation to reflect the innovations in contemporary poetry. After outlining Joyce's early foray into poetic appropriation, I will move to a close reading of his 2009 poem 'De Iron Trote' which aggregates material from a vast array of texts and contexts. Joyce's poem reveals the conceptual limits of contemporary definitions of appropriation by using a formally complex practice to produce a powerfully declarative poem. The purpose of describing Joyce's appropriative practice as declarative is to assert the articulate nature of his appropriations which interact with and respond to each other through rhyme, imagery, and the near-imperceptible changes Joyce makes to the text he appropriates. The word declarative also supports the concept of the poet writing which appropriation retains but that is denied by more intertextual

Irish University Review 46.1 (2016): 119–131
DOI: 10.3366/iur.2016.0205
© Edinburgh University Press
www.euppublishing.com/journal/iur

approaches to textual borrowing. The performative nature of the declarative presents Joyce's appropriations as articulate and meaningful, and sustains rather than effaces the individual poet writing. My purpose in selecting this word to describe Joyce's appropriative practice is not to suggest that the aggregation of text in his poems achieves an expository or didactic force. Instead I am using the word to assert the articulate nature of his appropriations; that is, to assert the potential for a phrase or line from one source to speak to a phrase or line from another. In this essay, I situate Joyce's practice within the current conversation concerning the relation between formal complexity and lyric expression in criticism. Aligning Joyce's appropriative practice with this discussion of the relation between formal complexity and expressiveness in poetry grants a clearer perspective on his work, and on the practice of appropriation in poetry.

INTERPRETING APPROPRIATION IN JOYCE'S 'DE IRON TROTE'
Joyce published his first collection, *Sole Glum Trek*, in 1967 with New Writers' Press, jointly run by Joyce, Michael and Irene Smith in Dublin. This first collection was followed by *Watches* (1969), *Pentahedron* (1972), and *The Poems of Sweeny, Peregrine* (1976), at which point Joyce stopped publishing poetry for nearly twenty years. *The Poems of Sweeny, Peregrine* could be read as Joyce's first engagement with appropriation. The poem sees Joyce carrying over the eighth-century myth of the Irish King Sweeny who was cursed by Saint Ronan to wander the woods deranged and alone until his death. Joyce subtitles *Sweeny* as a 'working' rather than a translation 'of the corrupt Irish text'. This subtitle acknowledges Joyce's reading of the original ancient Irish text alongside English translations by J.G. O'Keeffe among others, and calls attention to the many differences and discrepancies across the various manuscripts. *Sweeny* might be Joyce's first attempt at reusing the words of others in his writing, but it does not reflect the same appropriative style that we find in his more recent poetry. 'De Iron Trote' exemplifies Joyce's current appropriative practice. The poem is divided into two parts which variously challenge and respond to each other, and I will address each in turn.

'DE IRON TROTE': PART ONE
'De Iron Trote' appears midway through the 'Undone' section of *What's in Store* (2007) which is Joyce's twelfth collection of poems and is still his most substantial volume, running to more than three hundred pages. The two tables of contents which appear in the book, one at the front and a more detailed version to the back, list the many

translations or workings of European folksong, of Turkic and Finno-Ugric verses, and of the Chinese and the Irish. There are densely procedural poems, many variations on constraint, and an enduring negotiation with traditional lyric forms, both as a resistance to and a redefinition of that form. The 'Undone' section is comprised of five poems with dedications to Alison Croggon, Keith Tuma, and Fanny Howe. 'Causes of Affects', 'De Iron Trote', and 'The Peacock's Tale' are each appropriative in structure, while 'Dramatis Personae' mirrors the lyric sections of these three poems, and 'Elements' is a chiasmus. The title, 'Undone', might be read as reflecting the lack of intentional expression and sentiment in these densely aggregative texts while also suggesting the processes of unravelling and textual unmaking which characterize the poems.[2]

Joyce's use of conceptual rhyme and imagery and his modification of individual lines and phrases differentiates his appropriative practice from the Surrealist commitment to the unconscious, while also encouraging a more explicitly meaningful poetry that breaches the borders of lyricism. The first part of 'De Iron Trote' is aggregative in form, gathering together a multitude of diverse source texts. Part one runs over two and a half pages with paragraphs of varying length and begins as follows:

> As man, in deep and level sleep, periodically draws a
> long inspiration, song is learned and figured in the brain.
> Think of the way a musical box, wound up, potentially
> represents a slow or lively air.[3]

The opening image of a man inhaling a breath in sleep runs into the description of song learnt and manifest in the mind, and the paragraph proceeds with the instruction to consider a musical box which 'potentially / represents' song. The didactic, or declarative tone is carried over from the two source texts, Logan Clendening's *Source Book of Medical History* and T.H. Huxley's 'On The Hypothesis that Animals are Automata, and its History', and it contrasts with the peculiar nature of the proposition. The opening paragraph serves as an exposition of the tone, form, and themes of 'De Iron Trote', and the questions that arise indicate the difficulty of interpreting Joyce's appropriative poetry. Several conceptual rhymes emerge across the first section of the poem; the definition and distinction of the human as a cultural being in the first paragraph rhymes with the degradation of the human in the third; the Munster Plantation which is a primary image in the third paragraph parallels the imperial power manifested in the Ancient Chinese hunting parks invoked via E. H. Schafer's 1968 essay; and the apprenticeship of Ticket writers in the final paragraphs rhymes with Joyce's own practice as a poet and the writing of this poem. Joyce uses prepositions and adverbs to consolidate his sentences and sustain the block prose structure of the poem. These grammatical interventions help realise the declarative potential of 'De Iron Trote' by providing a centre-point of a rhyme or compounding the various meanings of a word to multiply relations between the lines.

The third paragraph of the poem exemplifies the expressive quality of Joyce's appropriative practice in 'De Iron Trote'. The first seven lines of the paragraph proceed as follows:

> Garments of silk, or thin dry wool, also give rise to a
> noise calculated to cause error, sometimes mitigating
> the production and carefully controlled cropping of live
> creatures for high ends. Else, from every corner of the
> woods and glens see them come creeping on their hands,
> for their legs cannot make fast, as in humans the larynx
> migrates down the neck since the age of eighteen
> months, from which arises the sound of voices.
> ('De Iron Trote', p.233)

The 'garments of silk or thin dry wool' that 'give rise to a noise calculated to cause error' become a 'mitigating' factor, literally 'alleviat[ing] or giv[ing] relief from the 'production and carefully controlled cropping of live creatures for high ends' in Zhou Dynasty China.[4] The following word, 'Else', 'like its synonym *other* admits contextually of two different interpretations: e.g., something else may mean 'something in addition' to what is mentioned, or "something as an alternative or a substitute"'.[5] Here, the word connects Schafer's description of the Chinese wildlife preserves from the second century B.C.E. in his essay on 'Hunting Parks and Animal Enclosures in Ancient China', with Edmund Spenser's description of the Irish 'creeping on their hands' 'from every corner of the / woods and glens' in *A View of the Present State of Ireland*.[6] Joyce's poem permits both interpretations, combining the Chinese and the Irish examples while also making them alternatives for one another. In this way, the 'production and carefully controlled cropping of live / creatures for high ends' compounds Spenser's representation of the Munster Plantation, while also becoming exchangeable with it so that the 'live animals', of the Chinese leisure parks are synonymous with the native population of the Irish colony. Joyce's use of the adverb 'else' to ground a conceptual rhyme about imperialism in Ancient China and sixteenth-century Munster serves as another example of the effects and techniques he uses to encourage the expressive or lyrical force of his appropriations. It is not only the changes that the poet makes to the text he appropriates which contribute to the declarative force of this appropriative poem. Joyce also incorporates a self-annotative element to his appropriations that grant 'De Iron Trote' a particularly self-conscious, articulate quality.

The comment on speech development which intervenes after the conceptual rhyme on imperialism is continued through the remainder of the third paragraph and supports the poem's declarative force:

> In time
> these come to speak of a political meeting, of market
> shares. Someone tells of a woman who murdered
> her lover. 'A chauffeur kills his wife', says another.
> All teetotallers like sugar. No nightingale drinks wine.
> Go figure. ('De Iron Trote', p.233)

After Clive Ponting's account of speech in infants, the poem introduces a cacophony of voices which itself invokes a longer history of poetic appropriation and aesthetics. These voices are drawn from the opening lines of Rosalind Krauss's 1998 study, *The Picasso Papers*, and refer specifically to Picasso's newspaper collages from the 1910s.[7] In effect, Joyce's poem directs readers towards its aesthetic influences and sources, with the obligatory degree of textual remove and dissociation via Krauss. The following lines describing Picasso's processes of composition from *The Picasso Papers* provide a critical correlative for 'De Iron Trote':

> Each newsprint fragment forms the sign for a visual meaning; then, as it butts against another, the sign re-forms and the meaning shifts ... [E]ach little paper piece submits itself to meaning, but never enduringly so. For the same piece, in another location, constellates another sign.[8]

These lines could serve as a description of Joyce's poem as easily as they do of Picasso's collage, and yet there is something discomfiting about the poet suggesting this analogy for his own practice. Picasso's status, alongside Georges Braque, as a creator of collage makes him a potent reference point in the analysis of Joyce's appropriative practice. The poet offers a more nuanced account of his practice in a series of emails from 2013.

In these two emails to me from spring 2013, Joyce articulates his assessment of the appropriative practices shaping 'De Iron Trote' and their function within his poetics.[9] Starting with his sources, Joyce explains that his selections tend towards older texts which are 'rancid with nostalgia' and 'almost fracturing already under the pressure of too much meaning'.[10] This pressure might be attributed to 'figures of speech (explicit or not) tearing [the texts] apart', or simply to the fact that they come from 'an older time or ... different sensibility'. Examples of Joyce's 'fracturing' texts are replete within the poem, notably Spenser's *A View* which comes laden not only with the specific social and literary contexts of sixteenth-century England, but also with the political and historical contexts of Ireland which are compounded for an Irish poet such as Joyce living and working in post-colonial Ireland. The reference from *Trades for London Boys* in the final three paragraphs could also be read as 'fracturing ... under the pressure', although the pressure impacting this text is different to that afflicting Spenser's text. The excerpts from *Trades for London Boys* provides an analogy between Joyce's practice as a poet and the formal training required of these apprentice ticket writers.[11] Meanwhile, the pressure that manifests itself in the middle lines of paragraph six where Joyce borrows from Peter Beckford's 1847 text, *Thoughts on Hunting*, regards the 'figures of speech' which are serve as a warning against idle chatter among the huntsmen. If the poet collates source texts which reflect an overbearing pressure of meaning, what is the effect when these texts are gathered together in a poem? Joyce offers his response to this question in his description of 'De Iron Trote' and similarly procedural poems as:

> [I]mmersed within language, and comprised of the elements of language, words, syntax, [and] register, ... which are often traceable, in differing granularities, to a variety of other texts, but they don't rely on those other texts being recognized and recalled to memory.[12]

For Joyce, then, these poems are a composite of language and literature which emerges at the local level of letters and syntax. The primary imperative for appropriating a text is the poem itself, and the texts appropriated must be 'traceable'. 'De Iron Trote' does not require that every text be revealed and recorded by the reader. The poet works with 'distinct methods' and 'local effects' to gather letters and words towards the constitution of a line of poetry, and this aggregation of text progresses in accordance with the immediate demands of the line.[13]

'De Iron Trote' is symptomatic of Joyce's 'many attempts to bring together diverse materials', but it is not enough to amalgamate various texts.[14] The poet demands that these texts 'mutually resonate', and this resonance manifests itself with Poundian force, 'transfusing, welding, and unifying', so that 'the whole assemblage constitutes a new meaning'.[15] Joyce's appropriations are declarative to the extent that they provoke language to unfamiliar and even unintentional patterns of association, and the resonance he finds in a successful poem does not delimit those patterns of association.

'DE IRON TROTE': PART TWO

The first and second sections of 'De Iron Trote' appear to assert opposing stances on appropriation; however, this second section does bear the marks of different poems and texts. It might illuminate a reading of this verse section to relate Joyce's 'train / of state' in the ninth stanza to the same phrase in Samuel Johnson's 'The Vanity of Human Wishes' ('De Iron Trote', p.239). The tenth stanza of Johnson's poem addresses Thomas Wolsey, a clergyman and politician who amassed a great fortune and lavish properties during Henry VIII's reign. Wolsey played an important role in the progressive redefinition of appropriation during the English Reformation. A 1743 biography of Wolsey asserts that contemporary historians charged the politician with 'sacrilege, on account of the dissolution of ... forty monasteries'.[16] In 'The Vanity of Human Wishes', Johnson dramatizes the King's turn against Wolsey and his alienation from Court by a retinue of courtiers and attendants:

> Claim leads to claim, and power advances power;
> Till conquest unresisted ceased to please,
> And rights submitted, left him none to seize.
> At length his sovereign frowns – the train of state
> Mark the keen glance, and watch the sign to hate. ...[17]

This reproach of Wolsey in Johnson's poem is followed by another of King Charles XII of Sweden which is read as 'skilfully includ[ing] many of Johnson's familiar themes' that echo the themes of 'De Iron Trote'.[18] These themes include 'repulsion with slaughter that aggrandizes one man and kills and impoverishes thousands, understanding of the human need to glorify heroes, and subtle contrast with the classical parent-poem [in Juvenal's Satire X] and its inadequate moral vision'. One could interpret Johnson's thematic influences as supporting Joyce's interest in the human consciousness expressed in the opening stanza in 'De Iron Trote' and the concomitant portrayal of colonialism in Ireland. That said, Joyce puts Johnson's 'train of state' to different use in his poem, demonstrating the difficulty of making assertions about the poet's intention in appropriating a text and its cultural and political resonances within the poem. 'De Iron Trote' extends the phrase beyond Johnson's regal ascription to accommodate a more literal meaning. The phrase is elaborated in the final stanzas of the second section:

> Let's catch
>   the track
>
> will lead us
>   to our train
>   of state,
> then venerably
>
>   process.'
>
> ....
>   *You've heard it's true.*
> *that by a snifting*
>   *clack*
>   *the air*
> *is expelled*
>   *from the*
>   *pickle-pot.* ('De Iron Trote', pp.237–38)

A 'snifting clack' is an old name for the safety valve on a steam engine that ejects air from the cylinder, and so the 'train / of state' in Joyce's poem recalls not just the royal retinue but also, through the 'track' and 'snifting clack', an actual train. The word 'process' compounds this interpretation by invoking the royal procession or 'train of state', and commenting reflexively on the procedural form of the poem. This term also suggests the mechanical process of the steam engine, and the 'process' or trial that Wolsey faced.[19] It is these final lines that present the second section of 'De Iron Trote' as the inverse of the first with regards to appropriation. Here, Joyce sets two separate stanzas in quotation marks, neither of which gives way to ostensible bibliographical sources.

There may appear to be little in the way of thematic connections between the two sections of 'De Iron Trote', and these opposed approaches to appropriation serve as evidence of Joyce's divergence from Picasso's collage practices. The form and structure of 'De Iron Trote' also problematizes received ideas of meaning-making and interpretation in poetry. Questions arise regarding Joyce's capacity to express himself through his appropriations, and about the possibility of there being anything meaningful or articulate within a poem composed in this way. These questions are addressed in recent essays and statements by Rachel Galvin, Keston Sutherland, and Andrea

Brady, and their responses are helpful in elaborating an alternative approach to appropriation.

REINTERPRETING APPROPRIATION IN CONTEMPORARY POETRY

In 2014, Galvin published an essay entitled 'Lyric Backlash' in *Boston Review* which responds to Calvin Bedient's essay in the same journal and argues for a critical interrogation of the opposition of lyric expression and formal innovation in poetry.[20] Galvin reads César Vallejo and M. NourbeSe Philip, two poets whom Bedient situates at opposite ends of the lyric/conceptualist spectrum, as 'both compos[ing] poetry according to formal concepts or constraints' such as appropriation, and yet both poets also 'strongly communicate affect'. Sutherland makes a similar argument for deconstituting the opposition of authorial expression and formal complexity in a blogpost for the 'Revolution and/or Poetry' conference at the University of California in 2013. According to Sutherland, '"Lyrical confession" versus "formal complexity" is a false contest whose function in literary critical culture is to blackmail poets and readers out of the formal complexities of subjectivity: the formal complexities of life itself'.[21] Galvin and Sutherland each articulate their arguments differently, and these differences reflect a broader divergence in critical opinions. Some critics emphasize a return to lyric poetry while others encourage a more expansive definition of conceptualist poetics, but these critics are united in absolving practices such as appropriation from the accusation of leading to meaninglessness in poetry, and of the anti-subjective, anti-lyrical imperatives that the Conceptualists attribute to such procedural practices.

Andrea Brady's 2010 poem *Wildfire* reveals the multiple meanings and interpretations of appropriation that exist, and demonstrates the necessity of redefining the practice for contemporary poetry and criticism. Brady's poem incorporates appropriation in terms which counteract the explicit de-subjectifying effect of conceptualist appropriation practised by Kenneth Goldsmith among others, and is indicative of the complexity of the practice and the divergence of an individual poet's engagements with appropriation.[22] *Wildfire* is subtitled a 'Verse Essay on Obscurity and Illumination' and the poem appropriates material from a vast range of texts. The sources of *Wildfire* include Ancient Greek works such as Theophrastus's *De Igne* and Marcus Graecus's *Liber Ignium*, as well as contemporary texts including Richard E. Threlfall's *The Story of 100 Years of Phosphorus Making, 1851–1951* (1951) and Ernest Volkman's *Science Goes to War* (2010). Brady's negotiation of appropriation must diverge significantly from the conceptualist approach to avoid replacing subjective expression with a 'mass of free-floating language' as conceptualism aims to do.[23] In her 'note on the text' which accompanies the poem, the poet details her intentions and motivations in writing *Wildfire*. Brady describes her difficulty appropriating text in an earlier poem entitled *Sweatbox* which she later abandoned, and this experience provides the impetus for *Wildfire*:

> The failure of my first effort to write such a poem, *Sweatbox*, showed me unable to cope with a rapidly unravelling history ... Epic fragments were transported by Penguin Classics to a nook in London then back out to a pixellated field sewn with cluster bomblets and the shards of the Nemean lion. I busied myself at the British Museum, reading the blurbs, constellating fragments as a melancholic formal reminder of the fractures and losses in real-time reporting and in the dispersal of a living culture. But I couldn't keep up with the news, couldn't fit that fast degeneration to an epic impasto worth thousands of years.[24]

The note describes Brady's engagement with appropriation and her intimate knowledge of the dangers implicit in borrowing texts. Brady differs from the conceptualists in the extent to which she acknowledges her own role in the selection of text and materials. Her reflection on the failed poem entitled *Sweatbox* shows the poet positioning herself as mediator of materials and text which are 'transported ... to a nook in London' where she lives or works, and then transferred out again 'to a pixellated field' (*Wildfire*, p.70). Responsibility for the poem rests solely with the poet and this is reflected in the acutely personal nature of her note on the text: '*my* first effort ... showed *me* unable', '*I* busied *myself* at the British Museum', 'But *I* couldn't keep up with the news' (emphasis added) (*Wildfire*, pp.70–1). Her sense of responsibility to and for the poem is entirely at odds with Goldsmith's orientation to composition as 'a perfunctory affair'.[25] Brady's account of the difficulties she experienced with *Sweatbox* serve as evidence both of her appreciation of appropriation as a uniquely declarative practice and of her awareness of the problems that surround it, problems which recur in Joyce's poetry and practice. Brady's introduction to *Wildfire* demonstrates that the ethical questions that problematize appropriation are not solely concerned with originality and meaning but also regard the 'appropriateness' of the materials aggregated and their orientation to the matter or concern of the poem.

One of the major problems in writing *Sweatbox*, which Brady sought to resolve in *Wildfire*, was that of authority, both her own authority to recount and respond to the atrocities of the Iraq War and the authority of her representations developed through the poem. In her note to *Wildfire*, Brady describes her struggle to overcome these difficulties in the earlier attempted poem:

> My appropriations showed through: the desire for wholeness implicit in the phrases airlifted from news bulletins; the desire for the right and the position to speak, for consensus and legitimacy of representation. The absence of those rights and places, the mourning echoes of the epic voice, turned the poem all tawdry ironic – better than a barbaric silence, but only just. (*Wildfire*, pp.70–1)

Brady's notes reflect the complex nature of poetic appropriation and issues of ethics and authority both in the appropriation of another author's text and in the practice of representation. Brady seeks to resolve some of these problems in *Wildfire*, or at least to become more acquainted with them. The fact that her 2010 poem was published coterminously with Place's *The Guilt Project* and *Statement of Facts*, and within years of defining conceptualist texts by Goldsmith, Caroline Bergvall, and Robert Fitterman, demonstrates that multiple meanings and interpretations of appropriation do exist simultaneously in poetry.[26]

This critical reinterpretation of appropriation encourages an alternative perspective on 'De Iron Trote', and on Joyce's practice more generally. It is Joyce's sense of responsibility to his materials and his belief that these various texts find some resonance through their alignment which distinguishes his appropriative practice from that of the Conceptualists. In 'De Iron Trote', Joyce invokes Spenser and Johnson to reveal the violent history of language, and the impossibility of escaping that violence in the use of language, whether in poetry, criticism, or conversation. Taken this way, appropriation is not an abstruse, abstracted practice intended to confuse and perplex readers and critics; it can also be a deeply meaningful form whose declarative force comes through in the many rhymes and concurrences that emerge across texts and contexts, as well as the clash and rupturing of individual lines and phrases within the poem. Joyce's poetry demands a more expansive interpretation of poetic borrowing for which the appropriation of text is not opposed to expression or meaning but actually enables a more explicit account of both the poet's and the reader's experience of the world. Joyce's poetry extends critical understandings of appropriation in poetry, and of Irish poetry more generally, by challenging the precepts and parameters of both categories and demanding more of critical readings of his work.

NOTES

1. Roger Fry, 'Review of Art Now: An Introduction to the Theory of Modern Painting and Sculpture by Herbert Read', *The Burlington Magazine for Connoisseurs* 64.374 (1934), p.2445.

2. The 'Undone' title also recalls Joyce's twin 2003 chapbooks, *Take Over* and *Undone, Say*, published by The Gig. According to Jeffrey Twitchell-Waas, the 'cover of the chapbook, *Undone, Say*, in which "The Peacock's Tale" was first published, give[s] a complete listing of the various word strings of "rhyme chains" Joyce incorporates into the lyric half of the poem, as well as those for "De Iron Trote"' (p.216). It is also notable, Twitchell-Waas says, that 'the aural rhyme chains are far more prominent in "De Iron Trote" than in "The Peacock's Tale"'.

3. Trevor Joyce, 'De Iron Trote', *What's in Store: Poems 2000–2007* (Dublin: New Writers' Press; Willowdale, ON: The Gig, 2007), p.233. Subsequent references are in parentheses.

4. 'Mitigate'. *The Oxford Online Dictionary*. 1989 http://www.oed.com/ [accessed 5 December 2015]

5. 'Else'. *The Oxford Online Dictionary*. 1898 http://www.oed.com/ [accessed 5 December 2015]

6. Edmund Spenser, *The Complete Works of Spenser: A View of the Present State of Ireland* (London: Scholartis, 1934), p.233.

7. The collage in question is Picasso's 'Violin and Newspaper' from November 1912 which includes a newspaper headline in the bottom left-hand corner of the canvas that reads 'Un Chauffeur Tue sa Femme'.

8. Rosalind E. Krauss, *The Picasso Papers* (New York: Farrar, Straus, and Giroux, 1998), p.1.

9. My thanks to Trevor Joyce for permission to quote from these emails.

10. Trevor Joyce, Private Email to Niamh O'Mahony, 1 March 2013.

11. In *Trades for London Boys*, the profession of Ticket and Showcard Writing is described as involving 'the writing of inscriptions and designs on shop window tickets, and all cards for advertisement and display which are not made in sufficient numbers to be worth printing' (*Trades for London Boys and How to Enter Them*. Ed. Apprenticeship and Skilled Labor Association of Denison House (London: Longmans, Green and co., 1908), p.32).

12. Trevor Joyce, Private Email to Niamh O'Mahony, 17 February 2013.

13. Trevor Joyce, Private Email to Niamh O'Mahony, 29 March 2013.

14. Trevor Joyce, Private Email to Niamh O'Mahony, 29 March 2013.

15. Ezra Pound, *Literary Essays*, intro. T. S. Eliot. (Norfolk, CT: New Directions, 1954), p.49.

16. Joseph Grove and George Cavendish, *The History of the Life and Times of Cardinal Wolsey: Prime Minister to King Henry VIII*, Vol. 3. 2nd ed. (London: Royal Exchange, 1743), p.430. *Google Book Search* < http://bit.ly/1Nz5bwd >, [accessed 5 December 2015]. The authors are careful to point out that Wolsey put the revenue of these monasteries to 'a spiritual use' (p.430).

17. Samuel Johnson. 'The Vanity of Human Wishes', *Samuel Johnson: Selected Poetry and Prose*. Ed. Frank Brady and William Kurtz Wimsatt. (Berkeley: University of California Press, 1997), p.60.

18. Howard D. Weinbrot, *Aspects of Samuel Johnson: Essays on His Arts, Mind, Afterlife, and Politics*. (Newark: University of Delaware Press, 2005), p.47.

19. My thanks to David Lloyd for elaborating the various meanings of this phrase in Joyce's poem.

20. Rachel Galvin, 'Lyric Backlash'. *Boston Review*. 11 Feb. 2014. Web. < http://www.bostonreview.net/poetry/rachel-galvin-lyric-backlash >, [accessed 4 Dec 2015].

21. Keston Sutherland, 'Statement for 'Revolution and/or Poetry' (*Revolutionandorpoetry*. 15 Oct. 2013.) [accessed 29 August 2014].

22. In his essay, 'Flarf is Dionysus. Conceptual Writing is Apollo', Goldsmith acknowledges the deconstitution of the poet writing under conceptualism: 'Come to think of it, no one's really written a word of it. It's been grabbed, cut, pasted, processed, machined. . . . With so much available language, does anyone really need to write more?' (Kenneth Goldsmith. 'Flarf is Dionysus. Conceptual Writing is Apollo', *Poetry*, 2014 <http://www.poetryfoundation.org/poetrymagazine/article/237176> [accessed 5 December 2015], n.p.)

23. Goldsmith, 'Flarf is Dionysus', n.p.

24. Andrea Brady, *Wildfire: A Verse Essay on Obscurity and Illumination*. (San Francisco: Krupskaya, 2010.), pp.70–71. Subsequent references in parentheses.

25. Kenneth Goldsmith, 'Paragraphs on Conceptual Writing,' *BuffaloElectronic Poetry Centre*, 2005 <http://epc.buffalo.edu/authors/goldsmith/conceptual_paragraphs.html> [accessed 5 December 2015].

26.. Goldsmith published *Traffic* in 2007 and *Sports* in 2008. Bergvall's 'Via' was published in *Fig* in 2005 and Fitterman published 'Notes to Conceptualism' with Place in 2011.

Marthine Satris

Codex Vitae: The Material Poetics of Randolph Healy's 'Arbor Vitae'

Experimental poets innovate formally in order to undermine expectations of what poetry should be. Many also do so in order to draw attention to the language and form of the poetry itself, highlighting the mediating work that language does and often playing down the referential elements of poetry. While such work can broaden conversations about what poetry is as a concept and a genre, those skeptical of this branch of the poetry tree have argued that the innovative turn in poetry is solipsistic, in that it separates writing from the material, lived world and from readers. However, Randolph Healy's 1997 poem 'Arbor Vitae' (Latin for 'Tree of Life'), shows how a formally innovative, difficult poem that is explicitly about language can also be a political, public act. Healy's poetic output since his first book was published in 1983 has been slim (two books and a number of chapbooks), but it includes several long poems and sequences that differ radically from mainstream Irish poetry. Early critics who attended to his work, including Robert Archambeau and David Lloyd, note that Healy, a long-time physics teacher, renovates poetic language by bringing in scientific terminology and frameworks.[1] But his long poem 'Arbor Vitae' does more than that. In exploring the experience of the deaf[2] in Ireland after teaching sign language in state-run schools was banned, Healy foregrounds language as mediation to show us the dimensions that are lost to our world if we do not allow for different forms of expression and meaning-making.

Healy's long poem is in three parts, with a 'Footnote' appended at the end. The poem was first published by Healy's press Wild Honey as a chapbook in 1997, at which point a concluding note was not included, though the 'Footnote' has appeared in each rendition of the poem since. In the following analysis, I am using the version of the poem that was published in Healy's 2002 book *Green 532: Selected Poems 1983–2000*, in which the three verse sections total seventeen pages and the 'Footnote' is four pages.[3] The first section

Irish University Review 46.1 (2016): 132–144
DOI: 10.3366/iur.2016.0206
© Edinburgh University Press
www.euppublishing.com/journal/iur

of 'Arbor Vitae' addresses the Irish Deaf experience specifically, the second section expands to look at the history of sign-based communication more widely, and part three begins to offer some solutions or hope for the future not through hearing aids or surgeries, but through social and cultural inclusion of the deaf. The footnote both explains the poet's personal investment in understanding his daughter's experience of deafness and notes the sources of the material that originates elsewhere.

The three verse sections are made of both newly composed and found language; each element is placed one below the next, usually separated by blank space, with no overt connections made other than sharing space on the same page. Healy assembles his text through a variety of procedures and constraints, including acrostics, which reveal how the body and language are interconnected, and how both are managed by the state. His poetic amalgamation of sign systems – he draws on computer languages, sign language, non-verbal signifiers, histories of deafness, and verbal puzzles – contributes the voices of the erased and repressed to Irish literature by defamiliarizing techniques and technologies of information management that we accept as natural. 'Arbor Vitae', in both form and content, communicates an appreciation for variation over conformity, and critiques the state by exposing its institutional enforcement of an ideology that devalues its own citizens and insists on the naturalness of one form of communication over all others for Irish citizens. The poem is a rare example of a contemporary Irish poem that uses formal innovation to exemplify what it calls on its readers to do: recognize that the line we draw between ourselves and those against whom we define ourselves is artificial, and that such a division separates us from lives that can only broaden and deepen our own experience of the world.

One of the challenges Irish lyric poetry has long faced is the demand on poets to write a bardic, public poetry, while they also feel drawn to write a private, individual poetry. In 'Arbor Vitae', the formal choice to corral the personal into the extensive 'Footnote' that follows the poem allows Healy's 'Arbor Vitae' to be both public and private, merging the two forms of writing without the worry of betraying poetry or betraying his people. I conducted an interview with Healy in 2009 in order to discover more about his poetry, since little criticism has been published on his work as a poet. Of his choice to append a clarifying note, Healy told me, 'There was a public element to "Arbor Vitae", and while I had to write in a particular way for myself with my own limitations as a writer, I felt it would be a shame if I managed to obliterate what were very important issues.'[4] This two-part structure contributes a thickness of meaning to the internally fragmented form of the poem, as well. The poem's driving purpose is expressed through a rhetoric of logos, and the pathos of intimate experience is reserved for the most academic of forms, the footnote, an irony I will explore further below. Therefore, the poem created is distinct from either of the expected genres of English verse, narrative epic or expressive lyric. Healy's use of assemblage breaks the hold of lyric expression on Irish poetry, as his poem and its lengthy accompanying note move toward an essay-like form. Because of the depersonalized focus in 'Arbor Vitae' on the *context* of his personal experience, the poem itself turns outwards, toward the cultural assumptions about language and citizenship that have gone unrecognized during the Republic of Ireland's establishment of itself as a nation-state.

The country of Ireland has long been figured as caught between English and Irish, between imperialism and nationalism, but when we reduce questions of language and identity to this black-and-white opposition, we ignore those in Ireland whose lived experience lies outside of this narrow spectrum. By starting from the experience of the deaf in Ireland, 'Arbor Vitae' brings together a critique of the state's use of its social institutions to repress its own citizens and an investigation of how we as embodied minds interpret the world and communicate that experience. In doing so, this poem moves aside questions of national boundaries that have so preoccupied Irish poets and critics to consider instead the effects of nationalist ideology on the lives and bodies of its citizens. Thus 'Arbor Vitae' contributes to a poetic tradition concerned with language and citizenship, but redirects the conversation away from authenticity or how language connects poet to nation and instead develops both a poetics and ethics of intersection. This poem examines ethics in society, but not the ethics of violence and tribe. It's an argument in the form of poem about the ethics of citizenship, and it argues for the value of difference.

In both form and content, Healy's long poem indicts the policies of the Republic for the hypocrisy of its treatment of disabled citizens and challenges the power of the state.[5] When the Republic's Department of Education took over the two main schools for the deaf (based in Cabra, near Dublin) in 1946 (girls' school) and 1957 (boys' school), all signing was banned, signing teachers were removed, and the students were taught lipreading and speech to better integrate with hearing society.[6] In 1979 the Irish Deaf protested this repression of their language and brought out a dictionary of Irish Sign Language, which evolved from the signs taught in the Cabra school for the deaf before signing was banned.[7] However, suggestions brought to the Dáil to make Irish Sign Language an official language of the State have been routinely denied.[8] 'Arbor Vitae' is premised on the notion that all systems of communication have equal value, and as a poem dedicated to examining communication itself, 'Arbor Vitae' has no choice but to engage the reader in thinking about the poem's own language even as she tries to parse the collaged text.

It's not hard to grasp the content of the poem, since the three verse sections are composed of neatly divided precise records of physical experiences or historical facts, mostly expressed without sentiment or excitement. The overall impression is of a matter-of-fact delivery of informative content, as is often true in Healy's poems. One example of a 'stanza' reads as follows: 'Paris 1779. / Pierre Desloges bookbinder / wrote *Observations of a Deaf-Mute* / denying that his native Old French Sign Language / lacked any grammar'.[9] This 'nonpoetic' character of Healy's language and form has been noted by many readers of his poetry, including fellow poet Trevor Joyce, as well as the scholars Peter Riley, Alex Davis, and David Annwn. Peter Riley, reviewing Healy's *Green 532: Selected Poems 1983–2000,* writes that Healy's poetry is a 'scientific exploration of the bounds and possibilities of language and existence', an approach that does not strip affect from language and communication, but refreshes it.[10] But the purpose in bringing all these facts and experiences together is what challenges the reader. Healy's tone is one common to a logic and research-based argument rather than to a lyric, and as introduced above, this poem moves into the genre of an essay by assembling information for the reader. As David Wheatley has pointed out, in countering Justin Quinn's dismissal of the poem for lacking cohesion and metaphorical imagery,[11] 'Any suspicion that this might be a poetic watering-down should be resisted; the essayistic poem-prose hybrid demands to be seen as a genre unto itself.'[12] This 'essayistic poem-prose hybrid' is especially associated with Modernism and has been contributed to by William Carlos Williams and Susan Howe, among others. The Modernist tradition to which these poets and Healy belong is also one of parataxis, difficulty, and intellectualism emerging from T.S. Eliot's reaction against the sensibility of Romantic poets and preference for the metaphysical poets' difficulty and conceit.[13] But more than just moving away from using poetry to distill a memory or to recollect a sensation, Healy's poem returns us to an older tradition of poetry where 'poem' was not assumed to mean 'lyric' but could be as rhetorically persuasive and as linguistically charged as Pope's 'Essay on Criticism'. Healy continues the buried line of poetry as persuasion, only this time amplifying the voices of the dismissed and oppressed.

Healy uses parataxis to assemble his poetry of persuasion, relying on the human instinct to find patterns and links, our cognitive leaps, to create the poem's throughline. In one small portion of the second section of 'Arbor Vitae', Healy lists several different non-verbal types of communication, implicitly challenging the reader to determine whether one is more complete or more authentic than the others:

dot dash   dash dot   dash dot dot

A cross inside a circle portrayed a sheep.
Cut a notch to make it into a ewe,
two notches and it is pregnant.

Wings thrash as a bird breaks cover.
One word, then another, and another
until the conversation fills the sky.[14]

This listing of Morse code, pictograms, and the non-verbal communication of animals asks the reader to consider what we expect language to be, and to consider the many different kinds of communication that rely upon senses other than hearing. Healy does not deny the ability of signs to convey meaning; rather, he emphasizes the socially constructed nature of communication, and our inability to read signs outside our normative systems. In each instance noted above, there is a code known only to those who have learned it or who innately understand it. These three instances of nonverbal language are followed by a quote and attribution: *'senseless and incapable of reasoning* / the "translated" Aristotle.'[15] Healy offers the philosopher's description and dismissal of the deaf as an example of the misunderstanding of deafness that has allowed societies to reject those disabled bodies as unproductive, and therefore valueless. It also alludes to a lack of communication across codes. The deaf appear to speaking people as unable to communicate, yet within their own community and language, the signals and symbols are understood. In assembling examples of successful communication and offering us the counter-assessment of the authoritative figure of Aristotle,[16] Healy allows the reader to struggle between accepting potential avenues of communication apart from orality and hewing to the established hierarchy of speech over all other forms of communication.

    That Healy makes his argument against the superiority of speech in a poem is also vital. Canonical Irish poetry, especially as represented by the Nobel Laureates of Irish poetry, W.B. Yeats and Seamus Heaney, is deeply premised on oralism. We can see this in Yeats's recitations and radio performances,[17] and in Heaney's reliance on his particular Northern Irish accent to create rhymes that do not quite exist in Received Pronunciation English.[18] Derrida writes that 'writing, the letter, the sensible inscription, has always been considered by Western tradition as *the body and matter* external to the spirit, to breath, to speech, and to the logos' [emphasis mine].[19] This historical connection of the written, visual sign to physicality, to the material, means that writing is seen as wholly external and of the body's interaction with the world, rather than emerging from the interior mind and spirit, for which the body is only an envelope.

Healy's accumulation of the different methods of communication in 'Arbor Vitae' builds on Derrida's work deconstructing the Cartesian hierarchy of mind over body. The form of Healy's long poem echoes this challenge to speech-based poetics as well, because this is a poem of reading and note-taking. It is an archive of research into sign systems and representations of deafness. Unlike the lyric, which, as its name suggests, has an ancient basis in song, Healy's poem does not include chiming sounds or carrying rhythms. His organizing patterns, like the acrostics and the repeated anagrams of chaos (an example from page eleven: 'Sohac, hasco, schoca'), rely on writing, and the words they encode cannot be heard when the work is read aloud. As he writes in the 'Footnote', 'No matter how good your hearing is there are things which you will not hear'.[20] In choosing a form of poetry that prioritizes the written form, traditionally the secondary form of communication, used to supplement the absence of speech, Healy aligns himself with those who choose non-oral means of communication, including those who use sign language. He also creates an experience, by introducing hidden codes and disjuncture, of imperfect interpretation on the part of the reader. This both highlights the mediating nature of all signifying systems and puts the reader in the position of not being in command of all the skills necessary to discover meaning so that we share the experience of those excluded from participating in the dominant form of communication.

By including the 'Footnote' in the text of 'Arbor Vitae', Healy, like many avant-garde poets, provides the reader with a paratext to which one can turn after working through the jarring mix of scientific terms, programming languages, and bursts of poetic constraint.[21] As discussed above, in a complete about-face from the depersonalized aesthetic of the first three parts of the poem, and their avoidance of the singular authorial voice, the 'Footnote' begins with an anecdote about the poet's daughter and his realization of her deafness. The note then moves away from the biographical to annotate the poem, in a continuation of a clear authorial voice. In the note, Healy offers an overt parallel between the denial of sign language education and the destruction of the Irish language; he also explains the reasons he uses anagrams of *chaos* and the sources of many pieces of information within the poem. At the end of the four page note, after offering answers to a final question in the poem and the keys to the final acrostic, Healy takes the reader back again to the daily situation of the Deaf in Ireland, and he gestures with hope to a future in which the Deaf are not denied their own language and 'in which the Hearing are not handicapped by the loss of the considerable talents of the Deaf ....'[22] This note situates a challenging, discomfiting poem in the personal experience and beliefs of the writer, and in doing so, it communicates to the reader that the language games of the poem emerge from the particular intersection of language, bodies, and the state that he and his daughter have experienced.

The autobiographical nature of the note also is of a piece with some of the confessional tendencies of Irish writing in the 1990s, when confession moved from the faltering Catholic church into the public eye in order to 'interrogate rather than bolster the state,' as Gerry Smyth puts it.[23] This demand by variant and schismatic citizens to be heard had long been seen as threatening the cohesion of the national body, and therefore the basis for Irish self-determination itself, founded on an essential claim of monolithic Irish difference from the British.[24] Healy writes about a hidden population whose presence undercuts the assumption that language aligns with nation, and against whose hands, mouths, and bodies the pressure of state institutions, including the church and the schools, is brought in order to suppress this alternative form of communication. Additionally, disability rights activist Corbett O'Toole points out that 'publicly naming one's relationship to disability' is 'mandated' within the disability rights community.[25] So Healy opening his footnote with his personal experience as the parent of a Deaf child contributes to making his poem a public, political, and confessional work within the rhetorical framework of disability rights. That he inverts the common expectation of the poem itself being the site of lyric self-expression while any notes provide background and context further emphasizes the weight of his formal choice of 'essayistic fragments,' which resists the assumption that the subject can find easy voice within established conventions. In fact, the note can also be read as an inventive rhetorical strategy that offers a link to connect the three poetic parts of 'Arbor Vitae' while avoiding the hallmark of lyric poetry, the metaphor.

To return to the poem itself, the conglomeration of information in 'Arbor Vitae' reaches far outside the bounds of Irish borders, allowing Healy to also write back against the coherence and unity of the national by demonstrating the global flows of knowledge. The Deaf are not contained within national borders, and the information that Healy gathers about Deaf history, from Martha's Vineyard to eighteenth century Paris, demonstrates an alternative way of forming a community and an identity, outside of national affiliations. The non-national structures of identity with which Healy is engaged allow connections to emerge that avoid hierarchal power structures. On the last page of the poem before the note, he gestures towards a rhizomatic structure: 'An aspen in Utah / by sending out shoots / has covered one hundred and six acres / the whole thing sharing a common root system.'[26] His paratactic form and the poem's interrogation of sign systems pull apart the static concept of nation without relying on globalized consumerism or detached cosmopolitanism to fill in the gaps.

Complementing the revelation of a global community, Healy also turns to the physical experience of the world to explore the ways in which we transmit and interpret the inputs we receive. An example of this element of his poem, which again offers an alternative to the social and political status quo, occurs on page twenty-three of the poem. On this page, Healy intersperses facts he has accumulated about efforts to restore hearing in the deaf through cochlear implants with a quote from Darwin, the history of the Martha's Vineyard deaf population, and the details of a wind rating scale (I have noted in brackets the origins of the quoted phrases):

> I have felt through the saddle
> the beating of the heart
> so plainly I could have counted the beats.   [Charles Darwin,
> *The Expression of the Emotions in Man and Animals*]

> That is, the auditory nerve, having twenty thousand synapses,
> is replaced with a device having twenty two electrodes,
> eight of which are functional.

> leaves and twigs rustle
> paper is raised   small branches move
> small leafy trees sway   [Beaufort scale]

> *Let us help you*
> *experience the brilliance of sound once again*
>   [Hearing aid advertisement]
> The first deaf islander arrived in 1692
> and was fluent in some kind of natural sign.

> Some patients are eventually able
> to use the telephone.
> What many hear is a series of clicks and squeaks
> which may help their lipreading.

Manufacturers publish

testimonials

not

continued numbness,
perceiving two voices instead of one
with a split-second delay
understanding men not women
headaches
sagging of one side of the face,
all voices sounding the same
some words from weather report
lipreading for all conversions still
confused in groups

The disjunctive assemblage reveals gaps and contradictions between the different assertions and experiences recorded therein. We understand from reading this page that the supposed binary choice between hearing with a cochlear implant and remaining deaf and silent is a false binary. Writing about constructions of disability, Bryan S. Turner sums up treatments like cochlear implants as 'normalization' and 'a form of governmentality that orchestrates various medical and welfare practices that aim to create the rehabilitated person' from the disabled body.[27] Rather than the choice being between exclusion from society or inclusion through speech, there are other alternative social formations that have not been explored and that do not require the alteration of the deaf body to conform to hearing social norms. For instance, 'the first deaf islander' refers to the disproportionately high number of deaf people who made up the population of Martha's Vineyard, off the Massachusetts coast. The island 'featured a dense social and kin network and this close contact between deaf and hearing people resulted in the evolution of a sign language that was widely used by both on a daily basis down the generations'.[28] This form of inclusive bilingualism is one solution Healy suggests in 'Arbor Vitae', one which is ironically ignored in a society that is officially bilingual.[29]

This false choice between silence and limited hearing also ignores the many other ways in which we fully sense the world. The entire body is a sensitive receptor for external stimuli. In the poem's emphasis on the body, it records and enacts the many translations our minds and bodies make in the world, revealing the multi-lingual existence of an ordinary person in both the form and content of the poem. When Healy quotes the Beaufort scale's evidence of thirteen to eighteen mile an hour winds – 'paper is   raised small branches move' – he is reminding us that our abstract concepts of speed are based in the physical world. And this transformation of a measurement into a physical experience exists on the same page with Charles Darwin's measurement of a horse's heart-rate, as felt through the scientist's body, presenting the reader with the many ways our bodies interpret data of the world through sensory organs other than our ears. Oral speech is itself a set of vibrations and movements within the body, which is elided by our focus on the sonic *effects* of that bodily movement. The embodiment of our consciousness and language in the world is conveyed through the different pieces of information Healy brings to bear, and the import of this is that instead of the self and identity being figured as an innate sensibility we express from within, who we are consists entirely of the interactions we have with the world, what vibrations we sense and how we respond to them. Healy's attention to the different ways in which information is transmitted in 'Arbor Vitae' keeps turning our attention to the exterior world, but that also frequently leads to an emphasis on the body that experiences the world.[30] Like Healy's use of scientific terminology, this phenomenological turn strips human experience of the common terms by which we understand it, allowing access instead to a shared experience of being in the world as packets of sensation-translating neural pathways. Healy's phenomenological approach offers an alternative to the traditional formation of community around cultural attributes. Yet the grounding of the poem in this physical experience of disability, a context in which the body and its limits are brought to the forefront, still shows the impact of discourse on the lives and bodies of the deaf. Healy draws from both post-structural and phenomenological philosophies in order to make a poem that is also a public intervention on behalf of those who have been defined as 'less than' by the institutions of the state.

In 'Arbor Vitae', Deaf sign language is the hinge for Healy's discussions of the many kinds of communication we ignore by focusing only on spoken and written language. A gesture-based language, based in bodily movement, not only does not move from interior to exterior like speech, but as Healy addresses, was seen, like writing, as a supplement, an addition we make to speech, but not enough in itself to communicate. However, 'if we allow that spoken meaning remains rooted in gesture and bodily expressiveness', as David Abrams urges in *The Spell of the Sensuous*,[31] then we find ourselves surrounded not by a silent world, but one that constantly has something to say. It's a matter of recognizing the commonality we have in our shared physicality. As disabilities studies scholar Tom Shakespeare has said, 'A situation where disabled people are defined by their physicality can only be sustained in a situation where non-disabled people have denied their own physicality'.[32] Once the embodied nature of existence and communication is acknowledged, it opens up spaces for reconsiderations of ideologies that are premised on such divisions. For instance, in Section One of 'Arbor Vitae', Healy writes, 'Home is an array of data arising out of / membranes, pressure, chemo- and light sensors / and, even more so, out of post-sensual processing'.[33] The human and its domestic surroundings are defamiliarized by figuring them as machines, sending signals, processing and categorizing – the body as computer. The sense of place that has been at the centre of national identity building in Ireland is here explored as a construction or interpretation of multiple signals firing within our bodies. This does not strip the meaning of 'home' from us, but by turning to the phenomenological experience of being in the world, asks us to rebuild our own meaning from scratch, just as 'Arbor Vitae' itself presents us with evidence in unfamiliar forms of language, and asks us to draw our own conclusions.

In 1997, when 'Arbor Vitae' was published, Ireland was just beginning the boom period that would be marked by an influx of immigration, rapacious property development, and an embrace of global flows of media and capital. While many traditional Irish pieties were becoming unstuck in 1997, the Celtic Tiger era of the next decade replaced them with faith in the autonomous individual above community, capitalism as freedom, and progress only through economic growth. Healy creates a poem that offers an alternative to this neoliberal focus on the individual yet rejects a nostalgic return to the past. Returning always to the impact of discourse upon the body, 'Arbor Vitae' keeps reminding us of our commonality with those who have been cast out and the need for skepticism of prevailing systems that rely upon exclusion and degradation of others to remain intact. With his note at the end of the poem, Healy builds on the many innovations of avant-garde Modernist and postmodernist poetry, and he infuses a personal, bodily instantiation into the poem while still foregrounding an understanding of language as artifice. Healy forgoes metaphor and the lyric voice in order to reveal through dissonant and often stark language the fact that citizens' lives are conducted in the language and terms of those in power; in Ireland, those terms are no longer dictated by an imperial government, but by a homegrown political class. As such, he gestures toward a writerly alternative to the oralism of the lyric, and to a poetry that can be both personal and political without relying on an individual voice to tell us only one story. Instead of conceptual poetry that exists only to shock or bore, Healy's poem makes something happen: he helps us see and hear dimensions of the world we have chosen to ignore and devalue. Healy abandons notions of authenticity rooted in the expressive subject or national culture, but does not become unmoored. 'Arbor Vitae' offers a path forward for both Irish poetry and avant garde poetry more generally, toward a poetry imbued with difficulty and with clear fealty to an international Modernist tradition, one which also turns to Ireland and its citizens, and asks them to look at what their hard won Republic has become.

NOTES

1. See Robert Archambeau, 'Not Heaney, Healy: Questions, Answers and Explorations at the Edge of Irish Writing', *Read me* 1 (1999), n. pag < http://home.jps.net/~nada/ healy.htm> and David Lloyd, 'Review: Chaos Theory', *The Poetry Ireland Review* 74 (2002), 110–18.
2. 'Deaf' with a capital D is used to signify the Deaf cultural community, and 'deaf' with a lower case d is used when referring to medical deafness.
3. Randolph Healy, 'Arbor Vitae', in *Green 532: Selected Poems 1983–2000* (Applecross, W.A.; Cambridge: Salt, 2002), pp.9–30. The footnote was not included in the original 1997 chapbook version of *Arbor Vitae*, but it was included in the *etruscan reader viii*, in which a selection of Healy's work, including 'Arbor Vitae', was published in 1998. It has been included in every reproduction of the poem since.
4. Randolph Healy, interview by Marthine Satris, August 29, 2009.
5. Michel Foucault argues that the era of 'bio-power' began with the government exerting control over life through schools and other institutions, the disciplines of which enabled the development of capitalism, and his work on the relationship of the body to power has been foundational to disability studies, as have phenomenological approaches to understanding the body. See *The History of Sexuality* (New York: Pantheon Books, 1978), pp.139–143.
6. Barbara LeMaster, 'School Language and Shifts in Irish Deaf Identity', in *Many Ways to Be Deaf: International Variation in Deaf Communities*, eds. Leila Frances Monaghan et al. (Washington, D.C: Gallaudet University Press, 2003), p.160; Áine Hyland and Kenneth Milne, *Irish Educational Documents,* vol. 2 (Dublin: Church of Ireland College of Education, 1992), p.474.
7. Sarah Burns, 'Irish Sign Language: Ireland's Second Minority Language', in *Pinky Extension and Eye Gaze: Language Use in Deaf Communities*, ed. Ceil Lucas (Washington, D.C.: Gallaudet University Press, 1998), p.248.
8. Claire McCormack, 'Deaf Community Roar for Recognition of Sign Language', *Sunday Independent*, May 3, 2015, sec. News.
9. Healy, 'Arbor Vitae', p.21.
10. Peter Riley, '"Anxious Fuchsia Ocean": The Accomplishment of Randolph Healy', *Chicago Review* 49.2 (2003), p.138.
11. Justin Quinn, *The Cambridge Introduction to Modern Irish Poetry, 1800–2000, Cambridge Introductions to Literature* (Cambridge, UK; New York: Cambridge University Press, 2008), p.110.
12. David Wheatley, '"And Cannot Say / and Cannot Say": Richard Price, Randolph Healy and the Dialogue of the Deaf', in *Modern Irish and Scottish Poetry*, eds. Peter Mackay, Edna Longley, and Fran Brearton (Cambridge, UK: Cambridge University Press, 2011), p.255.

13. T.S. Eliot, 'The Metaphysical Poets' in *Selected Essays, 1917–1932* (New York: Harcourt, Brace and Co, 1932), p.248.
14. Healy, 'Arbor Vitae', p.16.
15. Healy, 'Arbor Vitae', p.16.
16. It should be noted that Aristotle in fact, if one goes back to the original, did not phrase his assessment of the deaf quite in this fashion. This is a translation offered by K.W. Hodgson in his 1954 book, *The Deaf and Their Problems: A study in special education*, a translation that other translators and classical scholars dispute. See Christian Laes, 'Silent Witnesses: Deaf-mutes in Graeco-Roman Antiquity', *Classical World* 104.4 (2011), 451–73.
17. Emily C. Bloom, 'Yeats's Radiogenic Poetry: Oral Traditions and Auditory Publics', *Éire-Ireland* 46.3–4 (2011), 227–51.
18. Seamus Heaney, 'Feeling into Words' in *Preoccupations: Selected Prose, 1968–1978* (London: Faber & Faber, 1980), pp.43–45.
19. Jacques Derrida, *Of Grammatology* (Baltimore: Johns Hopkins University Press, 1998), p.35.
20. Healy, 'Arbor Vitae', p.27
21. Susan Vanderborg, *Paratextual Communities: American Avant-garde Poetry Since 1950* (Carbondale: Southern Illinois University Press, 2001). Vanderborg writes of the use of essays, notes, and manifestos by American avant-garde writers like Olson and Bernstein: 'Paratexts offer a forum in which the author can present ideological agendas more directly to an audience, ... or simply contextualize new poetry within literary and historical traditions familiar to a broad range of readers' (p.5).
22. Healy, 'Arbor Vitae', p.30.
23. Gerry Smyth, *Space and the Irish Cultural Imagination* (Basingstoke/New York: Palgrave, 2001), p.94.
24. M.K. Flynn, *Ideology, Mobilization, and the Nation: The Rise of Irish, Basque, and Carlist Nationalist Movements in the Nineteenth and Early Twentieth Centuries*, St. Antony's Series (New York, N.Y: St. Martin's Press, 2000), p.95.
25. Corbett O'Toole. 'Disclosing Our Relationships to Disabilities: An Invitation for Disability Studies Scholars' in *Disability Studies Quarterly* 33.2 (2013), para. 2.
26. Healy, 'Arbor Vitae', p.26.
27. Bryan S. Turner, 'Disability and the Sociology of the Body' in Gary L. Albrecht, Katherine D. Seelman, and Michael Bury, eds., *Handbook of Disability Studies* (Thousand Oaks, Calif.: Sage, 2003), p.253.
28. Annelies Kusters, 'Deaf Utopias? Reviewing the Sociocultural Literature on the World's "Martha's Vineyard Situations"', *Journal of Deaf Studies and Deaf Education* 15.1 (2010), 3–16 (p.3).
29. Muiris Ó Laoire, 'The Language Situation in Ireland' in Robert B. Kaplan, ed., *Language Planning and Policy in Europe. Vol. 3: The Baltic States, Ireland and Italy*, Language Planning and Policy (Bristol: Multilingual Matters, 2008), pp.193–262.
30. Also attending to the phenomenological implications of 'Arbor Vitae' is Alex Davis in 'Deferred Action: Irish Neo-Avant-Garde Poetry', *Angelaki* 5.1 (April 2000), p.85.
31. David Abram, *The Spell of the Sensuous: Perception and Language in a More-than-human World* (New York: Vintage Books, 1996), p.81.
32. Tom Shakespeare, 'Disability, Identity and Difference', in *Exploring the Divide*, ed. Colin Barnes and Geof Mercer (Leeds: The Disability Press, 1996), pp.94–113, archived at http://disability-studies.leeds.ac.uk/files/library/Shakespeare-Chap6.pdf, np.
33. Healy, 'Arbor Vitae', pp.12–13.

Kenneth Keating

Repetition and Alterity: Geoffrey Squires's 'texts for screen'

In 2004 Geoffrey Squires published a career-defining collection of selected texts and excerpts, *Untitled and other poems: 1975–2002*. Following this, Squires produced a number of digital texts which departed from traditional publishing processes and were disseminated online through various media. Gathered together in *Abstract Lyrics and other poems: 2006–2012*, a digital publication available only through Amazon as a Kindle Book, these pieces are described in the Acknowledgements as 'texts for screen'.[1] Squires's decision to embrace computer technology in the production of these digital texts represents a significant development from his earlier interrogation of issues of authorial control and the critical pursuit of singular meaning, while referring to these publications as 'texts for screen' reveals his understanding of the publications as ones that trouble classification. These texts amount to more than a digital conversion of an original text to an ebook, instead embracing the technology central to their construction. However, while sharing certain elements with emerging electronic literature, many of Squires's texts do not fully adhere to conventional understandings of what constitutes contemporary electronic literature either. Through examining the technical properties of Squires's 'texts for screen' and their relationship to the conventions of ebooks and electronic literature respectively, and subsequently offering brief close readings of a number of the poet's latest texts and a more extended engagement with the first of his .pdf texts *Lines* (2006), this essay will contend that in its form and content Squires's screen work problematizes the search for definition and demonstrates the progressively troubling force of indeterminacy.

Squires's earliest volume *Drowned Stones* (1975) first underlined his engagement with the avant-garde poetic tradition most obviously through the inclusion of excerpts from external texts such as John C. Lilly's *Programming and Meta-programming in the Human Biocomputer*,[2] and Manfred Stanley's essay 'Technicism, Liberalism, and Development'.[3] The presence here of non-poetic texts acts 'to reduce

Irish University Review 46.1 (2016): 145–157
DOI: 10.3366/iur.2016.0207
© Edinburgh University Press
www.euppublishing.com/journal/iur

the centrality of the lyric subject which, if not totally dissolved, finds itself displaced as the governing centre of the sequence',[4] a process conflated with the emergence of computer technology foregrounded in the specific texts Squires elects to feature. As examples of electronic literature, defined by N. Katherine Hayles as 'a practice that mediates between human and machine cognition. ... that inextricably entwines body and machine, without giving either absolute theoretical priority',[5] Squires's 'texts for screen' build on the poet's first introduction of computer technology in *Drowned Stones* to foreground more prominently the computer's mediation of the subject's experience of reality and its impact on the poetic act. As poetry created specifically through and for the computer screen, these digital texts do more than just reject the subject-object division as they progressively both reinforce and challenge the authorial control of a text and consequently the critical construction of stable, closed meaning.

The emergence of electronic literature has heralded what Jay David Butler terms 'the late age of print', a time in which our understanding of what constitutes a book, or in this context a poem, is under review due to the development of the digital age and its 'challenge to print as a technology for delivering alphabetic text and ... to the genres and structures that we associate with printed books'.[6] Resulting from this challenge are the numerous alternative genres specific to the computer which constitute the subcategories of electronic literature: 'hypertext fiction, network fiction, interactive fiction, locative narratives, installation pieces, "codework", generative art and the Flash poem'.[7] The common attribute of these subcategories is that they have been produced on and for the computer screen:

> Electronic Literature is born-digital. It is computational and processural, dependent upon the operations of the machine for its aesthetic effects. Electronic literature engages through a series of translations across machine codes, platforms, and networks; its resulting onscreen content depends upon algorithmic procedures, software, hardware, and (often) Internet compatibility'.[8]

Although primarily born-digital, many of Squires's 'texts for screen' do not easily fit into any of the listed subcategories of electronic literature, appearing as they do as static .pdf files. Rather than being a limitation, however, Squires's refusal to meet these established standards and his insistence on foregrounding authorial control firmly locates his work in an unstable middle ground between traditional print publishing and an emerging electronic literature. Occupying this middle ground mirrors Hayles's insistence that electronic literature gives theoretical priority to neither the human body nor computer technology and represents Squires's refusal to absolutely privilege either electronic or print literature in order to complicate reductive divisions between the two, frustrating the critical desire for singularity.

A number of Squires's 'texts for screen' are inaccurately listed on the publishers' websites as ebooks, but it is quite evident that these texts do not share any substantial characteristics with the static format of the ebook. Designed to be encountered through ereaders or standard ereading applications available on tablets or smartphones, ebooks are traditional print publications digitally converted into electronic files, but Squires's *Lines* (2006), *So* (2007), *Abstract Lyrics* (2011), and *Two New Poems* (2011) were produced solely for the computer screen. This difference is underlined in the format of the text as it offers groups of words on individual pages, rather than a linear progression of text horizontally and vertically on the page in line with the conventional print and ebook publication format. This key distinction is further underlined in the author's introductory notes, varying versions of which accompany all of the .pdf texts and of which *Lines* offers the first example:

Note on Reading

*Please click on Next Page each time
rather than scrolling down.*

*If you are using Adobe Reader version 7.0 or later,
click on the 'single page' icon, the second (from the left)
of the four layout icons at the bottom right of your screen.
Also, please ensure that you are using the 'Fit Page'
instruction, in order that the page will sit correctly
on your screen.*[9]

Terms such as 'click', 'scroll', and 'icon' evidence the computer-centred nature of this text, while the directions included here attempt to exert some authorial control over the reader's engagement with the text. Both these themes are brought together in Squires's expectation that the common, open-access software Adobe Reader should be the standard programme through which the text will be encountered, enabling him to foreground the importance of the appearance of the text on the screen, an emphasis rarely, if ever, found in conventional ebooks.

Matters of control and the troubling classification of such texts are further developed in Squires's three video texts published on

YouTube.com by the print publisher Wild Honey Press; *Repetitions* (2007), *Litany* (2008), and *Texts for Screen* (2008). Squires's short texts offer a consistent black background on which white text fades in and fades out at a steady pace with absolutely no interaction from the reader. Without sound or images other than the words, these texts are essentially Flash poems, 'characterized by sequential screens that typically progress with minimal or no user intervention'.[10] While criticism of electronic literature acknowledges that '[a]ll new media art works depend on the technology for which they have been conceived',[11] it is also recognized that '[t]he influence of software is especially obvious in the genre of the Flash poem'.[12] This obviousness foregrounds authorial control over the text and its appearance, and is due in part to the passive position of the reader who merely observes the software process the code and produce the images on the screen. Placing these seven 'texts for screen' together, it is clear that Squires has produced pieces which either evade categorization as ebooks or represent rather basic Flash poems, firmly establishing their uneasy position in relation to electronic literature as they embrace alternative technologies and the utilization of the screen while retaining the linearity associated with print publishing and the foregrounding of authorial control. Close readings of a number of these 'texts for screen' underlines the formal and linguistic instability in these texts and their rejection of stable categorization and meaning.

Squires's terse electronic texts feature only a small group of words on the screen at any one time and exemplify digital modernism, defined by Jessica Pressman as 'characterized by an aesthetics of restraint' which represents the use of minimalism 'as a conscious act of rebellion ... connect[ing] this movement to a longer tradition of similar rebellion, specifically, the modernist avant-garde'.[13] Squires's particular rebellion utilizes this minimalism to explicitly link production, or reproduction, to the problem of secure meaning. While the reader's encounter with these texts appears highly controlled, particularly in the Flash poems, the content of these texts challenges such possible singularity through suggesting alternative truths, suggestions founded on the insistent repetition which interrupts singularity. *Repetitions* foregrounds this interruption in its title and in the first four elements to appear in the video; 'Settled', 'settled', 'settled', and 'settled'.[14] The term suggests clarity, but its repetition complicates and destabilizes any singular and stable meaning. *Litany* reemphasizes this understanding of apparent stability simultaneous with an inherent counter-truth as it is composed of a series of lines which contain both the positive and negative forms of certain terms, opening, for example, with 'Having   having not'.[15] Two seemingly opposed assertions are presented on the screen at the same time, but while the positive appears first and may seem to thus be privileged above the negative form, the secondariness of the negative term may be disrupted if it be considered not a subsequent concept but a correction of the original positive form. In *Litany*, therefore, the repetition of the first phrase is altered through the addition of another element, but this element is negative in nature, conflating alteration, addition, and negation, underlining the instability of the seemingly stable text, as exemplified in the later screen image which places two occurrences of 'perhaps' above the negative 'not'. The negative term 'not' sits beneath the space between the two occurrences of 'perhaps', suggesting a permeation of the negative which disrupts even the propositions this text has previously established up to this point. This disruption is further underlined in the final screen image which appears to conclude on a wholly negative note; 'Never   never not', but this movement toward the negative is disrupted by the positive which grammatically emerges from the double negative in 'never not'.[16]

This troubling indeterminacy visually displayed on the computer screen in such a controlled fashion in these Flash poems appears again, though in a slightly different form, throughout the static .pdf 'texts for screen' as they once more highlight authorial control and the simultaneous presence of uncontainable meaning through the explicit foregrounding of alterity within repetition. *Lines*, the first of Squires's .pdf texts, opens with a number of pages each containing just a single line:

And as to   as   as to   as to

why we sometimes   why sometimes we

whether it is or not   whether it is   whether

which to us is   to us   which is

in this place   in this   this place[17]

Squires begins with 'And as to', the opening conjunction stressing the primary importance of addition, while the second section of this first page is simply 'as'. The removal of 'And' as well as 'to' in the move from the first to the second section underlines how the second section becomes a repetition of an element of the first section while marking its own alteration from this first section. '[A]s' then becomes 'as to', reintroducing the final element of the first section and finally the fourth section reproduces the third section exactly so that the four distinct sections of this first line represent the way in which repetition inherently complicates meaning through altering the original. This is further underlined in the fourth section which, in its exact repetition of the third section, appears identical, but through its occurring after the third section it exists as a repetition, a second version of an original of sorts, never a pure reproduction but always coming after, incapable of meaning the same as in the first occurrence.

Squires continues to emphasize the undermining of singularity in the pages which follow, evidencing various alterations or corruptions of the primary sections. Such alterations are so common that, as with the inclusion of negative forms after positive forms in *Litany*, the privileged position of the primary sections is destabilized. It becomes possible that what follows may not be altered or corrupted originals, but may in fact represent corrections, the second page, for example, containing 'why we sometimes' and 'why sometimes we' (*Lines*, p.6). That the exact same words appear in different formulations undermines any reductive conclusion over which is the primary version, but Squires's rearranging of the same words further highlights the potential for all phrases which compose a text to have multiple meanings outside of the poet's control, a condition underlined in the decision to move the first person plural 'we' from the centre of the phrase to a more peripheral position. This multiple nature of the pronoun disrupts singularity further and the only word which keeps its original position, 'why', stresses that the text poses a question, or in this case two seemingly identical questions though with different emphases. To these questions, no single answer may be offered, as the text evades any reductive singularity, instead embracing the loss of control which accompanies the removal of an organizing centre. The third page of *Lines* offers another example as 'whether it is or not' becomes 'whether it is' only to end with the simple 'whether' (*Lines*, p.7). The first of these sections includes the positive 'it is' only to end on the negative 'or not', the second section removing the negative elements 'or not', suggesting something more positive, but the decision to conclude with the single 'whether' removes all signs of positive or negative to leave only possibility. This process of reduction requires graphic reproduction of the one constant element, 'whether', but the meaning of this seemingly constant element is altered through all three sections so that the 'whether' that ends the line poses innumerable questions, setting up a contrast between positive and negative. Once again in line with *Litany*, the sequence here suggests a conditionality and a choice between at least two options, a choice which the poet once more refuses to make, preferring to embrace the openness, in a pattern which permeates the entire text.

Similarly alternative versions of this undermining of singularity through the alterity inherent within repetition occur in the fourth and fifth pages: 'which to us is   to us   which is' (*Lines*, p.8) and 'in this place   in this   this place' (*Lines*, p.9). In the single-sectioned sixth page 'where everything' (*Lines*, p.10), however, Squires interrupts this emerging pattern of alternative repetitions, complicating any reductive understanding of the poem's form. This complication is brought a step further through the blank page which immediately follows this (*Lines*, p.11), only to return to a similar, though perhaps more emphatic, demonstration of repetition in 'Because to because   because   because to' (*Lines*, p.12), repeating 'because' four times to suggest a multiplicity of reasons, or meanings. But any apparently developing pattern gets complicated once more through the subsequent occurrence of the first page composed of a single section whose elements combine to form an extended single clause: 'when there is no reason why it should not' (*Lines*, p.13). This momentary clarity is immediately undermined, however, as Squires returns to the repetition present from the beginning of the text, marking the simultaneous coexistence of stability and instability in order to disrupt any singular reading:

and all we can imagine   all that we can imagine

what it does   what it does   what it is in its nature to do

or   or

to see where   to see if

in this place   in this   this place

knowing   knowing of course   knowing

as if we were not surrounded   (*Lines*, pp.14–19)

Followed by another blank page (*Lines*, p.20), this segment thus presents itself as repeating the format of the first segment of the poem (*Lines*, pp.5–11), demonstrating similar developments between sections on each page: the removal or addition of elements which alter the meanings of each section, or the exact reproduction of one section as another, later section, again underline alteration even in what appears to be identical. This second segment is not an identical reproduction of the first segment, however, not only because it includes varying sections and elements. For while it repeats many of the features of the first segment, it also breaks new ground in various ways, the most notable regarding two different issues to do with length. Firstly, the second segment of *Lines* is longer than the first, and secondly, while the first segment is composed entirely of one-line pages, the second segment includes an aberration in the two lines: 'to see where   to see if / in this place   in this   this place' (*Lines*, p.17), further foregrounding potential similarity in repetition only to interrupt this with alterity.

This alterity within repetition is suggested more explicitly as *Lines* continues, for example in the third segment including 'and the difference   the difference in   the difference between' (*Lines*, p.23) and 'every   every moment   every   every' (*Lines*, p.30). Following the reference to 'the difference' (*Lines*, p.23), Squires addresses 'this constant' present in 'What we do   without thinking' (*Lines*, p.32) and underlines the necessity of this condition:

it is   it is in the nature of it   the nature of it   it is   it is
of the many possible   of the many   the many possible
as if from   from   or out of
for there to be   to be   for there to be   (*Lines*, p.37)

The 'constant' (*Lines*, p.34), associated with 'the difference' (*Lines*, p.23), therefore, 'is in the nature of it' and is indeed necessary 'for there to be' (*Lines*, p.37), implying once more instability under the surface-level stability of a text, as Squires's sparse pieces foreground the alterity within the repetition of identical elements and destabilize the search for secure meaning.

Squires may appear to complicate this toward the end of *Lines*, where a sense of permanence is suggested in 'and which cannot be altered   changed   altered' (*Lines*, p.86), but this line actively undermines itself in its movement from 'altered' to 'changed' and back to 'altered' as the claim that something 'cannot be altered' is itself altered through the suggestion of other elements in separate sections of this line. While the meaning of these sections which compose one line appears stable, insisting on the existence of something constant, the movement between the sections points toward instability through a multiplicity of terms suggesting the same idea, a complication which underlines multiplicity within that which appears singular. The absence of a coherent singularity is finally underlined in the last pages where Squires suggests the fluidity of meaning and its resting not in some transcendental truth but in multiple subjective positions when he writes 'what we make of it   what we make   what we   what' (*Lines*, p.88). Even such a conclusion is undermined, however, by the gradual dissolution of claims to subjective truths through the removal of elements in the progression of this line's sections from a point of understanding, 'what we make of it', to a point of acknowledging subjective creation in the making of truth, 'what we make', only once more to conclude with a term containing a simultaneous statement and question; 'what'. This undermining of truth, transcendental or subjective, questions itself, and reaches no conclusion as the poem finishes but does not end, highlighting the extent to which it is itself unsure of what it may be offering an ending to: 'of the end   the end of   of' (*Lines*, p.89). Thus *Lines* concludes with a non-conclusion which simultaneously suggests singularity and multiplicity through making moves in and out of certainty and uncertainty in turn to finally leave an openness which welcomes alternative understandings.

Squires's questioning of meaning in poetry is brought a step further in his two 2011 .pdf texts *Two New Poems* and *Abstract Lyrics*, both of which are markedly even more sparse than the earlier 'texts for screen'. *Two New Poems* contains two distinct texts, '1. Triptych' and '2. Text', the latter of which explicitly focuses on the control of meaning in texts as it begins with 'That it   that   that it',[18] a line of three sections which are produced through repetition and alteration similar to the opening of *Lines*, discussed above. This declarative 'that', however, becomes 'that what' (*Two*, p.46) to then become simply the question 'what' (*Two*, p.47), yet this question returns to the declarative in 'what it is   what it is that' (*Two*, p.48) as declaration and question share the space, neither privileged above the other. 'What' moves outside of this circular pattern, however, beginning with the focus on the search for singularity in 'what alone' (*Two*, p.50) only to once more open up to indeterminacy in 'what might' (*Two*, p.54). The text ends with an examination of the control of meaning as existence, or 'being' (*Two*, p.65) in a state of 'peace' (*Two*, p.67), is paralleled to being 'at the bidding of' (*Two*, p.71). The poem's conclusion highlights the extent to which the stability of an uncomplicated meaning and thus a stable existence is founded on being under the control, or 'at the bidding of', some other force, in this case an unnamed entity as the poem ends on a blank page (*Two*, p.72). This control is undermined through the inclusion of 'at will' (*Two*, p.69) between 'at peace' (*Two*, p.67) and 'at the bidding of' (*Two*, p.71), suggesting a possible freedom which may interrupt control, and the open-ended nature of the conclusion facilitates instability in the identification of the controlling force as singularity, control, and freedom simultaneously coexist to complicate any reductive meaning of '2. Text'.

Such problematizing alterity within repetition is brought once more to the fore in Squires's *Abstract Lyrics* which spreads seventy-nine words over seventy-five pages, many of them repetitions of earlier words, so that the poem becomes a collection of indeterminate but suggestive terms, emphasizing the instability that undercuts any apparent potential for meaning. Squires moves the lines from the middle of the page, as they were in his earlier electronic texts, to the top of the page, decentring these lines. Beginning with 'Some' on its first page,[19] the poem's second page repeats this word, though without the capital letter and indented on the page one space (*Abstract*, p.6). This technique of repeating with indenting is found throughout this text, utilizing the single-page view of Adobe Reader to physically move terms which appear identical to those which precede them in order to underline the alterity in the subsequent terms in each repetition; 'each time', for example, is included twice, first in line with the left margin, then indented a single space in the page which immediately follows (*Abstract*, pp.67–68); subsequently 'without' appears three times in a row, each one slightly more indented than the other (*Abstract*, pp.71–73), while 'so that' is repeated four times, first on the left margin, then indented two spaces, indented a single space, and finally returning to the left margin (*Abstract*, pp.75–78).

While the indenting of identical or near-identical terms or phrases foregrounds their alterity of meaning through recurrence in varying contexts, the content of *Abstract Lyrics* further emphasizes this undermining of singularity as it opens by referring to 'some / of which' (*Abstract*, pp.8–9), spreading out to suggest 'any' (*Abstract*, p.11) which soon becomes 'any / of such' (*Abstract*, pp.14–15) and this 'such' is then described as 'which to us is ... here / no not here' (*Abstract*, pp.21, 26–27). The indeterminate condition of two contrasting concepts existing alongside one another, in this case that of presence and absence, is highlighted in the subsequent 'or / or' (*Abstract*, pp.30–31) and in the later 'lastly or mostly / mostly / lastly' (*Abstract*, pp.38–40), as both are suggested as alternatives and neither is clearly chosen above the other. This emphasis on two conditions simultaneously coexisting suggests an undermining of singularity, but Squires interrupts such a conclusion through the use of so many blank pages, two of which (*Abstract*, pp.41–42) immediately follow 'lastly' (*Abstract*, p.40), while the nine pages immediately following them include the term 'because' four times (*Abstract*, pp.43, 45–46, 49), interrupted by five blank pages (*Abstract*, pp.44, 47–48, 50–51). The search for reason and meaning is not reduced to the simplistic conclusion that there is none, but the multiple uses of 'because' suggest multiple meanings while the predominance of blank pages at this point in the text suggest that these meanings are not simply multiple but also either unknowable or incapable of being reduced to a simplicity that could be conveyed through words on a page. *Abstract Lyrics* thus presents acts of communication as composed of something other than a reductive meaning, containing an unknowable and irreducible element which inherently complicates any supposed singularity.

The manner in which *Abstract Lyrics* once more leads the reader to an inability to conclude, to locate a stable end point and thus a permanent meaning, reflects one of the earliest traits identified in electronic literature, that is 'diminishing the sense of closure that belonged to codex and print'.[20] This suggests parallels with the endings of Squires's other electronic texts discussed above, *Lines* ending with 'of the end   the end of   of' (*Lines*, p.89), and '2. Text' also sharing this unfulfilled identification through finishing with an 'of' without qualifying who or what is the subject of 'at the bidding of' (*Two*, p.71). *Abstract Lyrics* also avoids qualifying or identifying the element it addresses, opting rather to remain open:

> so that
>
>   so that
>
> so that
>
> so that   (*Abstract*, pp.75–78)

Squires offers nothing further, implying that there is a reason for something, but only going so far as to begin explaining that reason in the 'so that', and its repetition alongside the use of indentation again suggests that there are multiple reasons, each one of them different from the other and possibly unnameable.

Squires's 'texts for screen', in their negotiation between the format of ebook and electronic literature, in their multiple presentations as Flash poems, .pdf files, and Kindle texts, and in their content which foregrounds repetition and the lack of singularity, represent the destabilisation of singular interpretation through the simultaneous presentation of stability and instability in form and meaning. While at times Squires appears to present an attempt to establish authorial control over the reader's encounter with the texts, the form and dissemination of these texts render any absolute control impossible. This lack of absolute control is conflated with the content of the texts as they often foreground multiplicity. Despite offering linear texts, ones which due to their format progress from a beginning of sorts to an end of sorts, Squires offers no coherent conclusions, explicitly evading such climaxes, opting instead for an indeterminacy which suggests that while a conclusion may possibly exist, it is not within the control of the author or the reader and will remain unknowable. Squires has produced 'texts for screen' which are neither ebooks nor electronic literature, but something in between, and the content of these texts repeat this formula, offering neither an absolute conclusion, nor an absolute rejection of such a conclusion, but something in between. This middle ground may appear to have its limitations, but by allowing new and traditional elements to simultaneously coexist Squires refuses to elevate one over the other. Coupled with the poet's refusal to provide a singular reading in the contents of the texts themselves, that combination of elements underlines the poet's utilization of the computer to construct unique 'texts for screen' which embrace troubling indeterminacy.

NOTES

1. Geoffrey Squires, 'Acknowledgements', *Abstract Lyrics and other poems 2006–2012* (Bray, Co. Wicklow: Wild Honey Press, 2012), Kindle file, 5%.
2. John C. Lilly, *Programming and Metaprogramming in the Human Biocomputer: Theory and Experiments* (New York: Julian, 1968).
3. Manfred Stanley, 'Technicism, Liberalism, and Development: A Study in Irony as Social Theory', *Social Development: Critical Perspectives*. Ed. Manfred Stanley (New York: Basic Books, 1972), pp.274–325.
4. John Goodby, *Irish Poetry since 1950: From Stillness into History* (Manchester: Manchester UP, 2000), p.128.
5. N. Katherine Hayles, *Electronic Literature: New Horizons for the Literary* (Notre Dame: University of Notre Dame Press, 2008), p.x.
6. Jay David Butler, *Writing Space: Computers, Hypertext, and the Remediation of Print* 2nd Ed. (New Jersey and London: Lawrence Erlbaum Associates, 2001), p.6.
7. N. Katherine Hayles, 'Electronic Literature: What is it?', *Electronic Literature Organisation*. Web 15 July 2014. < http://eliterature.org/pad/elp.html>
8. Jessica Pressman, *Digital Modernism: Making it New in New Media* (Oxford: Oxford UP, 2014), pp.1–2.
9. Geoffrey Squires, *Lines* (Exeter: Shearsman Books, 2006), p.3. All parenthetical references to Squires's 'texts for screen' which appear as .pdf files will refer to pages as numbered in Adobe Reader.
10. Hayles, 'Electronic Literature'.
11. Narvika Bovcon, 'Literary Aspects in New Media Art Works', *CLCWeb: Comparative Literature and Culture* 15.7 (2013), 1–12 (p.4). Web 23 April 2014. < http://docs.lib.purdue.edu/clcweb/vol15/iss7/17>
12. Hayles, 'Electronic Literature'.
13. Pressman, *Digital Modernism*, p.7.
14. Geoffrey Squires, *Repetitions* (Bray, Co. Wicklow: Wild Honey Press, 2007). Web 11 July 2011. < https://www.youtube.com/watch?v=wPI8SxNtXvQ>
15. Geoffrey Squires, *Litany* (Bray, Co. Wicklow, 2008). Web 11 July 2011. < https://www.youtube.com/watch?v=g7diRzHes6o>
16. Squires, *Litany*.

17. Squires, *Lines*, pp.5–9. All further page references for this text will be made parenthetically. For the purpose of this discussion the various parts of these texts will be addressed as follows: 'page' will refer to a single page in the .pdf file as viewed in Adobe Reader as demanded by Squires; 'segment' will refer to the identifiable groupings of pages as set apart from one another through the inclusion of blank pages; 'section' will refer to a single piece of a line as set apart from other pieces of the same line through significant space between each piece; 'element' will refer to the words or phrases which compose each section.
18. Geoffrey Squires, '2. Text', *Two New Poems* (Bray, Co. Wicklow: Wild Honey Press, 2011), 42–72 (p.44). All further references for this text will be made parenthetically.
19. Geoffrey Squires, *Abstract Lyrics* (Exeter: Shearsman Books, 2011), p.5. All further references for this text will be made parenthetically.
20. Butler, *Writing Space*, p.79.

James Cummins

'The history of Ireland he knew before he went to school': The Irish Tom Raworth

Tom Raworth is an elusive poet. The syntactically disconnected nature of Raworth's poetry actively resists traditional critical interventions. Moreover, Raworth is a poet who is not easily categorized because he exists outside of all the various poetic schools. As Keith Tuma points out, Raworth has 'managed to avoid being altogether claimed by one or another of the factions or pseudo-factions in alternative British poetry, while being respected by all of them'.[1] Raworth not only resists association with poetic schools; he also resists issues of national identity. Raworth is an 'English' poet who is more at home as part of an American poetic tradition, having connections to and being influenced by both the first and second generation New York school, Beat and Black Mountain poets while also acting as 'a kind of elder statesman to the Language movement'.[2] Raworth's dual poetic nationality is evidenced by his inclusion in the 1986 anthology *21 + 1 American Poets Today*, with Raworth being the plus one.[3] To further complicate Raworth's national identity it is important to point out that since 1990 Raworth has been an 'English'/'American' poet with an Irish passport. Raworth's Irish heritage is never fully explored by critics and it is my intent in this essay not only to elucidate contextual elements of Raworth's Irishness but also to examine how his sense of national identity plays an important role in his poetry.

Raworth's mother, Mary (May) Moore, was originally from Dublin and for a time lived upstairs from the Irish playwright Sean O'Casey. The connection between the Moore family and O'Casey is supported by a letter from O'Casey to James O'Connor where the matter of a faulty will is discussed, and which as the editor David Krause states

Irish University Review 46.1 (2016): 158–170
DOI: 10.3366/iur.2016.0208
© Edinburgh University Press
www.euppublishing.com/journal/iur

'provided the plot for the Boyle family in *Juno and the Paycock*'.[4] O'Casey writes:

> Mr. Moore will have great difficulty in sustaining his contention unless he throws all energy possible into seconding my efforts … Please ask Mr. Moore, therefore, to get hold of those witnesses and you should give him the benefit of your advice as regards getting some information from the schoolmaster.[5]

Mr Moore also appears in O'Casey's autobiography *Inishfallen, Fare Thee Well* where he 'walked by himself, shaking his head with annoyance when neighbours had surrounded him to try to shield him from some of the worst weather'.[6]

During this turbulent time in Irish history, Raworth's mother joined the women's republican paramilitary organization, Cumann na mBan, and, according to a first-hand report, took part in the 1916 Rising. The exact details of her involvement are not clear but from Nora (Gillies) O'Daly's various accounts, May Moore was stationed in St Stephen's Green. O'Daly writes:

> As I was finishing a tardy breakfast on Easter Monday morning two girls came to me with the long-looked-for Mobilisation Order, instructing me to call for two more of our members on route. [,] Miss Bridget Murtagh and Miss May Moore. We were to report to the South side of Stephen's Green without delay.[7]

According to Raworth, his uncle Liam was a member of Tom Barry's Flying Column and was arrested for tunnelling into Mountjoy prison. In *A Serial Biography*, Raworth quotes from a letter sent from his uncle to his mother: 'I am enclosing the form and would be glad if you would get it sent along to Sean Price or Frank Daly to fill in as I have forgotten the dates. I have written to Sean McEntee about being arrested in the tunnelling into Mountjoy jail'.[8] Both Raworth's mother and uncle emigrated sometime after the Civil War (1922–23), Mary Moore to England and Liam to Australia. It is not clear if their choice to leave Ireland was a political one, with the anti-treaty side being defeated and Ireland continuing as a divided Free State as opposed to a full republic. However, the fact that both Raworth's mother and uncle were involved in organizations that opposed the Treaty may well indicate that these decisions were linked to strong political convictions. Raworth's descriptions of his mother's first visits

back to Ireland further imply the importance of his family's political
history:

> Shortly after the war we all went to Dublin and I know this was
> the first time she'd been back. I have memories of being dragged
> around Eden Quay, St. Stephen's Green, The GPO, the Four
> Courts.[9]

The importance of showing her young son the sites of resistance
indicates that the history of Ireland's political struggle and her
involvement in it were vital aspects of her sense of self.

The importance of Raworth's childhood visits to Ireland can be seen
in the early poem 'Notebook' where he describes visiting his aunt's
cottage in 'corduff, lusk, county / dublin. beside it the stone
schoolhouse where ashe taught'.[10] This refers to Thomas Ashe who
was a teacher, a founding member of the Irish Volunteers, member of
the Irish Republican Brotherhood, member of The Gaelic League and
also commanded a battalion during the 1916 Rising. For his
revolutionary actions, Ashe was imprisoned in both the UK and
Ireland. While on hunger strike seeking political prisoner status, Ashe
was force-fed and in September of 1917 died from his injuries. The
poem allows the reader access to Raworth's past but through Ashe we
are also introduced to the cultural history of Raworth's Irish heritage.
Ashe exists as a folk hero, particularly for people who would identify
with his political cause. His name introduces issues of imprisonment,
confinement, and struggles against an oppressive system in order to
reassert a sense of national identity. The history of Ireland's colonial
struggle is echoed in Raworth's poem where 'my cousin pat and i
argued, english / bastard he said, what / could i do but call him /
irish pig and fight?'[11]

Speaking more broadly about his mother's national and cultural
identity, Raworth states:

> For identification, my mother certainly never thought of herself as
> other than Irish .... her brogue [Irish accent] remained until the
> end ... My father was away during the war so I had a strange
> Irish accent before school. My mother tended to keep herself to
> herself, though she was friendly with a Mrs Murphy one street
> away ... and with other people at the church ... Culturally? Well,
> she sang all the time so I got a lot of that embedded. And
> I remember ... overhearing about the Abbey Theatre when I was
> small ... I don't think she tried to assimilate .... my sense
> thinking back is that she didn't want to draw attention. And
> I certainly never got any anti-English sentiment ..... after all,

she married my father who was either a protestant or a nothing, but converted.[12]

The importance of this heritage to Raworth can be seen more specifically in two sections of his 1969 prose book *A Serial Biography*. In the first section he describes his mother singing traditional Irish songs such as *Glen of Aherlow*: 'My father died / I closed my eyes / outside the cabin door. / The lawyer and the sheriff / had been the day before'.[13] Other ballads, such as Thomas Moore's *She is Far from the Land*, are half-remembered but sung none the less. The common denominator between these songs is their political intent, arising from a 19th-century desire to promote an independent Irish nation. The history of this rise of nationalism is traced in *A Serial Biography* by Raworth who recounts the popular narrative of Robert Emmet:

> who would never have been caught but for his love for Sarah Curran. Instead of escaping he went back to see her. Let no man write my epitaph he said. Hanged drawn and quartered. And when they held up his head in St. Thomas Street in the hush the only sound was of a locket falling from his neck. And in it a strand of hair from Sarah Curran.[14]

Raworth then links this to his mother's generation by jumping in time 'up to [James] Connolly and the GPO. So the English took him out, on the stretcher, tied him to a chair to keep him upright, and shot him'.[15] Despite a clear interest and connection to his mother's history, Raworth regretfully admits 'he never got the whole story from her, and never asked'.[16]

Another cultural influence on Raworth's work which stems from his mother's Irish heritage is that of religion. Raworth's mother's spiritual belief, as with most people who are raised in a theocratic state, was a matter of habit as much as a deeply rooted belief system. As Raworth states in *A Serial Biography*: 'my mother being Irish, a Catholic from birth, there was no real zeal behind her religion. A thing you just did. If you missed mass one Sunday, God would understand'. He goes on to say that 'her conversation was sprinkled with God Willing's ... Jesusmaryandjosephprotectus she would say as the bombs fell'.[17] This form of transcendental subservience also extended towards her relationship with her only son: 'in 1964, when we were in real trouble, evicted from our flat, no money, my wife and I went down to see her. Without thinking, after hearing the story, my mother said Ah well, God is good'.[18] What makes religion such a lasting influence on Raworth's work is the fact that his 'father was a convert, with the missionary fervour. He could never see how I could so easily throw away something it had taken him thirty years to reach'.[19] The seriousness of Raworth Senior's belief in and worship of God can be seen through the use of his most common sign-off in letters to his son: 'May God bless and direct you'.[20] In a letter to his son, dated 21st February 1977, Raworth Senior demonstrates how belief can create self-righteousness which can either stifle, or at the very least place pressure on, family relationships. With only one side of this conversation available to us it is impossible to know the exact intention of these words but what is clear from this letter is that Raworth and his family are in some doubt as to their legal position regarding residency in the US. Raworth senior writes:

> we are comforted by your words that you are not idiots to travel 6000 miles without knowing you have a place to stay, and hope that you will have ample time to make arrangements if the authorities should direct that you must leave. Please let us have your address whenever you make a move.

This implies that Raworth, worried about where his family would live if deported, enquired about the possibility of staying with his parents. Refusing his son and his family respite, Raworth's father explains that 'at our age we need peace and quietness for physical and mental reasons, and we are entitled to pursue them as much as others are entitled to the pursuit of happiness'. This refusal seems to have prompted Raworth to remind his father of his Christian duties: 'Thank you for drawing our attention to the Sermon on the Mount and the Seven Corporal Works of Mercy. Certainly they are worth rereading and taking to heart'. Raworth Senior responds by asking forgiveness while still refusing his son and his family a place to stay:

> I see that there are also Seven Spiritual Works of Mercy, including such things as forgiving offensives and bearing wrongs patiently. You must pray for us. We have prayed for you so long and now perhaps you will spare a prayer for us that we may be given the grace and means to exercise these corporal and spiritual works and become worthy of the promises of Our Blessed Lord.

He ends the letter by stating 'one of the most difficult works for us is to harbour the harbourless as we haven't much harbourage here'.[21] It is clear that a religiously derived morality was an important part of Raworth's upbringing and that the contradictions he, rightly or wrongly, saw relating to these beliefs caused much tension between father and son.

In order to reinforce the argument that religion plays a vital role throughout Raworth's poetry I want to suggest a number of other examples. Firstly, we should consider the title of *Ace* and the order in which value is ascribed to certain cards and how a traditional deck places royalty at the upper echelons, starting with the Jack or Knave (royal servant), then the Queen and finally the King. The only card assigned a higher value is the 'Ace' and so we could look upon the ace card as a representation of God, 'my father / is alive / and in / "heaven"',[22] who has the power to appoint the divine right of kings. I do not want to go as far as to claim that Raworth is religious particularly considering the section of *Writing* which reads 'REFORMED CHURCH // my company was / founded on dirty money'.[23] Nonetheless, lines such as 'he stalked off / over the water',[24] referring to the episode in the bible where Jesus walked on water, or 'we three / he i and she / on meeting / in the cemetery / agreed to be / one separately',[25] which echoes one of the main tenets and mysteries of the Christian faith, The Holy Trinity, more than imply a certain religious education and understanding. These lines indicate that Raworth's life was lived through a language saturated with religious reference, even if it was not a life rooted in the religious belief system itself.

Raworth's mother appears throughout the poem 'West Wind'. By the early 1980s, she was in the later stages of her life and had been hospitalised due to the onset of Alzheimer's or another form of age-related dementia; she asks her son 'are you audrey's sister?'[26] It is painfully clear that watching his mother's 'gangrene / shuddering / flecked with yellow / red-rimmed eyes'[27] is difficult for Raworth, an only child, as she is left in the care of a health service under attack by Thatcher's conservative government. Raworth now acts as a care-giver to his elderly mother and this role reversal is not lost on the author, who by now has five children of his own, and writes: 'no breast-feeding / no sleepless nights / who made you?' Raworth's responses – 'god made me / no / my parents made me'[28] – show not only that he has rejected his parental faith, but also how instinctive and automatic a belief system can be.

A second, more cryptic, reference to religion also appears in 'West Wind' where early in the poem the line 'or guss *teen*' sits uncomfortably within the overall context of the poem:

you drove splendidly
a long stretch
at the sorting centre
forms across the board
good help

reflection on the coating
or guss *teen*
the past was always
not quite right
give me more sound
copying
marks of teeth[29]

I quote such a long section so as to be able show how little this line interacts with the lines around it and to elucidate my argument in relation to its elusive meaning. Firstly, this line does not cohere syntactically, which is very much at odds with Raworth's usual practice and that of 'West Wind' in particular. To clarify, the only possibly unknown word in the three-word line – *guss* – is a local British West Midlands term for a rope which was used by young boys to pull coal in mines. The italicised *'teen'* reinforces this and could be seen as a critique of child labour or a reference to the mining industry — 'send'm into / dead volcanoes / proud / to be neanderthal'[30] — which Thatcher was in the process of decimating during the early eighties. However, the combination of words is still 'not quite right' until you consider how this combination of words might register aurally. Repeating the line out loud the possibility arises that 'or guss *teen*' is a word play on Augustine, the early Christian theologian who, like Raworth's father, was a convert. This point is reinforced by the fact that the first epigraph to *A Serial Biography*, in which Raworth discusses his mother's and father's faith, is a quotation from Saint Augustine. Whether or not Raworth's line 'or guss *teen*' is directly referencing Saint Augustine is not fully clear. What we do know for certain is that throughout his life and career his mixed cultural heritage has been an influence on his writing.

Turning now to an early uncollected poem by Raworth entitled 'An Island to the East of Ireland' I will demonstrate how his mother's heritage influenced his sense of self and how these themes manifest themselves in his poetry from the beginning of his career. The relevance of this forgotten poem is only fully felt when considered alongside the fact that it was only published as part of *The English Intelligencer* and appears nowhere else in Raworth's published oeuvre. *The English Intelligencer*, which I will refer to as *TEI* from here on, was a poetry worksheet which appeared between January 1966 and April 1968, first under the editorship of its founder, Andrew Crozier, and, later, Peter Riley.[31] This worksheet was an attempt to echo the poetic communities that built up around certain strands of

American poetry, most notably Black Mountain and would, at least for a number of young poets, act as vital nexus of poetry and criticism in England.

Peter Riley states that *TEI* was born out of a 'need to share something more than private correspondence can cope with ... the language we can use has to be worked out in common, among however many will allow themselves to trust, respond, risk, REACT, move outside their private worlds'.[32] Despite this talk of being 'more than private' or of a desire to 'move outside their private worlds', *TEI* was never made for public consumption; instead, it was distributed by post 'to a loose-knit group of collaborators and bystanders'[33] whose names and addresses were published regularly as part of the journal. This act of printing the names and addresses allowed Raworth and Anselm Hollo to produce the now infamous 'spoof' issue containing both poems and prose credited to the main figures associated with the journal. As Raworth explains:

> There's nothing much complicated to say about *The English Intelligencer*. At that time Anselm and I found the stance too solemn and Little England and much of the work boring. I say 'at that time' and 'much' as there was some I liked then, and others whose later work interested me. In one issue they foolishly printed the names and addresses of all recipients. So Anselm and I dashed off a copy with (I think) the next sequential number and mailed it off a couple of days before the official one was due.[34]

This in itself shows at best a whimsical approach and at worst a total disregard for the journal. I will not focus on the entirety of the 'spoof' issue of *TEI*, but will use sections of the mock letters to support my overall argument that Raworth, despite being a recipient of every issue and being close friends with a number of its key contributors, intentionally positions himself in opposition to the main drives of *TEI* and that this opposition is directly related to his mother's Irish heritage.

In his introduction to *Certain Prose of The English Intelligencer*, Neil Pattison states that 'one of the mistakes most frequently made about the *Intelligencer* is that the apparent parochialism of its title represented authentically the group's mission'[35] and in some ways he is right to suggest that we cannot think about the writers involved as a coherent group. Many of the writers had well-established and deep connections to their American and European counterparts but, intentionally or not, this issue of nationalism and Englishness was and would remain central to the way *TEI* was perceived. In fact, it was one of the first key issues raised by participants, with Elaine Feinstein stating:

> I like much of what is in the *Intelligencer* and what I know of the people it should reach. But I wanted to say about the Englishness: in our present context it makes sense to put some force into the need to make things here, but I should be unhappy to give any strength to the <u>kind</u> of nationalism you parodied ... surely the language of the island belongs to whoever lives here and uses it ... let's not have any fictional 'Englishness'. What could be nastier?[36]

The issue of national identity and outside influence was raised again by Gael Turnbull when he writes:

> but i just don't see the point of such near parody of Olson ... I mean, I am interested to see what [John] Temple can do with his 'roots' etc. – but must he swipe the means so obviously ... surely, somehow, there <u>are</u> ways of being 'for the island and its language' without merely parroting what certain Americans have done.[37]

It is clear, then, from these passages, that from the outset that *TEI* was expressly intended to create something wholly English, albeit something which was emulating aspects of American poetry scenes, but the fact that *TEI* was not publicly available suggests that it was not, in fact, 'for the island and its language'.[38]

Turning now to Raworth's poem 'An Island to the East of Ireland' I will demonstrate how Raworth, like Feinstein, had reservations about the project as a whole. Firstly, by naming Britain via its association with and proximity to Ireland, Raworth reverses the domineering role Britain has played in the history of both countries. Moreover, by using the language of the Intelligencer he calls into question the still-present imperialist attitudes. Using Ireland as the central defining landmark by which to identify Britain highlights Raworth's sense of dual nationality. This poem does not try to trace the 'roots' of Raworth's Irishness, Englishness or Britishness, but rather explores issues surrounding identity, influence, friendship, accents, and other geographical markers. The poem opens '(said teddy unto bobby well / what do you think about things / <u>here</u> & they went off into questions of / idiom'.[39] The question 'what do you think about things / <u>here</u>' implies that at least one, if not both, of the characters are not from 'here', the island east of Ireland, and it is this conversation about idiom that prompts Raworth to ask 'so how do we do it?',[40] highlighting the fact that it is his accent and his way of speaking that they are discussing.

It is Raworth's accent which comes from 'the south london of my youth' which is central to this question of idiom and his sense of identity. It is through this sense of geography and its:

> turn of phrase bleedin
> rainin stair-rods   those
> interrogative endings so
> i'm down there, inn'i? an
> e ses t'me, dunn'ee?[41]

Raworth directs the question 'how / in fact do we speak' at Andrew Crozier who 'also knows [the south London of my youth] the railway running / through the wooden stations'. Raworth aligns himself with Crozier by stating 'we / were the dandies then' and declares that it is not merely a similar geographical background that they share, but also 'our / south london voices a flattened cockney'. However, this is as far as Raworth can go with this plurality: he then begins to distance himself from shared experiences, choosing instead to continue with the singular: 'even now i feel most at home in the / obscenities splitting words bee / fuckin yootiful springing the rhythm'.[42] Raworth here could be making an allusion to Gerald Manley Hopkins whose sprung rhythm technique was based on the natural speech patterns of the English language and was an important precursor to free verse. As Peter Riley states in an early letter to *TEI*, 'the important thing is to hear the sounds that people are speaking around you, and (more difficult) that you yourself speak, and make these relate to the poetic diction you are forging'.[43] It is clear from this poem that Raworth wants to demonstrate the particulars of his speech. However, this is a way of speaking that Raworth does not feel fits with *TEI*'s particular brand of Englishness, instead it is a type of speech that has emerged from a working class and multicultural London.

Raworth further distances himself from an insular England and English poetry by stating that 'of live people / i learned most from an american of french / descent, a german finn, an american jew and an Italian / polish jewish american'.[44] For Raworth it seems, at least ostensibly, English poetry does not register nor does it have anything to teach him. Instead, he looks to a form of multiculturalism that has for the most part found a home in the American experience of multiple immigrations. In an interview with Barry Alpert for the magazine *Vort*, Raworth states that 'for a long time after I left school all the writing I saw bored me' and it was not until 1957 when he 'bought a copy of the San Francisco issue of *Evergreen Review*' that his interest in poetry began.[45] For Raworth this poetry was a far cry from 'that English insular sense that I sometimes feel oppressed by … that I don't see any point in … I don't really see any reason in terms like "English Poet"'.[46]

The above quotation seems, albeit covertly, to be directed at magazines such as *TEI* with its closed distribution and its self-entitled Englishness. If we look for a moment at the spoof issue, we can see in a more direct manner some of Raworth's concerns about the *TEI* project. The very act of making a spoof issue containing both poems and prose credited to the main figures shows the disregard in which Raworth held the project. This can be seen in the mock letter from John James to Crozier, which states:

> You see, what depresses me more than anything else is the list of names at the back of the 'Intelligencer'. Are they all to be trusted? In fact are 50 or so of us enough? Certainly Hitler started with fewer, but the English mentality, deplorable though it may seem to us, is unlike that of the Germans in the late '20's or even early '30's. I must confess to some misgivings.[47]

It is clear that Raworth and Hollo believe that *TEI* is a journal built not only on an exclusive coterie but one defined by nationality, and that this form of nationalism is both worrying and dangerous. This point is subtly reinforced early on in the same piece of prose when they write: 'Berkeley asserted that the only things that exist are ideas. But he was Irish – do we admit him?'[48] It is clear then from this poem and its placement in *TEI* that Raworth is sceptical of the label 'English'. Raworth states: 'I can see some sense in the energy you draw from where you are … But to want to be like "the best English poet" is so totally ludicrous'.[49] This is not to imply that Raworth is rejecting his English heritage in favour of an Irish national identity. Rather, I wish to highlight how his mixed nationality influences his thinking and how his sense of distance from a singular national identity is why Raworth could never endorse an 'English' poetry scene or a journal like *The English Intelligencer*.

What is clear throughout Raworth's poetry is that biography and family play an important role in his work. The very fact that Raworth published *A Serial Biography*, which includes a slew of information relating to family and friends, indicates that Raworth's sense of his own biography is irrevocably linked to the histories of others. The social, cultural, and political histories that are attached to Raworth's Irish heritage have a crucial impact on his sense of self and his poetry. Raworth does not reject Englishness by replacing it with some imagined sense or Irishness; instead, throughout his career

Raworth has resisted the idea of single national poetic traditions, opting instead for a multinational set of influences. Culturally he is both English and Irish but poetically he remains elusive.

NOTES

1. Keith Tuma, *Fishing by Obstinate Isles: Modern and Postmodern British Poetry and American Readers*, (Evanston, Ill.: Northwest University Press, 1998), p.234.
2. Marjorie Perloff, *The Dance of the Intellect* (Cambridge: Cambridge University Press, 1985), p.234.
3. *21 + 1 American Poets Today*, edited by Emmanuel Hocquard/and Claude Royet-Journoud, (Universite Paul Valery, Montpellier, Delta, 1986).
4. Sean O'Casey, *The Letters of Sean O'Casey*, ed. David Kraus (Washington DC: Catholic University of America, 1975), pp.92–93.
5. O'Casey, *Letters*, pp.92–93.
6. Sean O'Casey, *Innisfallen, Fare Thee Well*, (London: Macmillan, 1949), p.100.
7. Nora O'Daly, 'Nora (Gillies) O'Daly Eye Witness Account of 1916'. *The Unmanageable: Revolutionary Women of Ireland*. Web. 27th Dec. 2014.
8. Tom Raworth, *Earn Your Milk: Collected Prose*, (Cambridge: Salt, 2009), p.21.
9. Raworth, 'Collages'. Message to the Author. 5 Nov. 2013. E-Mail.
10. Raworth, *Collected Poems*, (Manchester: Carcanet Press, 2003), p.11.
11. Raworth, *Collected Poems*, p.11.
12. Raworth, 'Collages'.
13. Raworth, *Earn*, p.20.
14. Raworth, *Earn*, p.20.
15. Raworth, *Earn*, p.20.
16. Raworth, *Earn*, p.21.
17. Raworth, *Earn*, p.32.
18. Raworth, *Earn*, p.32.
19. Raworth, *Earn*, p.32.
20. Raworth, *Earn*, p.91.
21. Letter from Raworth Snr. to Tom Raworth, 21st Feb 1977, Box 3, Tom Raworth Papers, archives and special collections at the Thomas J. Dodd Research Centre, University of Connecticut Library, Storrs.
22. Raworth, *Collected Poems*, pp.203–204.
23. Raworth, *Collected Poems*, p.255.
24. Raworth, *Collected Poems*, p.272.
25. Raworth, *Collected Poems*, p.311.
26. Raworth, *Collected Poems*, p.367.
27. Raworth, *Collected Poems*, p.368.
28. Raworth, *Collected Poems*, p.368.
29. Raworth, *Collected Poems*, p.356.
30. Raworth, *Collected Poems*, p.356.
31. Neil Pattison, Reitha Pattison and Luke Roberts ed. *Certain Prose of the English Intelligencer*, (Cambridge: Mountain Press, 2012), p.i.
32. Pattison, *Certain Prose*, p.37.
33. Pattison, *Certain Prose*, p.i.
34. Raworth, 'Re: Catch up'. Message to the Author. 6 March 2012. E-mail.
35. Pattison, *Certain Prose*, p.xii.
36. Pattison, *Certain Prose*, p.3.
37. Pattison, *Certain Prose*, p.4.
38. Pattison, *Certain Prose*, p.9.

39. Raworth, 'An Island East of Ireland', *The English Intelligencer* Series 1, Issue 14, p.224. The Teddy and Bobby in this passage refers to Edward Lucie-Smith and Robert Creeley.
40. Raworth, 'An Island . . .'.
41. Raworth, 'An Island . . .'.
42. Raworth, 'An Island . . .'.
43. Pattison, *Certain Prose*, p.50.
44. Raworth, 'An Island . . .'.
45. Raworth, 'An Interview with Barry Alpert'. *Vort* issue 1 1972. p.29.
46. Raworth, 'Interview', p.36.
47. Pattison, *Certain Prose*, p.112.
48. Pattison, *Certain Prose*, p.112.
49. Raworth, 'Interview', p.36.

Rachel Warriner

Image and Witness in Maggie O'Sullivan's *A Natural History in 3 Incomplete Parts* and *POINT.BLANK.RANGE*

The visual aspects of Maggie O'Sullivan's practice are a point of focus for the emerging critical work on this important poet. Mandy Bloomfield, Peter Manson, Nicky Marsh, and Frances Kruk have all considered the question, forming a provisional consensus that suggests that O'Sullivan's poetic form is inherently visual, using the page to create a material, visceral, and embodied space.[1] O'Sullivan is a poet known for her sonorous landscapes, dense and intriguing texts that appropriate language and interrogate words, their meanings, but also their sounds and appearance as artifacts on the page.[2] However, in two books from the 1980s, written while she was based in London – *A Natural History in 3 Incomplete Parts* (1985) and *POINT.BLANK.RANGE* (1984) – O'Sullivan introduced a different kind of visuality, one that used appropriated images, collaging them onto the poems so that they either obscure language, as in *A Natural History*, or replace it, as in *POINT.BLANK.RANGE*. It is these visual practices that are the focus of my examination of O'Sullivan's work, ones that I propose are suggestive in terms of how we can understand her appropriations more broadly, pointing to a particular type of subjective poetic politics.

The use of appropriated imagery was unusual in O'Sullivan's works of this time. *A Natural History* and *POINT.BLANK.RANGE* were among a number of short chapbooks created by the author during the mid 1970s to the late 1980s, developed amongst the creative community surrounding Writers Forum in London and later published together in the 2006 collection *Body of Work*.[3] Most often, the visual aspect of these works, as Bloomfield states, highlights the materiality of texts in a practice that 'acknowledges and employs the physical, visually and acoustically embodied dimensions of language in a 'production' of meaning that critiques the logic of instrumentality and consumption'.[4]

Irish University Review 46.1 (2016): 171–182
DOI: 10.3366/iur.2016.0209
© Edinburgh University Press
www.euppublishing.com/journal/iur

Using diacritical and asemic marks, colour, emboldened and underlined words, and typographical interventions in her practice, O'Sullivan's visuality is most often not referential and instead seeks to inscribe something of the writer into the page, existing as an indexical trace of making. The visual aspects of O'Sullivan's work are most often interventions into meaning, standing as evidence of an alternative layer of significance that is made invisible in mainstream textual practice.[5] In *A Natural History* and *POINT.BLANK.RANGE* by contrast, appropriated images are incorporated as representational artifacts. Amongst the evocative references that O'Sullivan incorporated in *A Natural History*, for example, exploring the natural world, her Irish heritage, portraits of her parents, descriptions of violence and protest in the three sections 'Incomplete', 'More Incomplete', and 'Most Incomplete', the images are the most straightforwardly legible of O'Sullivan's inclusions. Not offering an alternative to the referentiality of language, they are instead clear in their inferences. For a poet who so carefully dissects the interrelation between meaning and language, direct reference stands as markedly unusual in O'Sullivan's practice.

This seems important: why would a practitioner so adept at creating a play with meaning, using new and evocative forms of sound and image in language, include objects that are so straightforward in their implications? Set against the subtle and suggestive linguistic plays, the images are blunt and legible. The page in *A Natural History* that includes a map of Greenham Common – site of important all-women protests against nuclear weapons – and a list of people killed by rubber and plastic bullets in Northern Ireland provides a good case in point. The text that is not obscured by the image includes certain discernible words: 'The Moon's w/', 'w/BLACK black', 'Vanilla Scent', 'the. The Body', 'wringing odd', 'fuschia lacewing:', and

Fire, as in
the Sun.[6]

This text seems to be a facsimile of a previous page included in the first section of the poem, titled 'Incomplete'. The first page in the book that is not a title page, the similarity of text and layout suggest that it is a repetition that forms the basis of the collaged page in the section 'More Incomplete'. This original form, then, highlights the effect that the collaged images have on the text, it reads:

The Moon's w/BLACK BLACK eye of wasp/BLACK black
Vanilla Scent. Skin of Open Fields, the. The Body
wringing odd skittish foreign public, fuschia lacewing:
Credentials Green, very floated lilac axle

pennyfans, filth-fold. addled quackery. lash capitals.
bonnets crinkle beat, lemon root shell bandeau
matched w/sand twinkle, seam: cheeky pulse & cheery
vertigo worn w/remix, Diffusion. Face prow. Bubbles.
Baffled Carne, cleeze w/fire echo. Vomica, primary
tea, see Skipping X. Flagjar, frecklebed, wintergreen
anyway, look . . .

Boulevard.

Fire, as in
the Sun[7]

It is possible to make inferences from this section of text; the phrase
'Credentials Green', for example, could suggest some kind of political
inclination, the 'addled quackery' might suggest a frustration with
professional incompetence. However, these are extremely unsecure
interpretations, falling away in the clash of other connections and
associations. Words seem as though they have been extracted from
elsewhere, 'Diffusion' for example is capitalized without context
suggesting that it could have been directly quoted from an original
source. The obscure-but-suggestive terms such as Vomica, part of the
name *strychnos nux-vomica*, a poisonous tree, or the neologisms such as
'cleeze', create a language that is sonorous and splintered by
allusions.[8]

By contrast, the collaged elements operate in an almost exactly
opposing way. The map of Greenham Common, although relying
broadly on knowledge of the political association of the place, suggests
a fixed meaning. This meaning is not one that dissolves in relation to
other elements on the page, but instead is secured and bolstered in
relation to the other signifiers that are included. The list of people
killed by rubber and plastic bullets is entirely uncomplicated. Even a
passing knowledge of the political situation in Northern Ireland
during the 1970s and '80s allows us to understand this as a document
of State violence and innocent death. Both situations were the focus of
broad media coverage, making the collaged elements into
straightforward political ciphers. What is being represented on this
page is a leftist position that is supportive of peaceful protest and
against government oppression. Furthermore, rather than silencing the
texts below, the collaged elements secure meaning onto a page that
was otherwise elusive. The text 'The Body / wringing odd' is inflected
by the description of the cruel deaths of the mostly young victims of
rubber and plastic bullets, the phrase 'BLACK black', which echoes the

black of the background of the text on which the list of those killed is printed, suggests mourning. The final phrase 'Fire, as in / the Sun.' speaks both to the firing of bullets and to the nuclear blast that the women of Greenham Common protested against. Instead of blocking the flow of the text, the images on this page seem to decode it.

In fact, when taken as a whole, this sequence of collaged images seems to create a stable argument that pictures the result of violence and oppression. Prefaced by a page that reads as an inter-title made up of the words 'Moral Conditions.' placed between two lines that emphasise the text and its inference, there are six images on the five pages that follow, collaged over the texts.[9] These elements sit on top of the pages below. Separated by the strong black lines that border each of the collaged fragments, the sections look more like they have been affixed to a scrapbook, overlaid without regard to the meanings of the works that they cover. If the words had overlaid the image or intruded on their support then perhaps this would feel more relational. However, the integrity of the original image, painting or newspaper cutting is retained; words do not intrude onto their space. Instead, collaged elements cut into texts, leaving them half-legible or obscuring them completely. That these are in all cases texts that we have read before adds to this sense. Their being obscured does not deny the reader access to them as they are all present as whole texts in the preceding section. There is no struggle for dominance over meanings here; the collaged elements blankly override the texts below as though they were affixed to scrap paper.

Therefore, the meanings that are brought out in the interaction seem more to be a coincidence of proximity than a deliberate foregrounding. After all, we do not need the words 'The Body/wringing odd' to describe the victims of rubber bullets when immediately adjacent is the image *Striking Worker, Murdered* by Manuel Álvarez Bravo (1934) which is overlaid onto the text.[10] Although the image is specific and therefore its context is describable, collaged in as it is it represents brutal death, the trail of blood that escapes the obviously dead body seeming to illustrate the murder factually described on the facing page. Again, certain words are brought into significance by this visual interjection. As Kruk points out, the 'i' that appears so rarely in *A Natural History* seems now to be the voice of this murder victim with the words 'i bleed & soak & pool olive'.[11] Manson, too, points to the way in which 'describe. / Thunder. Bleeding. The Sky Confessing It. / & being / jobless' is brought to the fore with the image, as Manson says it is 'altered by its new context'.[12] However, the most important connection on the page is not between the word and the collaged elements, but instead between collaged elements themselves. The text fades behind the image of violence, the list of murdered protestors made more poignant by the blank detail than by its interaction with the texts beneath.

The images together build a picture of mourning and violence creating a legible and recurring theme for this section. The inclusion of Edgar Degas's crayon drawing *Old Roman Beggarwoman* (1856) as the first image of the work – one that is also used for the cover image of the book – creates an immediate impression of grieving.[13] The woman, pictured weeping into her hand is a vision of victimhood; the choice of this image, which shows an older, but not elderly, woman dressed in a headscarf, her face obscured in a way that suggests absorbing sorrow, alludes lightly to the Virgin Mary and maternal grief. Placed sideways on the page in order to align with the flow of the words which are also turned to a landscape format, the image seems to override them, not silencing them, but instead picturing a figure overwhelmed by sorrow, unable to interact. Here, grief overrides meaning.

The violence of the pages that refer to Greenham Common and protestor deaths is then introduced as the explanation for grief. This creates a context for the image of devastating sadness that precedes it. The final two pages that are collaged over contrast the screaming headlines of the media with the rather contemplative image of a woman writing at her desk by Josep Cardona entitled *Girl Writing in Cafe* (1903).[14] The headlines that read 'Man killed after RUC "go berserk"' and 'Man dies as police fire in IRA riot' are illustrated with the grainy image of what looks like a hand holding a grenade or pipe bomb.[15] In this image, violence is depersonalized; its mediation by newspapers becomes the focus. Cardona's image of the woman writing, put into landscape format, is in comparison quiet and uncertain. This woman is hunched over a desk, her face like that of Degas's woman is obscured. This looks more like illustration of the text. The page that the image is collaged over is made up of two parts, the landscaped text is entirely legible and the text that is formatted in portrait is almost entirely obscured, the words '(towards the)' are the only remaining evidence of the passage and they are cut off so that only the lower half of the letters is visible. The headlines clearly identify men as those actively involved in violence: it is a male worker that lies dead, men who die in the police brutality that the newspapers record, men and boys who form the majority of victims of the police use of plastic and rubber bullets – 12 males compared to 3 females. These images, and the reference to the Greenham Women's camp, create a legible narrative of women responding to male violence in grief, protest, and thought.[16]

As part of her useful wider examination of violence and identity in poetry, Kruk posits a way of interpreting Cardona's drawing in *A Natural History*. She states: 'This writer might be the recorder of historical events as seen from a paused moment in the present: the "I" as witness to the exploration and exposure of unofficial histories'.[17] Seeing this image as an analogy to the way in which O'Sullivan dissects official histories through a practice that resists meaning-making and instead highlights the violence of official stories, Kruk points to the notion that the writer offers up a form of testimony. This brief reference to witnessing points to a way of interpreting how O'Sullivan's collaged images suggest the means by which the poet presents her reader with evidence of social and political violence. Thinking about the way the writer builds a legible narrative through images in *A Natural History*, I want to examine the idea that what O'Sullivan evokes here is a mode of witness.

I invoke the term witness in this context due to the relationship it implies between evidence and experience. As Günter Thomas outlines in his 2009 essay 'Witness as a Cultural Form of Communication', witnessing implies both legal evidence and religious testimony.[18] In this interaction between two registers of information, one that implies a factual account of true events, and the other that attests to the strength of faith of the witness, a tension between the language of official systems and the authentic account of belief creates something that speaks to O'Sullivan's oeuvre. Alluding, too, to the register of trauma that Bloomfield identifies as marking O'Sullivan's texts, considering the poet as witness allows a reading of her work that accounts for the way in which even in an obscured form, there emerges a sense that we are being presented with abstract evidence not only in the images she includes but also through recurring themes and the flicks and flickers of connotation.[19] If we consider O'Sullivan as witness to those subjects that she explores – in *A Natural History* insect and plant life, 1980s politics, violence, and portraits of her parents and in *POINT.BLANK.RANGE* violence and horror, gender, death, close up shots of arms and legs, smiling faces, and animals, children's drawings – then her attentive gaze and careful selection not only of words, but also of images, builds a picture that witnesses not a specific set of events, but instead a violence that is inherent in society, one that infests the mind and intrudes on the body.

Turning back to *A Natural History* with this in mind, a reading can emerge which sees the narrative that these images present as a means of providing objective evidence to complement the subjective record of thought and experience that the rest of the text obliquely describes. The collaged elements and their narrative of grief and violence introduce something that seems to refer away from the poet's interpretations and selections and instead towards cultural and political forces that shape our experience. Only the newspaper articles from which headlines are taken are fragmented; the rest of those elements that are collaged in are whole, they are not manipulated or intervened into by the poet in the same way as the texts that she includes. Furthermore, their original sources are cited at the end of the book: the reader is not to understand these as O'Sullivan's drawings or photographs, but instead as complete transcriptions of other works. By placing the section that contains the collaged elements after the first appearance of the pages that lie underneath, O'Sullivan does not erode the meaning of the original texts. Instead, by scrapbooking these elements in on top of already existing previous pages, the collaged elements seem to be objective and meaningful, included so as to evidence something wider that inflects the poet's subjective sense of violence and trauma. Public discourse overlays personal experience creating a tension between types of evidence, O'Sullivan's personal attention to violence in language interacts with the language of reportage in journalistic reports and the idea of expression that exists within the discursive system of art. Rather than either a faith-based testimonial or an objective account, these systems merge and are complicated by O'Sullivan in their interaction, both interwoven and juxtaposed. Evidence of oppression – the documents, reports and photographs of death accompanied by an image of the grief that such violent silencing incurs – contrasts to the more subtle markers of the texts: the breaks, allusions, and violent interjections that inhabit a language that presents itself as a dissection of 'the natural world' and its relationship to the poet's memories. O'Sullivan's description to Scott Thurston of the process of composing *her/story eye* demonstrates exactly this kind of interweaving of the subjective with the external. She describes how 'both my mother and Bobby Sands were dying at the same time – she in Lincoln and he in Belfast – and both were buried on the 7th May 1981. I remember each day visiting hospital to be beside my mother's bedside amidst a flood of news coverage on Bobby Sands and his hunger strike'.[20] In this way the public events become fused with the private, the grief of one deeply personal loss is with another that is political.

This merging and nuancing of the relationship between personal and objective testimony can also be seen in the visual poem *POINT.BLANK.RANGE*. The book was first seen as a whole in *Body of Work* published by Reality Street in 2006 which brings together O'Sullivan's nine booklets of London-based work made between 1975 and 1987. Although the planned original booklet was not produced (as O'Sullivan explains 'it was an accident of fate that it was never published at its time of making'), sections of this source material appeared publicly before during the 1980s in two places.[21] Firstly, an extract was included in the 'Interface' volume of *Reality Studios* in 1984 in which O'Sullivan details the sources for the images used.[22] Secondly, the material is included in a visual piece also entitled *POINT.BLANK.RANGE*: a triptych of three large banners, each composed of three pieces of blue material hanging from a baton with the images presented like a roll of film unfurled and stitched to the support. These were adorned with blue, yellow, black, and red ribbons which trail down underneath the rows of hanging filmstrips. Although some of the material is repeated, this booklet is a different piece: despite the repetition of the images, the carnivalesque affect of the banners does not translate to the poem, and although the groupings of four images remains the same, their order is different. The reference to television in the booklet is clear. At this point, O'Sullivan was working as a researcher for the BBC and this influenced the composition of this piece; as she describes, 'it seemed natural to extend my working with images in my BBC work to my own poetic practice'.[23] Here, it is as though we are being made witness to something; the images feel like screenshots of culture, our view zoned in so as to focus on important details: in O'Sullivan's words '*POINT.BLANK.RANGE* is big close up, very close indeed, at close quarters'.[24] Almost like unravelling a clue, the images suggest to the reader something sinister and hidden at work beneath the surface of media representation.

Although *POINT.BLANK.RANGE* is unusual in O'Sullivan's oeuvre in being made up entirely of appropriated images, the formal plays and visual rhymes are consistent with her textual practice. A section printed on page 240 of *Body of Work* provides a good example of the way she extends this play. In the stack of four images different versions of close up representations of hands are framed. The first, a detail taken from Tony Palmer's *The People of Providence*, seem to be those of an old woman: resting on floral material they are withered and knotted. Below is the lifeless hand of a dead American gunner, the picture taken after his ship has been torpedoed in the Second World War. Only the hair of the figure and their arm and hand are visible, but there is something in the pose that implies death, reminding us of the image of Álvarez Bravo's murdered worker. This contrasts to the image below, which was as O'Sullivan states 'from Col painting by my friend, Alex Crawford, aged 6, of School', cropped so as the top of the face is missing, the simple, semi-circular smile still clearly visible.[25] Finally there is a detail of Fred Astaire's hand as he dances with Ginger Rogers, the fingers trail almost romantically along a surface that is hard to distinguish. The harsh cropping of images, which leaves so little of the original subjects intact, directs our scrutiny at parts of the images that would usually go unnoticed; we are led to compare the shapes and folds of the hands, looking at the shadows that surround them. The child's drawing of a hand, which reads as a troublesome afterthought to the main representation of the smiling face and scribbled hair, looks unrealistic in its five, equally sized and spaced rounded lines. However, it also looks remarkably similar to the fingers below, which are a much more elegant and evocative construction. The contrast of youth, age, and death is brought into sharp relief, the conflict between the apparent elderliness of the hands at the top of the image making the youth of those that lie lifeless below more poignant. The child's drawing, immediately below the image of the dead body reminds us of a naive innocence that seems threatened by the realities of violence pictured above. These are images that skirt the boundary between the personal and the public. The image of the dead soldier immediately suggests something from the public realm, an image clipped from a newspaper perhaps, and the child's drawing suggests something personal, a gift from a young friend as O'Sullivan so affectionately describes it. However, these are not certain designations; the child's drawing could conceivably have come from the public realm, and the image of the dead soldier, while unlikely to be a personal picture could have been a fictional one, taken from a film or illustration from a book. Furthermore, the other two are ambiguous. They could have been taken from personal photographs or stills from films, they could imply something deeply personal such as a cropped portrait of a loved one, or they could be arbitrary markers of popular culture. What is important is the way in which they are brought into interaction to create meaning, one that suggests both a subject existing between the personal and the public, but also the relationship between systems such as the media, the state, and militarism. At the heart of this is the poet who selects evidence to suggest something pertinent about this complex set of interactions, something about the feeling of living in amongst these competing coordinates. In this way, the voice of the witness does not suggest that the child's drawing, for example, is violent, but that it reminds the adult subject of violence. The personal and the public interrelate to create a reading of the world that is at once subjective and objective, an interpretation that draws on the evidence both of feeling and of knowing to create a picture of endemic violence.

This is further evidenced in the facing pages 232 and 233 which contrast mundane images that are reminiscent of the kinds of photographs you would discover at home – things that look like images of uncles and aunts and the line ups of old school photographs – to a violent and militaristic landscape of barbed wire, soldiers, and barely visible characters lurking in the undergrowth. The photographs to the left of the double page show snapshots of people posing for the camera. Not slick, instead they seem like those images that were more common before digital cameras, captured when people were not quite prepared, their smiles in the process of forming or their gaze off in the slightly wrong direction. They are a recognizable type of imagery; they feel old, unthreatening, and familiar. By contrast, the militaristic images on the right are aggressive and alienating. Images of Greenham Common taken from *City Limits*, they are far starker in their contrast of black and white, the barbed wire is a dark shadow against a light sky, the images of soldiers are silhouettes. The figure who lurks in the third image, a still from F.W. Murnau's 1927 silent film *Sunrise*, is almost ghostlike: it is hard to gather anything more than the sense that someone threatening has fixed you in their gaze. The final image of this sequence is a detail from a postcard of Paula Modersohn-Becker's painting *Poor-House Woman With Glass-Balloon* (1907). The poor-house woman's serious gaze is fixed on smiling men at the bottom of the left-hand page, making her look like she is standing vigilant, waiting for an attack.

This play is constant throughout the piece: on page 239 an image of a plastic spider is disturbingly contrasted to a biological diagram of a woman's uterus; on page 252 a monkey and a wooden horse both stare out at the reader with a frightening attention; on page 256 a tarantula stands above the soldiers who stand above a man-made geometric web, all looking ready to pounce on the figure who is trapped behind bars at the bottom of the page. Although the series of images contains many shots that are not in themselves threatening, the combination of these smiling children, family portraits, animals, and drawings with the images of death, the skulls and bodies, the preying spiders, the military and police in riot gear, and the snippets of language such as 'or dead animals/please put in/plastic bags' makes the piece feel like a visual thesis of threat and violence. The close attention in itself feels aggressive, made the more pertinent through the pun in the title of *POINT.BLANK.RANGE* which connects the shot of the camera to a gunshot that cannot miss. It is as though close attention is revelatory, that the audience is being given testimony to society's hidden violence.

Both *POINT.BLANK.RANGE* and *A Natural History* work to reveal an aggression that lurks amongst the familiar and the beloved. The portraits of the poet's parents in *A Natural History* and the personal portraits in *POINT.BLANK.RANGE* feel like we are being given access to something precious and private. However, the way in which they are contextualized amongst violent fragments creates an ambiguous relationship between the vulnerable and the threatening. Page 242 of *POINT.BLANK.RANGE* provides an example. A young child is placed in relationship to the staring, closely cropped eye of a tiger, the inanimate eye of a wooden horse and the same pair of withered hands that appear on page 240. In this context, the child looks somehow menacing, despite the tumbling curled black hair, the focus on detail of the other image turns our attention to the quality of their gaze and the edges of their smile. Instead of an image of an innocent, this child looks mildly dangerous, threatening the reader with the intense and ambiguous stare. In amongst this accumulation of imagery, nothing can remain unmarked by it. However, this marking does not feel directed by a poet manipulating through her selection. Instead, because these are documents presented in the context of a gridded informational format, mediated only in the degree to which they are cropped for our attention, it feels like we are being presented with evidence, asked to draw our own conclusions from the material that is collated.

In this way, the notion of witness in these texts points to a way of thinking about O'Sullivan's wider practice. Rather than the postmodern archaeological process that Bloomfield identifies in her discussion of *that bread should be* and *A Natural History*, witnessing allows for an understanding of a political work that foregrounds the subjective experience of the writer not as a means to examine the individualized subject, but instead in order to interpret broader political and cultural concerns.[26] Adopting a mode of testimony, the collation of snippets of language, found and imagined, evidence the experience of living in a particular system at a particular time. O'Sullivan's attention to the bodily, visual, and the sonic – what Dell Olsen describes as her 'synaesthesic practice' – is part of a sincere testimony to an alternative way of perceiving and interpreting the world.[27] These texts that witness and convince use carefully selected references to build a case against violence, discrimination, and sadism that is constructed both from objective citation and from the strongly held conviction of the author. This practice is, for O'Sullivan, one that exists in relation to the language of culture. In a 2007 interview with Charles Bernstein in response to a question about the integration of different forms she describes 'the words working as part of all this kind of radical shifting'.[28] This stands as a good metaphor for the practice that her appropriated images and collaged elements contribute to; a work of ever shifting, ever radical poetics.

NOTES
1. See Mandy Bloomfield, 'Maggie O'Sullivan's Material Poetics of Salvaging in *red shifts* and *murmur'*, in *The Salt Companion to Maggie O'Sullivan*, ed. by Chris Emery (Cambridge: Salt Publishing, 2011), pp.10–35; and '"Dragging at the haemorrhage of uns – "': Maggie O'Sullivan's excavations of Irish history', *Journal of British and Irish Innovative Poetry* 1. 1 (2009): 11–36; Peter Manson, '*A Natural History in 3 Incomplete Parts*' in *The Salt Companion to Maggie O'Sullivan*, pp.71–79; Nicola Marsh, 'Agonal states: Maggie O'Sullivan and a feminist politics of visual poetics', in *The Salt*

Companion to Maggie O'Sullivan pp.76–93; Frances Kruk, *Violence and Identity in the Poetry of Danielle Collobert, Maggie O'Sullivan and Raúl Zurita*, Ph.D. thesis, (London: Royal Holloway, University of London, 2012) pp.50–91.

2. See *The Salt Companion to Maggie O'Sullivan*.
3. A number of these were collated and reprinted in *Body of Work* (Hastings: Reality Street, 2006).
4. Bloomfield 'O'Sullivan's Material Poetics', p.29.
5. O'Sullivan includes almost diagrammatical collages of musical notation and texts in various languages cut so as to transform these semantic practices into visual forms in *From the Handbook of That & Furriery* and also includes an image of her mother in *Un-assuming Persona*. However, this is part of a dedication and therefore does not intervene into the text. See O'Sullivan, *Body of Work*, pp.133–186.
6. O'Sullivan, *Body of Work*, p.100.
7. O'Sullivan, *Body of Work*, p.72.
8. For more on O'Sullivan's neologisms see Peter Middleton, '"Ear loads": Neologisms and Sound Poetry in Maggie O'Sullivan's *Palace of Reptiles*' in *The Salt Companion to Maggie O'Sullivan*, pp.97–122.
9. O'Sullivan, *Body of Work*, pp.98–103.
10. O'Sullivan, *Body of Work*, p.101.
11. Kruk, p.69.
12. Manson, p.77.
13. O'Sullivan, *Body of Work*, p.99.
14. O'Sullivan, *Body of Work*, p.103.
15. O'Sullivan, *Body of Work*, p.102.
16. O'Sullivan's interest in feminism is made clear in a number of publications during the 1980s and '90s, not least the editing of the anthology of women's writing *Out of Everywhere* (London: Reality Street Press, 1995). Marsh ties this directly to an interest in the visual aspects of writing and interdisciplinary practice in 'Agonal States'.
17. Kruk, p.70.
18. Gunter Thomas 'Witness as a Cultural Form of Communication: Historical Roots, Structural Dynamics, and Current Appearances' in *Media Witnessing* ed. by Paul Frosh and Amit Pinchevski (London: Palgrave Macmillan, 2009), pp.89–111.
19. Bloomfield draws on Dominick LaCapra's suggestion that trauma 'does not disappear; it returns in a transformed, at times disfigured and disguised manner'. See 'Maggie O'Sullivan's excavations of Irish History', p.27.
20. Scott Thurston, 'Interview with Maggie O'Sullivan', in *The Salt Companion to Maggie O'Sullivan*, p.244.
21. O'Sullivan, 'Query', email correspondence with author, 3/4/2015.
22. See *POINT.BLANK.RANGE* in 'Interface' *Reality Studios* 6, 1984: pp.58–67.
23. O'Sullivan, 'Query'.
24. O'Sullivan 'Query'.
25. O'Sullivan, *POINT.BLANK.RANGE* in 'Interface', p.67.
26. Bloomfield 'O'Sullivan's excavations of Irish history', p12.
27. Redell Olsen, 'Writing / Conversation with Maggie O'Sullivan' in *The Salt Companion to Maggie O'Sullivan*, p.207.
28. O'Sullivan and Charles Bernstein, '"Writing is a body-intensive activity" Close Listening with Maggie O'Sullivan', in *Jacket 2*, http://jacket2.org/interviews/writing-body-intensive-activity, accessed 16/04/2015.

Maurice Scully

Key Dance
[sheet music]

listen
ing to a
tick
&

the that the
that termite
in its tunnel
electrical

fizzle be
tween comm
unicating
pairs

skip prior check

then

Irish University Review 46.1 (2016): 183–188
DOI: 10.3366/iur.2016.0210
© Edinburgh University Press
www.euppublishing.com/journal/iur

hop

   stick

      do

ceiling sky
glass vent splashed
air framed by
keys that

lock to bare
laws things turn
not into what
you did/

cut/vast ratchets
to instil in wait/

      do

      but

do what you
could not help
but do (speckled
& looped &

pointed parts
pushed through)
to play

prior (tig skip & then
then a/then a/)
to the piece
you can

play

when truths
not a usefully apt
notion
skim quick blue oceans
in a pre-built sieve

to get to/get used to/get by it
set by get it
be- buy it lest it
let
lost
live

loose no lets see
unlock it
& across
then down
(amen)
I mean
grey chalky surfaces
of the inside of
the conduit

dash see what
or do I dash
what you mean
& could not

help but do
comes through yr
means (two) not
the same cramped

keep to lock
small bright
glass skies that
slide/check/all

the way/past/
framed by
keys that stick
to blank

ways things turn
not in to what
you did/cut
do but what

you could not
help but do –
looped & scooped
& scarred & parts

pushed through –
to play prior
(tig skip & then
dash-back)

to the piece
you can play
or

or one sharp arc
yr choice take
it or pick or
take it

or carp or
a dog by
a car park
where all's

mapped
marked out
sparks or
one bird

busy at the top
of a blossoming
appletree

or that thin
bar circling
on its tiny pivot
on yr wrist

been there been
there done done
that

Trevor Joyce

Stone Master
For Owen

1

The markets, in the early light, are crowded
with inedible loud blooms going for a song.

Of confectioners, where sweet destructives
are luminously spun, you will find no lack
in the king's shadow. Patrons throng and haggle.

It is one thing to see, but quite another
to discern the wholeness of what's seen;
the fountain's clogged, the sun obscured,
the silver tarnished, and the parched
seed chokes amongst the rubbish
of these blinding thoroughfares.

By the wall of the inner palace,
faint memory, all conserved and candied out,
serves for a welcome pick-me-up.

2

The trapping and onward selling of faces
was once a flourishing trade. No more, alas,
and complete sets now rarely reach the market.

Large families were more challenging
and therefore more precious than smaller ones;
the vendor's temptation was, therefore,
artificially to extend, augmenting
thereby the associations, and his yield also.

Irish University Review 46.1 (2016): 189–193
DOI: 10.3366/iur.2016.0211
© Edinburgh University Press
www.euppublishing.com/journal/iur

So we arrive into a confused legacy:
bitterness laced with coma; nests
of bright amnesia fledge unfathomable grief.

Nowadays we accept this cut and shut of faces
as displaying the varied masteries of knowledge;
the true fancier never must shun strange.

3

The dwellings being constructed mostly in wood,
fires are frequent, sometimes of such ferocity
as to threaten the entire fabric of the city.

If such conflagration be not quickly reduced,
the high officers are bound to attend and force the hunt.
Their Carfax of Light and Winds has sightways all sides,
and stands on permanent watch lest fire break free.

Be alert always among such sundries
so no treasure escape; by exercise of due discretion
and an educated eye, even the most unpromising
filth may yet resolve to fine collectibles.

Should one abscond, the sentry beats an immense drum,
and shouts at the top of his voice, *Fire there is!*
Fire there is! to set nets and lift citizens from dreams.

4

By day, flags are unfurled out
to indicate the colour, arrangement
and direction of the fire, whereas at night
minor incendiaries serve as indices
or symbols of the great.

The first imperative is to make smooth,
and to keep closed all surfaces;
any slight crevice may conceal
the starting up of a violent outbreak;
slightest error give the game away.

A serious conflagration in this capital is rendered
more terrific than in other human cities
by the loose singing and speaking
of the multitudinous throats in the streets.

5

I discovered in many family groups
individual faces which did not resemble
their siblings. Subtle discrepancies,
to be sure, but determinative.

I start a tale, you finish it;
you switch into a funny story,
and I duly laugh; so are we near familiars.
It is the unmotivated howling through the hours
of darkness unsettles both of us.

Check the relevant licences, and sometimes
the signature differs from that of the majority.
Distrust is duty, and always this decision:
a genuine clerical error, or does it suggest worse?

Kith binds to kin. Klaxons hold in close reserve.

6

These gullets, notwithstanding the culling
of thousands by late majesty, now gawp
and gape as before, and scavenge abroad,
guzzling offal from the victuallers, and the brains,
pluck and sweetbreads of the accidental dead.

None own them, but all protect them.
They are never admitted into houses,
miscellaneous as they are, and against them
the groves are tight; but the streets
are surrendered to them as a kind of rightful domain,
while some consider it a sort of duty
to furnish housings for their stray
utterances, with comfort of vocables,
paper, script and pabulum.

7

They are of a peculiar race, somewhat like
the inside neck of a sheep,
and are said to be susceptible
of a deep quinsy, though not of outright
and conspicuous madness.
They maintain also among themselves
a hierarchy of minute distinctions;
so should any vagrant stray
from his familiar turf, he is at once
snacked upon by maws, jaws, and pitiless
incisors; those whose place is sacrosanct.

It is commonly remarked, that they know
an alien by his swank, and cannot help
but utter when they see a hat.

8

One story told of the master may be apocryphal.
A dutiful investigator was received one day
by one of his children, who abruptly answered
"Oh Daddy's upstairs constructing families".

Sounds of unsuccessful machinery drowned out
the remainder, and it felt like being in a church.

Wholesome, despite occasional wheezes
and stretching noises, like the effort
of a good yeast proving. Later, it was found
that the face of prophecy had been abstracted
and substituted with the appearance of an actuary
which had eyes painted on it to mimic vision.

Though a very crude fake, it had evidently
deceived many experts for many years.

9

Until recently, the streets were all unnamed,
houses sans cypher. Districts alone
were designated, generally by some prominent landmark
in each: this chic boutique, that wen,
yon bloody shambles. Much stayed indiscriminate.

Orders now have issued to remedy this inconvenience;
which facilitates establishment of barracks
in those divers suburbs which were often disturbed
by alien populations, that refuse.

Numbered, chaos wanes. By night now,
in the heart, the ways are still. Every
human voice quiesced by evening; were it not
for the laughing of throats, and the footfall
of the patrol, speaking silence would reign absolute.

10
There were suggestions over the years
that the Stone Gallery was so treacherous
that it should be destroyed. Impossible!

The Gallery is now so vast, so held in awe,
that it can be neither countered nor ignored.
Inhabiting its cabinets and vaults, many there
are made acute example of.

One can but examine it with right exactitude, noting
fault and slippage, hurting here, domesticating there.

A clutch of weazands sighs by the wall, faces
still attached; they will be taken away
and conspicuously destroyed.

Were they suffered to survive
who knows how they might sing.

Fergal Gaynor

The Octagon

The Octagon

*When the wind is southerly, I know
a hawk from a hand saw.* Hamlet

Irish University Review 46.1 (2016): 194–204
DOI: 10.3366/iur.2016.0212
© Edinburgh University Press
www.euppublishing.com/journal/iur

I

On the hillside
the house is empty –
where is the shepherd?

In the fold
the flock shifts –
where is the one
who brings calm to the sheep?

In the wilderness
in the place of wild beasts
he searches the ravines.

Gripping his staff
he stares in the fissures –
night is not far off.

In the hillside house
the fire is unlit,
the sheep unwatched –
where is the shepherd?

II

Our bastards anointed

on such bodies possessed
never laid hands

thought's bright foot
stubbed on the horizon

from shaping tongue
inarguable forms

the womb mistaken
for a multitude of infants

made of light

Matchless Lucifers

by divine numbers' stream
strike quick silver

plumb jobs in the underworld
the angels underpaid

reach of bronze Mars
into compound and wedding crystal

further change of state
to license the Lawgiver

for a limited future

Frantic bondsmen

bind quick nets
for careering bees

Beelzebub dust
in the songster's gullet

dung-rollers pile
unsoil the olive

ungovernable rise
ephemera to be fed on

like children

Jet you higher airs!

Stream over tonguing winds!
Re-stitch the cloven peoples!

Purge low circulations!
Draw up all purer drops!

Un-herald the striking flash!
Stir opiate clouds!

Cut stars from their ether!
Douse earth with fiery seeds

without germ

Start

intimate
shoots

reconstitute
the borders

bloom
uncontained

mature
the fantastic

nursery

Doctor

the patient
accounts

disprove
pastorals

plot
loyalty

incorporate
the fabulous

decline

For the fat decade

has splayed the lord
that cries and culls

for the bank-holing martins
have tracked the ore

for the unknown voice
has benighted the pawns

for the stranded eel
has slipped through the grass

into sand

And clubbing jacks

have heaped black drift
against the heart's door

and hide has been sought
by the ruler of game

and the enveloped outed
to lights of exposure

and the cosmos reflected
in a bubble's iridescence

swelling swelling

III

Light dims,
Aldebaran, alone,
starts up the slope.
Night will fall with violence.
Now eyes widen
seeing less –
and the ear opens,
listening
for a footstep,
for a hand on the latch.

Irish University Review 46.1 (2016): 205–209
DOI: 10.3366/iur.2016.0213
© Edinburgh University Press
www.euppublishing.com/journal/iur

Sarah Hayden

this   load-bearing wall
this   floor, that shines
this   elliptical paraboloid concrete shell
this is where i live

when i draw it: four windows, one chimney and a door

the drawing is a lie
it is an occasion of forgetfulness

the door is red
it is an accident
        it is not my house.

this is where i live

                        this   is my house.
                this   is where i live
                            the floor shines
the walls—unclad, unmullioned and dreaming of spandrels—
                            are curtains.

Pale green. The palest.
7000 twisted, tufting strands.
Velveteen savannah over which bare soles,
in all seasons,
happily can pass___
pressingly.

Hands sweep its richness and
[barring heat and the presentiment of a crackle]
turn up none the richer.
No   sough,
no sur/plus,
is imparted.
'Everything was orderly and prearranged'.
At every edge, a quiet closing, its ends
definitive.
Its surface is entirely flat.
    or look, look closer___
<peeks>   peaks and troughs. wonderment.

One grey line, all about it. This grey: Near green. Grey as a stone [amidden] its kin. As the sky over it.
Grey as the architect's seagreen sagegreen eyes. As the silvered underscreen. [notwithstanding the
marine citation, no thing ripples]

And four grey rectangles, diagonally set, a/cross the xy.
Within their boundless bounds, the strands might be shorter___
Or perhaps it only looks that way___There are tricks of the lights [sometimes set ajangle].
Tricks of the forms and their proportions. Tricks of the colourplay.
But no flourishes.
Shaking its sleeves clean out, it discloses not a thing.
Between unimage and ground, unfigure and forms,
via the discoursing of 16 shimmering vertices a gentle oscillation is established.
                                        'Rhythm can be obtained'
                                            for everyday use.

Once, people danced. Faintly damp, strap-printed feet and other, still shod toes pressed upon it.
The maths was off___but the mood was high. Notwithstanding provisions made, some
mouthwarm flakes
drifted down. Barely bigger than
their more organic analogues, they fell
meltingly troughward.

<vibration>

Another, other
enervated the multitude. This was not
immediately perceived but felt____   only
as a layer of animation. en extra. A premonition past
of the world becoming live-er,
in fest of life.   Webby stuff silently engaged its crampons.   Everyone remained vertical
At least until such a time as further   submission to gravity was sought.
Beneath and on all sides, a   tree made tesselate.

<average footfall>

And once: a dog: joyed to find a such in which to snuffle: to feel it insinuate itself—fleetingly even—
between digital pads. Skating across the hardsoftwood perimeter unmindful, unminded____
then,
finding this grassless green underpaw, nosing forward____
bringing itself low to give the tickle to a soft stomach,
pulling along langorouslike, but too fast. A bath hopped into though
not yet enough cooled. Then head again to the ground as paws [clean] mime the upscuffing of an
underwards that is not there. Or not for dark dense metres yet. [and that, even, long quieted].
Nap set all awry, a bare   pinch   of pointy hairs shook free. a sigh. Some crawling crouching,
bending and picking, some sweeping and
smoothing but No
Harm Done.

The cat too, of course. Here until the second boy. Then never again. After 8 years, 8 years or 9.

Otherwise, it is not of the occasion. Nothing here is.

Breath comes harsh
varistranded.
It sounds of a reaching towards
and of a falling away.
Limbs approach the machinic
—a pongean model thereof.

<They do because they can because they do they do>

Melt away___
No___
evanesce, to float above

a hanging gas, a feline dream. I
see the whole

shape [form] below me.

Time asserts itself intramuscularly. Daily submission:

A grudged deliverance.

Billy Mills

The City Itself

words for this space
a space to frame them
concord of sorts

a book to hold them
here it is
& it is so

Irish University Review 46.1 (2016): 210–212
DOI: 10.3366/iur.2016.0214
© Edinburgh University Press
www.euppublishing.com/journal/iur

after such wandering
to come to this: urban landscapes
made possible the sign says
seen from the road in a field
not a field yard rather the road goes
to the city itself held in mind

as once it was imperfect & lovely
as it still is & will be
in instants enduring what is
& is not different in time
only always & never
now garden a quiet corner

echoes of selves distant gods
of lesser wars distrain these streets
walked daily in search of nothing
other the next place a shadow
familiar corner the need
to seem occupied as the city

evolved in undistinguished strategies
a non-binary series unfolding
whose shades are various
& few a river bisects it
moves uncertainly forward
& opens no further steps required

no single purpose served is
unresolved immerse yourself
climb the streets and see an underlay
which is shared which is money
& time & what we do between them
& it has been itself so long now

an imperturbable process of moving
to leave here now the city itself
again its tidal pull gathers
all that has happened   that flows
under time & that which is not
buried a river streets buildings

unknowing agents of change
night is not & day is not
clustered against hostility
of memory & change listen:
it is never still silent
at rest never content

in water
slowly
morning

tiny
& endless
rises

bird
glides
the sun

reflects
nothing
air

lifts us
follow
wing

what it is
to be
what is

there is
this thing
that moves

& turns
& dips
again

& is
evening
even

turn
& go
again

Catherine Walsh

barbaric additions

from *Barbaric Tales*

Irish University Review 46.1 (2016): 213–218
DOI: 10.3366/iur.2016.0215
© Edinburgh University Press
www.euppublishing.com/journal/iur

barbaric additions

how   not

 turn your head

  look right

  (way up)

    left (back)

time it

these actual doldrums

 approaching

sky   held in

your hand

this sit   is it actual

attended   width of

no chance Permian permeate

this it what stark

domain chutes infinities

as easily concepts of

mathematical finitude

pervade former sets

nonchalences of

permeability   glyphs

sliding layers multi

tasking in cellular

dihesion coherent

testimonials to

doubt we are here

entering experience as

having a finite understanding

of finitude regardless of

any exact change where
cohesive divergent entities
appear structureless
void   blinkered by   light

a rationality exudes
malefluences efflorescence
commands nicities of
attention demanding prime
time slots in our over
institutionalised
scaffoldings our primitive
egos warped scales
all that fall oh wise
a coming up episodes
of fire outside the act or
main stage performancing
serialised festivities as
scapes not scarps why
make this posit outcome when
all cracks are entities
fields of information

exchange irresolute containers

of non defined change

faulting a plasticity

superficies of

what is condoned

less any stark how

not turn your head

look a rationality exudes

another set of nonchalences

sloppy joiners careering

domains foreclosing

discourse collective

amputation

ether where

mind heart part

grieving attached

to a future already

relegated toeing

lines past

ineptness

since conditioning

matters structure

when even if

subjunctively

discharging anomalies

sound real which

actual play skids

along interrogating

its own fear unreleased

caches crack snapping light

since when even if

a rationality exudes

malefluence on the

extreme outer surface

of any superficies

attends a fungal

latching a chain gang

backed up in the

pressurised survive

grow mutate relate

replicate parasitic

mash of thrive

rugged you go rugged

you come rugged you

stay rugged you

remain rugged

hemmed individuals

courting spark

where tough get

going past

issues of bankable

power when any rationality

exudes complacence

I'm scared

List of Books Reviewed

Christopher Murray, *The Theatre of Brian Friel: Tradition and Modernity* (Scott Boltwood)

Richard Rankin Russell, *Modernity, Community, and Place in Brian Friel's Drama* (Scott Boltwood)

Paul Delaney, *Seán O'Faoláin: Literature, Inheritance and the 1930s* (Brad Kent)

Robert Tobin, *The Minority Voice: Hubert Butler and Southern Irish Protestantism, 1900–1991* (Benjamin Keatinge)

Aidan O'Malley and Eve Patten (editors), *Ireland, West to East* (Benjamin Keatinge)

Stephanie Schwerter, *Northern Irish Poetry and the Russian Turn: Intertextuality in the Work of Seamus Heaney, Tom Paulin and Medbh McGuckian* (Michael McAteer)

Irish University Review 46.1 (2016): 219
DOI: 10.3366/iur.2016.0216
© Edinburgh University Press
www.euppublishing.com/journal/iur

Book Reviews

Christopher Murray, *The Theatre of Brian Friel: Tradition and Modernity*.
London: Bloomsbury, 2014. 299 pages. £18.99 GBP.

Richard Rankin Russell, *Modernity, Community, and Place in Brian
Friel's Drama*. Syracuse: Syracuse University Press, 2014. 317 pages.
$39.95 USD.

Brian Friel is the living Irish author whose work consistently elicits the
most scholarship in Irish Studies, not just in Ireland, but throughout
the Continent and North America as well. In the forty years since
D.E.S. Maxwell's *Brian Friel* (1973), two dozen books and essay
collections and well over one hundred articles and chapters have
analyzed the playwright's use of language, music, memory, politics,
and place, along with many other topics. During the current decade,
the flow of book-length studies of Friel's work has, if anything,
increased, with notable titles by such scholars as Anthony Roche and
Geraldine Higgins beginning the decade. 2014 saw the publication of
books by two of the field's most recognizable, though quite different,
literary scholars, Christopher Murray and Richard Rankin Russell.

After decades of recognition as one of Ireland's most established
theatre scholars, Christopher Murray has supplemented his
indispensible, earlier work with Brian Friel on *Essays, Diaries, and
Interviews: 1964–1999* with *The Theatre of Brian Friel: Tradition and
Modernity*. Conversely, the American scholar Richard Rankin Russell
has departed from his usual focus on contemporary Irish poetry and
fiction to produce his first study of a playwright with *Modernity,
Community, and Place in Brian Friel's Drama*. As even the cursory glance
at these two titles reveals, the concept of 'Modernity' is essential to
both approaches; however, any similarity ends there, for the works are
distinctly different.

For Murray, Friel's modernity has diverse conceptual points of
contact with the early twentieth-century literary movement associated
with 'Chekhov and other experimenters such as Pirandello, O'Neill
and Tennessee Williams'. Indeed, throughout the book, Murray is
attentive to Friel's engagement with such foundational Modernists as
Eliot, Beckett, Brecht, Ibsen, and Yeats. In contrast to Murray's reliance

Irish University Review 46.1 (2016): 220–238
© Edinburgh University Press
www.euppublishing.com/journal/iur

on shared, albeit amorphous, assumptions regarding the nature of Modernism, Russell uses the term with several specific references in mind. Indeed, the distinction between the two works is nowhere more succinctly conveyed than in the manner that each author treats 'modernity' in his book's index: while Murray provides no page references to important occurrences of 'Modernism' or 'Modernity' in his book, Russell lists two dozen, divided into nine subtopics within 'modernity', including 'defined': 'that philosophical program that had developed a dogmatic emphasis on rationality thanks to Descartes ..., and which dominated philosophy, science, and other areas of knowledge until at least the mid-twentieth century by pushing for a generalized account of everything through abstract intellectualizing that often jettisoned particularity and local culture'. Likewise, in stark contrast to Murray's use of the founders of literary Modernism as the important context for Friel's plays, such figures as Yeats, Eliot, Brecht, O'Neill, and Ibsen are virtually absent from Russell's book. In short, despite any nominal similarity, these authors establish distinctly different strategies for discussing Friel and Modernity.

Finally, if their articulations of modernity establish no overlap, so too the plans for the two books resist simple comparison. Murray's design is to consider sixteen plays in less than two-hundred pages in thematically organized chapters that usually treat two or three plays. Thus, Murray produces a nearly comprehensive survey of Friel's career from *Philadelphia, Here I Come!* (1964) through *The Home Place* (2003), with the only major plays to escape treatment being *The Enemy Within* (1962), *Lovers* (1967), *The Mundy Scheme* (1969), *The Gentle Island* (1971), and *The Communication Cord* (1982). By contrast, Russell's book focuses on a mere five in two-hundred-fifty pages: *Philadelphia, Here I Come!* (1964), *The Freedom of the City* (1973), *Faith Healer* (1979), *Translations* (1980), and *Dancing at Lughnasa* (1990). Indeed, the book is so focused on this handful of plays that even the drama widely considered important to appreciating Friel's achievement – such as *The Loves of Cass McGuire* (1966), *Volunteers* (1975), and *Aristocrats* (1979) – are barely mentioned. Thus, we have two fundamentally different books in approach and scope which need to be considered separately.

Overall, Murray has written a valuable addition to Friel criticism, and its greatest value is in the numerous and diverse instances in which he contextualizes the plays not within past Friel criticism, but within each play's production history and historical context. For example, in grappling with *Give Me Your Answer, Do!*, Murray's discussion of Friel's advice to the actors of the New York premier guides the book to a nuanced reading of the play's ambiguous ending. Likewise, his discussion of the evolution of the play's reception allows his readers to understand why this important play has not received the recognition it deserves. Similarly, when discussing *Faith Healer*, Murray's book is at his best when he provides details of the New York premiere and the subsequent Abbey rehabilitation; this material reminds the reader that sometimes our very understanding of a play's meaning and significance is bound up with its staging and casting history. Often combined with acute scenographic analysis, Murray brings such production-specific insights to his readings of such plays as *The Loves of Cass McGuire* (1966), *Freedom of the City* (1973), *Living Quarters* (1976), *Wonderful Tennessee* (1992), and *Molly Sweeney* (1994).

Moreover, Murray follows Anthony Roche's earlier *Brian Friel: Theatre and Politics* (2011) by exploiting the wealth of material available to the researcher in the Friel Papers, the massive archive housed in the National Library of Ireland. Murray's ability to discover and meaningfully interpret elements of Friel's working documents adds considerably to our understanding of such plays as *Volunteers* (1975), *Translations* (1980), and *Give Me Your Answer, Do!* (1999). Murray is a scholar who started working with Friel's archive well before the playwright donated it to the Irish state, and his intimate familiarity with it are clearly evident in his apt exploitation of it. Finally, Murray is able to skillfully and intelligently contextualize the plays, whether that be by comparing *Philadelphia, Here I Come!* or *Wonderful Tennessee* with other lesser known Irish plays, or by situating such plays *Dancing at Lughnasa* or *Volunteers* in their specific moment in Irish cultural history. In short, Murray often produces arguments displaying great knowledge of Friel's artistic development and Ireland's cultural milieu.

All this deserved praise is not to say that Murray's book is perfect; too often he rushes through his ideas and incompletely articulates the relationship of his work to past Friel criticism. For example, in his discussion of *Philadelphia, Here I Come!*, Murray claims that the play's main character 'Gar is an ironized version of Hamlet'. Although he also equates Katie Doogan to Ophelia and Gar's comrades to Rosencrantz and Guildenstern, all this is done without convincing explanation or analysis, and such free-floating assumptions are too frequently provided without argument. Similarly, by attempting to discuss so many plays in less than two-hundred pages, Murray forces himself to rush through the critical context of each play, and he routinely focuses only on material from monographs and bound essay collections, almost entirely ignoring even influential journal articles. Thus, too often he omits important criticism that should have guided his arguments. For example, it has been thirty years since Ruth Niel first discussed the reliance of Friel's *Volunteers* on *Hamlet*, and the nature of this relationship has since been developed in articles and chapters by half a dozen scholars, but by ignoring this past work, Murray repeats too many past assumptions and adds little new to this topic. Likewise, in his discussion of the relationship of Friel's *Translations* to Shakespeare's *Henry IV*, Murray fails to use Anthony Roche's lengthy discussion of *Translations* and the Henriad in his 1994 *Contemporary Irish Drama* as his starting point. While Murray adds an additional example to supplement Roche's many details, Murray's observation can best be appreciated within the broader context of Roche's sustained analysis. In short, the demands of both summarizing the criticism and offering his own interpretations in the short space allotted each play undermines his ability to achieve either goal very well.

This brings me to the idiosyncratic nature of Murray's project: *The Theatre of Brian Friel* is part of the Bloomsbury series of Critical Companions, which obliges the author to include three or four articles in the volume. This requirement to reserve fifty pages of the book to reprint past articles is certainly the reason that Murray's own arguments are frequently rushed. Such articles are intended to cover representative topics, as can be found in the volumes on Harold Pinter and Sean O'Casey, where a playwright's broad relationship to women, class, or memory are the subject of essays. By this standard, two of the essays chosen by Murray to represent Friel criticism are valuable. Shaun Richards's essay, 'Placed Identities for Placeless Times: Brian Friel and Postcolonial Criticism', remains one of the most important, wide reaching, and influential journal articles to have been written on the relationship of the playwright to postcolonial criticism. Similarly, Csilla Bertha's 'Memory, Art, *Lieux de Mémoire* in Brian Friel's *The Home Place*' is a rather wide-ranging and useful introduction of the importance of memory in several plays, not just the one mentioned in the title. Ultimately, both are articles by established figures in Friel criticism and among their best work.

Conversely, Murray's choice of David Krause's 'The Failed Words of Brian Friel' is quite odd. In it, Krause offers a caustic reading of *Molly Sweeney*, *Wonderful Tennessee*, and *Dancing at Lughnasa*, claiming that characters are 'stillborn', scenes 'embarrassing', and character dynamics 'ineptly' presented. In the twenty years since its publication, Krause's work has had no perceptible impact on subsequent scholarship; indeed, it may be notable for how many critics ignore or dismiss this article by a critic never known for his work on Friel. If Murray's intention had been to provide an essay that represents the vital importance of language theory to Friel's oeuvre, there are many excellent examples, not the least of which would be Richard Kearney's 'Language Play: Brian Friel and Ireland's Verbal Theatre' of 1982;

Kearney's work changed the direction of Friel criticism by introducing a brand of language theory that continues to influence the field.

Richard Rankin Russell has set a distinctly different challenge for himself in *Modernity, Community, and Place in Brian Friel's Drama*: he must justify devoting an entire book to only five of Friel's plays: *Philadelphia, Here I Come!* (1964), *Freedom of the City* (1973), *Faith Healer* (1979), *Translations* (1980), and *Dancing at Lughnasa* (1990). Clearly, the plays chosen by Russell constitute almost the core of Friel's canon and perhaps each could be used to argue that Friel had indeed fulfilled his youthful ambition 'to write the great Irish play'; nonetheless, this selection omits such canonical plays as *Aristocrats* (1979) and *Molly Sweeney* (1994), not to mention such important plays as *The Loves of Cass McGuire* (1966) and *Volunteers* (1975), and plays somewhere between the important and the canonical, like *Give Me Your Answer, Do!* (1997) and *The Home Place* (2005). While it has not been unusual for monographs published after 1999 to treat a handful of plays as secondary, or even tertiary, to Friel's career, many readers may find it unfortunate that Russell offers a sustained analysis of only one play from the second half of Friel's career, despite the importance of other plays to his work's thesis.

However, Russell does not intend to write a conventional monograph on Friel, in which a study seeks to mark the artistic trajectory of the writer in relation to a specific theme over the course of his career. Rather, a more accurate way of describing Russell's project would be that he uses Friel's plays as a way to illustrate a slightly different critical goal, which, I believe, would be to '[study] place and space within Irish writing and culture by exploring the impact of modernity on communities', using Brian Friel's plays to illustrate his points. This is best seen in Russell's chapters on *Philadelphia, Here I Come!* and *Translations*. In both plays, Russell convincingly argues that the audience sees Ireland caught between two cultural modes. In *Philadelphia*, we see Ireland on a technological cusp characterized by American film and the accelerating speed of travel worldwide, which is, in Russell's interpretation, a mediascape that Gar has already mastered, even though the Ballybeg community around him lags behind both technologically and conceptually. Likewise, in the book's dissection of *Translations*, Russell explores the multifaceted points of contact between the Irish rundale community of early nineteenth-century Ballybeg and its English empiricist, industrial counterpart. By adopting this interpretive framework, Russell is able to turn to some of the touchstone scenes of the play and tease out new interpretive shadings and perspectives. Moreover, his long-chapter analysis for each play allows him to tease out the details and nuances of his interpretations, which often yield complex and rewarding arguments.

One of the strengths of Russell's book comes from his broad knowledge: he frequently scaffolds his readings of Friel and Irish culture on a surprisingly diverse and apt assemblage of cultural theorists, ranging from Walter Benjamin to Una Chaudhuri, from Benedict Anderson to Gaston Bachelard, and from Jacques Derrida to Wendell Barry. Indeed, it is one of the rewards of the book to see how such a disparate group of critics can be used to pry open Friel's plays. However, this is not to imply that Russell's book is weak in its relation to Irish criticism, quite the opposite. As one would expect, Russell displays his intimate familiarity with the broad theoretical discussions of such major staples of Irish Studies as Joe Cleary, Elizabeth Butler Cullingford, Seamus Deane, and Richard Kearney.

Thus, Russell presents slow readings of a select group of Friel plays where he tries to run to the ground every major facet of his triple focus on modernity, place, and community. Sometimes this patience produces a rewarding chapter, as in his forty pages on *Faith Healer*, where he explores Ballybeg's geopathology and the multiple aspects of ritual woven throughout Friel's drama. However, sometimes the freedom of writing long chapters on a single play tempt Russell down one or two dead ends that leave the reader wishing that the book project had forced concision on the author. This is apparent nowhere more than in the fifty pages on *Translations*, where the chapter gets off to a slow, muddled start which includes a curious complaint against the play's inclusion in the most recent *Norton Anthology of English Literature* in its 'Nation and Language' section. However, for this reader, such moments of lost focus were surprisingly rare, while the book offered much to interrogate, much to dwell upon, and much to benefit from.

Overall, though both Murray and Russell set out to explore Modernity in Friel's plays, their fundamentally different books manifest just how diverse Friel Studies remains. Rather than having settled into a repetitive focus on the themes articulated by the early scholarship, Murray and Russell, along with the leading critics writing on Friel today, have broken away from the monotonous reliance on love, memory, religion, and language that defined much of the early criticism. In their distinct ways, each book offers substantive and ground-breaking forays into Friel's extensive career.

SCOTT BOLTWOOD
Emory and Henry College
DOI: 10.3366/iur.2016.0217

Paul Delaney, *Seán O'Faoláin: Literature, Inheritance and the 1930s.*
Dublin: Irish Academic Press, 2014. xi + 280 pages. €24.95 EUR.

Seán O'Faoláin is one of those writers who is rarely read and yet
everyone seems to have an opinion of him. He has been variously
charged with being a proto-revisionist, a liberal nationalist, a snob, and
a frustrated republican. The problem is that all of these labels can be
shown to be equally right and off the mark. While O'Faoláin's
polemical work – for which he is now best known – is in the main
unequivocal, there are significant moments in which he straddles
fences. At times he claims that situations are considerably more
complex than they might appear and he often revisits his past
arguments in later writings, sometimes revising his views to account
for new contexts, for his own changed perspectives, and for different
audiences. If there is an overarching argument to be found in Paul
Delaney's wonderful new study, it is this: O'Faoláin is more equivocal
than he is often depicted to be.

The power and joy of Delaney's book are elicited through his
rigorous and sensitive readings of O'Faoláin's work and his patient
contextualization. One of the appealing features is the brisk biography
of O'Faoláin's early years in which Delaney challenges a number of
accounts. For one, O'Faoláin claimed – and many critics have since
echoed – that the 1916 Easter Rising converted him wholesale from
being loyal to Empire to becoming an IRA volunteer, but Delaney
makes the case that this conversion would have been a more gradual
process. As well, Delaney traces the rise of the budding polemicist
who was finding his voice in the 1920s, first as a propagandist with
Sinn Féin and later as a contributor to the *Irish Statesman*, the periodical
whose liberal ethos came to inform much of O'Faoláin's later thinking.
In many ways this earlier period was O'Faoláin's apprenticeship.

Delaney's focus on one decade – the 1930s – is entirely justified.
This was the time in which O'Faoláin came into his own as a writer,
carving out a national and international reputation. His production in
these years is impressive: four biographies, an edited autobiography,
two novels, two short story collections, a play, and a ream of essays.
While there has been an upswing of scholarly interest in O'Faoláin's
work, much of this has been on his essays published in *The Bell* in the
1940s and 1950s, meaning that there has been a terrible neglect of the
earlier publications. Similarly, there has also been more sustained
attention to Ireland in the 1940s, but relatively little on the prior
decade, which is often dismissed as an uninteresting time marked by
conservative politics and having a stagnant culture defined by
censorship and radical disillusionment. As Delaney argues, there is a
great deal in O'Faoláin's work in this period to suggest that a liberal

Catholic intelligentsia was actively engaged. If there is a shortcoming in Delaney's approach, it is in the marginalization of even broader concerns, such as the rise of totalitarianism on the continent – which is central to understanding O'Faoláin's polemical positioning in this period – and of O'Faoláin's ties with networks of writers who were more to the left of the political spectrum than he was.

Following the template of some of the earliest studies of O'Faoláin's work, Delaney's book has a bi-partite structure, with a section on the biographies followed by a second on the fiction. The effect of this could be interpreted as granting primacy to the biographies at the expense of the creative writing. But this is not the case. Delaney instead demonstrates that while the biographies might be regarded as polemical interventions, the fiction is less programmatic and far more nuanced than is allowed by a number of critics.

Biographies have long been one of the more popular genres in the publishing trade. In post-independence Ireland, however, their popularity was regarded as intertwined with a need for the people to make sense of their recent revolutionary past. In this context, biographies and autobiographies have been understood as a concomitant writing of the individual and a writing of the nation and indeed O'Faolain's biographies very much shadow his relationship to Ireland. The first of these, *The Life Story of Eamon De Valera* (1933), was largely a puff piece, written as Fianna Fáil came to power after the 1932 election. It was something that O'Faoláin regretted almost immediately afterwards; indeed, he appears to atone for it in his later, more critical biography, *De Valera* (1939). While the two books offer similar descriptions, the latter is rather muted in tone: de Valera appears as more heroic in the first, but is decidedly more calculating and complicated in the second. The new biography also allowed O'Faoláin to speak on the recently passed 1937 Constitution: while he applauded its stabilizing effects, he criticized its conservative ethos and treatment of women. The latter is particularly interesting given O'Faoláin's misogynistic biography of Constance Markievicz that appeared in 1934.

While the subjects of these biographies were contemporary, the more distantly historical *King of the Beggars: A Life of Daniel O'Connell* (1938) is arguably O'Faoláin's most direct intervention in current politics. Delaney opens his discussion of this biography by tracing the well-known debates between O'Faoláin and Daniel Corkery. Corkery's influential *The Hidden Ireland* (1924) was ostensibly a study of eighteenth-century Irish poetry, but it was also a recuperation and positive revaluation of native literature that rejected colonial denigration and pointed towards a culture on which the newly independent state could be based. In some ways, *Synge and*

Anglo-Irish Literature (1931) was Corkery's further repudiation of anything that smelled of English culture. O'Faoláin was immediately critical of these works, writing a scathing review of the latter in T.S. Eliot's *The Criterion*. In his essay on Corkery, published in Seamus O'Sullivan's *The Dublin Magazine* in 1936, O'Faoláin unleashed one of his most polemical criticisms, suggesting that much of what Corkery stood for and proposed was already well under way in Nazi Germany. O'Faoláin's concern with Corkery's views might seem rather late in coming, especially as the essay was published five years after Corkery's book. But O'Faoláin worried that Corkery's ideas were now actualized in the Irish education system and were being promoted by politicians, and so they held far too much sway for his tastes.

King of the Beggars is a continued and more sustained response to Corkery, opening with a proem that criticizes the romanticist claims in *The Hidden Ireland*. O'Faoláin saw the collapse of the Gaelic order as not a simple result of colonial forces, but as the native culture's inability to adapt to modernity; however, he downplayed the fact that much of that modernity was brought by colonizing forces. O'Connell was for O'Faoláin the father of Irish democracy, the one who took a half-dead Irish culture and dragged it into the modern era, in the process amputating from it those bits not fit for modern life. Aside from his explicit jousting with Corkery, *King of the Beggars* also shares in some of the hero-worshipping of Victorian biographies and can be read as an implicit measuring up of contemporary politicians – notably de Valera – to the greatness of the former leader. Yet O'Faoláin also remains critical of O'Connell's selling out of the masses in favour of the bourgeoisie who came to have more power under Catholic Emancipation and whose descendants ruled post-independence Ireland. His introduction to the abridged edition of *The Autobiography of Theobald Wolfe Tone* (1937) offers a further reading of the past as a commentary on the present. However, for all of O'Faoláin's criticisms of Corkery, his own work should be held up to the same scrutiny: his biographies are notably free of documentation and so while one might admire his narrative power and larger arguments, the evidence upon which they are based is sorely lacking, leaving him open to those same charges that he levels at Corkery of skewing or imagining the past to fit his outlook.

Perhaps given that O'Faoláin's non-fictional writing in this decade was so consumed with recuperating the past, it is perhaps natural that his stories are rooted in the genre of historical fiction. Like his biographies, these works set in former times comment as much on the past as they do on the 1930s. Yet the strength of Delaney's study of O'Faoláin's fiction is not in the assessment of its polemical value, but rather of its achievements as literature. He carefully structures his arguments based on close readings of grammar, syntax, and verb tense, distinctions between author, narrator, and character, and explorations of dominant themes and leitmotifs. With such attention to detail, Delaney counters several of the dominant critical paradigms and the consensus on much of O'Faoláin's oeuvre in this period. He also delights in the complex and the ambiguous; for example, he views O'Faoláin's treatment of violence in his short story cycle *Midsummer Night Madness* (1932) as too contradictory to be defined. Similarly, the effects of historical forces and inherited memories are teased out through analysis of the divided protagonist of *A Nest of Simple Folk* (1933). And the rebellion of the narrator of *Bird Alone* (1936) – who, like Joyce's Stephen Dedalus, is supersaturated in the religion against which he struggles – is shown to be hopelessly incomplete.

Nowhere does the latter issue of the place of the Catholic Church and its habitus in Irish culture become so focused as in O'Faoláin's second short story collection *A Purse of Coppers* (1937). Priests and the theme of the Church are threaded through thirteen of *A Purse of Coppers'* fourteen stories. While the overall depiction of contemporary Ireland is decidedly depressing – as signalled in the title of the opening story 'A Broken World', which is more emphatic than 'Broken World?', its title when it was first published in *The London Mercury* in 1936 – the people of this bleak society are rendered as something more than caricatures. Indeed, the many priests are often drawn in sympathetic lines that distinguish them from the Church hierarchy, who, O'Faolain charged in many of his essays, were authoritarian and life-killing.

Paul Delaney breathes some much needed fresh air into O'Faoláin studies, offering new and sensitive readings of his work that ceaselessly probe, refusing to close off debate or offer simple conclusions. It would be nice to see a similarly considerate study that follows as intensely O'Faolain's fate from the 1940s to his death in 1991, set against the backdrop of a slowly liberalizing Ireland that, for better or for worse, gradually took on some of the contours of his vision.

BRAD KENT
Université Laval
DOI: 10.3366/iur.2016.0218

Robert Tobin, *The Minority Voice: Hubert Butler and Southern Irish Protestantism, 1900–1991.* Oxford: Oxford University Press, 2012. 301pp. £71.00 GBP.

Aidan O'Malley and Eve Patten (editors), *Ireland, West to East.* Oxford and Bern: Peter Lang, 2014. 297pp. €55.60 EUR.

The general acclaim with which Hubert Butler's essays have been greeted since the publication in 1985 of *Escape from the Anthill* by Lilliput Press up to *The Appleman and the Poet* (2014), might lead us to overlook the anomalous position of Butler within the wider fabric of twentieth-century Irish and international letters. In an age of the professional academic, Butler was an amateur scholar; in an age of the tightly-argued monograph, Butler preferred the essay form; in an 'age of extremes', Butler was a liberal, Protestant intellectual and, as Robert Tobin reminds us, Butler fell foul of the clerical constrictions of Irish intellectual life in mid-century Ireland. He has appeared, retrospectively, as 'a voice in the wilderness', but we have belatedly recognized and applauded his persuasive, gentle rhetoric. Butler seems almost to be Ireland's answer to Isaiah Berlin, but without the academic regalia, and whose corpus is still being rescued from the often obscure original journals in which it was first published.

The time is undoubtedly ripe, then, for a full-length biographical study of Hubert Butler and Tobin has gone some way towards answering that need. Tobin's book, however, is not a conventional biography since it seeks to contextualize Butler's career within a broader framework of southern Protestantism since independence. As Tobin demonstrates, although educated in England (Charterhouse and Oxford), Butler was influenced in his youth by several socially-minded, Protestant intellectuals seeking to steer the Irish Free State in a culturally and economically enlightened direction. Tobin identifies the intellectual and social activism of Standish O'Grady, Horace Plunkett, and George Russell (AE) as crucial influences on the young Butler. The efforts of this trio to do some good in their immediate community chimed with Butler's own deeply–ingrained sense of social duty and his own decision, while still at school in England, to follow his ancestors by residing at the Butler family home, Maidenhall in Co. Kilkenny which he would do, aside from foreign travel, from 1941.

As befits a scholarly monograph published by Oxford University Press, Tobin's study is meticulously argued and carefully documented. The appendices of Butler's own extensive list of publications and the list of Kilkenny Debates he organised from 1954 to 1971 will be very useful for future scholars. And Tobin makes judicious use of a range of unpublished letters and archival materials which are highly illuminating. One may occasionally quibble with the sheer volume of references contained in the footnotes – for example, whether we really need reference to four separate publications to substantiate Horace Plunkett's involvement in the co-operative movement – while also being grateful for the scholarly precision which Tobin displays.

Nevertheless, in spite of the welcome light which this volume sheds on Butler's important contribution to Irish intellectual life, there are certain methodological issues and points of emphasis which may need to be reconsidered. Chief among these is Tobin's perception of Butler's Protestantism as the framework for interpreting his resistance to the pressures of mid-century Catholic conformity in Ireland. As Tobin acknowledges, 'by the age of twelve [Butler] concluded that he did not believe in God', and although his Protestant identity remained important, his approach towards the faith was non-doctrinal. More importantly, Tobin's monograph underplays the myriad ways in which Catholic Irish intellectuals resisted the pressures of de Valera's vision of a frugal, Catholic nation at ease with itself. Indeed, the satire and critique of writers like Patrick Kavanagh and Flann O'Brien is all the more powerful because it speaks from direct 'insider' experience of the clichés and pieties of the 'dark circumscribed forties' (and fifties), as John Jordan famously described them.

More seriously, there seems to be a certain sleight of hand in places whereby Butler's Protestant identity becomes the morally privileged centre of resistance to a monolithic, Catholic and theocratic Irish polity. By quoting a letter from Hubert Butler to his wife Peggy in which he suggests that 'Unless some effort is made to stop all this hate and stupidity[, it] will certainly be directed against the few remaining Anglo-Irish, as there are no Jews, Communists, Freemasons, etc. to be used as scapegoats' (letter, June 1939), Tobin is endorsing an injudicious analogy, made here by Butler, in private correspondence, between the situation of Protestants in southern Ireland and the very grave situation of Jews and other minorities in continental Europe. Similar rhetorical slippage can be found elsewhere in the volume, as, for example, Tobin's characterization of the term 'non-Catholic' (a phrase disparagingly used in the 1940s and 1950s about the Protestant minority) as 'an attempt to reconstitute Protestants as "non-matter", a demographic blank space in Irish life akin to the empty fields where destroyed Big Houses had once stood and which nature would in time reclaim' which is an emotive way of comparing Protestant isolation in the Irish Republic with the far more serious 'demographic blank space[s]' left by the Famine, Cromwellian wars, and other displacements across Irish history. These false analogies arguably render the terms of Tobin's argument and cultural framework somewhat tenuous, if not occasionally offensive, to 'non-Protestants'.

There is thus, arguably, a sectarian undercurrent running beneath the chosen interpretative framework of the study which equates Protestantism and liberalism a little too readily. In spite of some discussion of Butler's 1941 essay 'The Barriers', issues of partition and majoritarian Protestantism in northern Ireland are barely mentioned. Meanwhile, the suggestion by Butler, endorsed by Tobin, that Irish people and politicians should avoid the 'compulsion to compare [Ireland] to England' and 'dispense with British imperialism and Catholic universalism alike' seems hardly reasonable or realistic. Indeed, Tobin's criticisms of Irish 'xenophobia and insularity', attributed here to 'an ongoing preoccupation with England and the urge to develop an Irish identity undefiled by English influence', seem a little harsh in the circumstances. One struggles to think of a post-colonial society that has not experienced an agonistic relationship with their imperial power, especially in the aftermath of a decolonial struggle. While one may applaud Butler's historical and geographical range and the scope it offers for cultural comparison and critique, it is perhaps idealistic to expect a supranational detachment or transcendence of Ireland's polity from England's shadow in the immediate aftermath of independence.

In other areas of the study, Tobin displays admirable balance and adopts some striking formulations. Thus, for example, he acknowledges that Butler's 'role as a public controversialist placed him at odds with his co-religionists as often as it did with his Catholic opponents thus providing greater nuance to his occasional tendency to attribute enlightenment exclusively to the Protestant class. In such instances, Tobin elucidates a more truly Butlerian vision of 'non-dogmatic Christian communion' which exhibits 'localist idealism' and is closer to 'the essential moderation' of Butler's positions. The heroism of Hubert Butler is, of course, non-sectarian and is demonstrated by his numerous acts of philanthropy and active humanitarian intervention, reflected also in his writings. Indeed, he once claimed to have been 'happiest' in helping Jewish families to escape from Vienna via acts of 'indiscriminate humanitarianism' while working with the Quakers in 1938. Despite the slippages in Tobin's account, Hubert Butler still emerges as a clear-eyed idealist whose 'sober consideration of avoidable follies' in Irish and European history did not overwhelm his consciousness or dampen his much-admired 'liberal-humanitarianism'.

Although Tobin's study deals admirably with the local/international dichotomy in Butler's thinking, one needs to turn to the three essays on Butler contained in *Ireland, West to East* to get a fresh perspective specifically on the Balkan Butler. Aidan O'Malley provides an admirable account of Hubert Butler's explorations 'In Europe's Debatable Lands' of Yugoslavia while Stipe Grgas attempts to account for 'Hubert Butler's Non-Presence in Croatia'. Meanwhile, Michael McAteer's important intervention, in an essay titled 'From Ireland to Croatia: Hubert Butler and Alojzije Stepinac' suggests that there are important qualifications which must be made to Butler's well-known account of genocide in wartime Croatia.

As Chris Agee has suggested in his essays on 'The Balkan Butler' (1999) and 'The Stepinac File' (2000), two pivotal moments in Butler's career centre on his experiences in Croatia. The two moments in question are the 'moment in the library' in Zagreb in June 1947 where Butler discovered the 'hysterical adulation' in the wartime newspapers towards the regime of Croatian fascist dictator Ante Pavelitch which he found 'profoundly disturbing' given Pavelitch's wartime record of mass extermination of Orthodox Serbs and other minorities. The second moment is the famous 'Papal Nuncio Incident' in Dublin in 1952 where Butler achieved momentary notoriety for challenging, at a public meeting, the defence by the Catholic Church of Archbishop Aloysius Stepinac whose wartime collusion with the Ustashe regime of Pavelitch had exacerbated the massacres in Croatia. Butler's outspokenness led to a walk-out by the Papal Nuncio and to Butler's vilification in the media and ostracization in Kilkenny.

However, the whole rumpus of the 'Papal Nuncio Incident' was only possible, argues McAteer, because 'Croatia became a free signifier, connoting pro-fascist clerical Catholicism for Butler, and Communist-persecuted Catholicism for mainstream Irish Catholics' all of which 'demonstrated a poor grasp of the region itself at the time'. McAteer's careful reconstruction of some of the pre- and post-war contexts for Stepinac's conduct leads him to conclude that 'the further into the question of Butler, Stepinac, and Tito's Yugoslavia one travels, the more confused and messy the historical narrative becomes'. This is important because it reminds us that Butler's own historical analysis of wartime Croatia is not infallible and that even the historian endowed with an 'ethical imagination' (as Chris Agee has termed it) may, on occasion, misconstrue or misinterpret the available evidence.

Hubert Butler is perhaps the best-known Irish intellectual to have engaged with the cultures of Russia and eastern Europe in his writing, but he is by no means unique. While Butler explored pre and post-war

Yugoslavia without the benefits of modern transportation, but equipped with proficiency in Serbo-Croat, which he used to good effect, more contemporary authors have ventured forth to explore the 'new Europe' which has opened up since 1989, leaving clear imprints in contemporary Irish poetry and fiction. The volume of essays *Ireland, West to East* edited by Aidan O'Malley and Eve Patten provides a welcome survey of what the book's subtitle terms 'Irish Cultural Connections with Central and Eastern Europe'.

In his assessment of 'Hungarian Affinities in Contemporary Irish Poetry', Philip Coleman finds the fruits of cultural exchange in work by Dennis O'Driscoll and Hugh Maxton, among others, while pointing to the range of Hungarian authors available in English translation, partly thanks to the translations of Anglo-Hungarian poet George Szirtes. Unexpected connections are also identified by Guy Woodward in his essay on 'John Hewitt and Eastern Europe' between Ulster poet John Hewitt and Hungarian and Czech authors showing that 'rootedness' and cultural exchange are not incompatible. Indeed, many of these essayists find in common a dilemma between the apparently mobile and permeable boundaries of contemporary Europe and the specificities of language and tradition in specific corners of the continent.

As John McCourt reminds us in his essay on 'Eastern European Images in the Irish Novel from Charles Lever to Colum McCann', 'Irish writing has traditionally looked West and allowed the East only marginal attention'. If 'the East' has sometimes been manifest in terms of cliché-ridden atavism, as for example in the nineteenth-century Irish Gothic novel, recent literary texts deal with more realistic and pressing issues of emigration, displacement, cultural belonging, and estrangement. A common theme here is what the editors refer to, in their 'Introduction', as 'peripherality' and so, as several contributors note, Ireland's position as a small nation on the western fringes of Europe has historically found common cause with the emerging nations of Eastern Europe. Indeed, as Lili Zách reminds us in her essay on 'Ireland, Czechoslovakia and the Question of Small Nations', the early development of Irish foreign policy and neutrality was predicated on the notion of small nations and their need to preserve their independence and identity against larger, imperial neighbours.

This volume is itself a testimony to academic exchange between scholars at Trinity College Dublin and scholars at the University of Zagreb and thus reflects the possibilities of scholarly co-operation 'against a backdrop of continuing geopolitical redefinitions of "Europe" itself', as the editors suggest. It reveals that it is time, perhaps, to take the opposite direction to Gabriel Conroy and to set out on a journey eastwards to enjoy further cultural enrichment within the new Europe.

BENJAMIN KEATINGE
South East European University, Macedonia
DOI: 10.3366/iur.2016.0219

Stephanie Schwerter, *Northern Irish Poetry and the Russian Turn: Intertextuality in the Work of Seamus Heaney, Tom Paulin and Medbh McGuckian*. Basingstoke: Palgrave Macmillan, 2013.

Stephanie Schwerter's *Northern Irish Poetry and the Russian Turn* is, in many respects, a unique and remarkable study. She brings her fluency in Russian and her proficiency in translation to three of the most significant figures from Northern Ireland since the 1970s: Seamus Heaney, Tom Paulin, and Medbh McGuckian. The most interesting question that her book addresses is that of the poet's responsibility at a time of political violence. Although this is not resolved, one of the striking features of the book is the way in which 'the Russian turn' highlights a notable anxiety among those Northern Irish poets selected; one that this turn may have been intended to dispel. Heaney, Paulin, and McGuckian look to Russian literature in the Soviet era because it was poetry written out of violent political circumstances; at the same time, they admire it for what Viktor Shklovsky once called *literarnost* (literariness). With varying degrees of emphasis, the contrast between a literature attentive to violent political circumstances and a literature that proclaims its own autonomy as art shapes the representation of Russia in Heaney, Paulin, and McGuckian as they respond to the situation in the North from the 1970s to the 1990s. Schwerter cites Heaney's essay 'The Government of the Tongue' in which he argues for the poets' obligation to articulate injustices without taking sides (p.12). Yet much of the information that she brings to light about many of the Russian writers with which Heaney, Paulin, and McGuckian have engaged shows just how absolutely the Russians took sides, predominantly in opposition to the Soviet regime. As Schwerter notes, prisoners once smuggled poems out of Soviet labour camps on bars of soap, so important was poetry regarded as a mode of resistance under Stalinism (p.3). With perhaps the exception of Republican poet Bobby Sands – an unsettling shadow behind this book – Northern Irish poets never found themselves in this predicament.

The problem is best exemplified in Schwerter's treatment of Tom Paulin's translation of Marina Tsvetaeva's poem 'André Chénier' which he published in his 1987 collection, *Fivemiletown*. Written under the most extremely abject circumstances, Tsvetaeva's poem was a belated rallying call for the White Army in their fighting against the Bolsheviks during the Civil War that followed the 1917 Revolution. Paulin completely changes the imperative in Tsvetaeva's poem: from militant resistance to the Bolshevik terror, to getting beyond the bitter sectarian violence of Northern Ireland in the 1980s. Schwerter downplays this dichotomy by emphasizing instead how both the original and the translation are testimonies to the horror of war. Her argument also slips rather egregiously in reading Paulin's translation as an allusion to 'political fanaticism' of fathers who would allow their sons to join the paramilitaries or the British Army during the Troubles (p.80). Famous Scottish comedian Billy Connolly once did a tour of duty in the North with the British Army Parachute Regiment, for example, returning years later to perform a comedy show in Belfast.

One of the impressive features of the book is its treatment of exile. Schwerter's reading of Heaney's 'Chekhov on Sakhalin' from *Station Island* (1984) illuminates the extent to which Chekhov's posture of observing the inmates on this prison island in Tsarist Russia gave expression to conflicting desires in Heaney after the 1981 Hunger Strikes at the Maze Prison: to express the guilt of 'collusion' with Chekhov's literary disinterest and, at the same time, to get away as far as possible from the North. In this way, the line that Schwerter picks from Heaney's description of Sakhalin island – 'That far North, Siberia was South' – is as confessional as it is isolationist: as she points out, Sakhalin is not north but east of Moscow, where Chekhov lived from 1879. The work on Heaney's engagement with Osip Mandelstam's poetry and his translations of poems by Joseph Brodsky in Schwerter's study is exemplary. Particularly instructive is the attribution of the phrase 'inner émigré' to the Russian secret police as a term used for both Mandelstam and Anna Akhmatova as dissident poets. Heaney uses the expression in 'Exposure', one of the poems in *North*. Equally significant is her scrupulous reading of Mandelstam's presence in poem XX in the 'Squarings' section of Heaney's *Seeing Things*, mediated through Clarence Brown and W.S. Merwin's translation of the Russian's work. Here, the pressing image of Moscow's Red Square that is drawn from Mandelstam's reflections upon space and power are ventriloquized in Heaney's exploration of order and power within poetic form itself (pp.32–33).

Heaney's deep admiration for Mandelstam and his close identification with Joseph Brodsky, who was forcibly exiled from the

Soviet Union in 1972 (Heaney left Belfast in 1972 for a new life in the Republic of Ireland) and who eventually secured a teaching position at the University of Michigan, raises the important issue of Cold War geopolitics in relation to Northern Irish poetry during the course of the Troubles. The turn to Russian poetry of the Soviet era carries implications for socialist-republican influences on poetry from the North during the worst years of political violence. Schwerter's reading of Paulin's 'The Other Voice', written in 1980 during the IRA/INLA dirty protest in the Maze Prison, brings a sharp contrast with Heaney to the fore. It is telling that the Marxist influences in Paulin's poem originate in an urban working-class locale, a Trotskyite 'cell' that met in a back room off the Donegall Pass, a staunchly British loyalist district controlled by the Ulster Defence Association in the seventies. In 1980, that word 'cell' could not but conjure in Northern Ireland the Republican protesters in the Maze Prison cells, even if Paulin was thinking of the original Belfast Presbyterian cell in his poem, from which the United Irishmen emerged as a revolutionary movement at the end of the eighteenth century. Schwerter picks up on Paulin's Marxist tendencies – alert as they are to the precedence of Mayakovsky – in the allusions to Plekhanov and Trotsky in 'The Other Voice'. She sees the signature of the July 12th Orange Order marches in Ulster in the image of 'long marches' in Paulin's poem, but misses the major revolutionary undercurrent here: the Long March of October 1934 to October 1935 that would inaugurate Mao Zedong's assent to power over the Chinese Communist Party, leading the way for the cultural revolution of the 1960s.

In many ways Schwerter's reading of Russian literary references in Medbh McGuckian's poetry is the most impressive feature of this book. Not only does she advance on Alcobia-Murphy's pioneering work on McGuckian's sources to bring hidden allusions to light, she accounts for the distinctive effect of McGuckian's poetry: communicating love and suffering profoundly through language and imagery that appears to border at times on incomprehensibility. We see this in Schwerter's reading of McGuckian's 'The Man with Two Women' (1992) that Alcobia-Murphy has taken simply as a poem reflecting discreetly on a love-affair. Schwerter advances beyond this to show how the poem takes its cue from the *ménage à trois* in which Mayakovsky lived for fifteen years with Lily Brik and her husband Osip. She convincingly traces McGuckian's gender reversal of this arrangement in the title of her poem (a man with two women rather than Lily Brik with two men) to the character, 'Man with Two Kisses', in Mayakovsky's 1913 avant-garde farce, *Vladimir Mayakovsky: A Tragedy*. The theme of three-way love features also in Schwerter's discussion of Boris Pasternak's long-term love-affair with Olga

Ivinskaya while he was married to Zinaida Nikolayevna, narrated in Ivinskaya's autobiography, *A Captive of My Time: My Years with Pasternak*. Ivinskaya was the inspiration for Lara in Pasternak's most famous work, *Doctor Zhivago*. Schwerter advances beyond Alcobia-Murphy's identification of this work as a source for McGuckian's 'Gráinne's Sleep Song' and 'Little House, Big House' from her collection *On Ballycastle Beach* (1988). Her reading shows not only that *A Captive of My Time* is the source text for these poems, but *why* this is so. The poems are not only informed by emotional conflicts of the extra-marital affair but by Olga Ivinskaya's incarceration in a Soviet Labour camp and consequent miscarriage of Pasternak's child. It is unfortunate that Schwerter does not follow her reading through in relation to the old Irish mythical love-triangle of Diarmuid, Gráinne, and Fionn MacCumhaill. The title, 'Gráinne's Sleep Song', clearly indicates that McGuckian absorbed Ivinskaya's *A Captive of My Time* into the Irish legend in expressing the psychological captivity imposed by the reality and the threat of paramilitary and state violence in Ulster from the 1970s.

Schwerter approaches the matter of translation by providing the original Russian verse together with her own literal translation and the Ulster poets' literary translations. While it is very useful to see these alongside one another, it requires condensing the space available on the page, losing the original spacing arrangements of the poems in the process: both of the original Russian poems and of their English translations. This may be an unavoidable necessity with the standard format of Palgrave volumes, but it is still obtrusive, given how important the physical layout of a poem on the page is to our reactions to verse. Partly as a consequence of covering so much material in such close detail, Schwerter's interpretations of some poems lack nuance, particularly with regard to rhyme structure, and to the specific circumstances of Northern Ireland within which Heaney, Paulin, and McGuckian absorb and express the Russian influences that are examined in the book. This being granted, the wealth and detail of information provided in Schwerter's vibrant study opens up a whole new perspective on Northern Irish poetry and how it has been received during the era of Troubles. *Northern Irish Poetry and the Russian Turn* is a vital resource in understanding the Russian literary influence on poets from the North during the dark days of the Troubles.

MICHAEL MCATEER
Pázmány Péter Catholic University, Budapest
DOI: 10.3366/iur.2016.0220

List of Books Received

Balinesteanu, Tudor, *Religion and Aesthetic Experience in Joyce and Yeats*. Basingstoke: Palgrave Macmillan, 2015. 216 pages. £55 GBP.

Bielenberg, Andy, John Borgonovo, and Pádraig Óg Ó Ruairc, *The Men Will Talk To Me: West Cork Interviews by Ernie O'Malley*. Cork: Mercier Press, 2015. 224 pages. No price given.

Bolger, Dermot, *That Which is Suddenly Precious: New and Selected Poems*. Dublin: New Island Books, 2015. 228 pages. €14.99 EUR.

Brady, Ciaran, *Shane O'Neill*. Dublin: UCD Press, 2015. 112 pages. No price given.

Carville, Conor, and Mark Nixon (eds), *Samuel Beckett Today/Aujourd'hui: 'Beginning of the murmur' – Archival Pre-texts and Other Sources*. Leiden: Brill/Rodopi, 2015. 244 pages. No price given.

Clare, David, *Bernard Shaw's Irish Outlook*. Basingstoke: Palgrave Macmillan, 2016. 207 pages. £60 GBP.

Dawe, Gerald, *Of War and War's Alarms: Reflections on Modern Irish Writing*. Cork: Cork University Press, 2015. 194 pages. No price given.

Dennison, John, *Seamus Heaney and the Adequacy of Poetry*. Oxford: Oxford University Press, 2015. 245 pages. £55 GBP.

Devlin, Kimberly J., and Christine Smedley (eds), *Joyce's Allmazeful Plurabilities: Polyvocal Explorations of Finnegans Wake*. Gainesville: University Press of Florida, 2015. 323 pages. $74.95 USD.

Ferriter, Diarmaid, and Susannah Riordan (eds), *Years of Turbulence: The Irish Revolution and its Aftermath – In Honour of Michael Laffan*. Dublin: UCD Press, 2015. 322 pages. €40 EUR.

Irish University Review 46.1 (2016): 239–241
DOI: 10.3366/iur.2016.0221
© Edinburgh University Press
www.euppublishing.com/journal/iur

Flanagan, Frances, *Remembering the Revolution: Dissent, Culture, and Nationalism in the Irish Free State*. Oxford: Oxford University Press, 2015. 249 pages.

Gibbons, Luke, *Joyce's Ghosts: Ireland, Modernism, and Memory*. Chicago: University of Chicago Press, 2015. 286 pages. $45 USD.

Hanna, Adam, *Northern Irish Poetry and Domestic Space*. Basingstoke: Palgrave Macmillan, 2015. 188 pages. £55 GBP.

Healy, Dermot, *Fighting with Shadows, or Sciamachy*. Ed. Neil Murphy and Keith Hopper. Victoria, Texas: Dalkey Archive Press, 2015. xxv + 387 pages. £12 GBP.

Healy, Dermot, *The Collected Short Stories*. Ed. Neil Murphy and Keith Hopper. Victoria, Texas: Dalkey Archive Press, 2015. Xxxviii + 239 pages. £10 GBP.

Kenna, Shane, *Jeremiah O'Donovan Rossa: Unrepentant Fenian*. Sallins: Merrion Press, 2015. 296 pages. €19.99 EUR.

Kent, Brad (ed.), *George Bernard Shaw in Context*. Cambridge: Cambridge University Press, 2015. xxxii + 384 pages. $120 USD.

Kirkpatrick, Kathryn, and Borbála Faragó (eds), *Animals in Irish Literature and Culture*. Basingstoke: Palgrave Macmillan, 2015. 270 pages. £58 GBP.

McDiarmid, Lucy, *At Home in the Revolution: What Women Said and Did in 1916*. Dublin: Royal Irish Academy, 2015. 285 pages. €25 EUR.

McGee, Owen, *Arthur Griffith*. Sallins: Merrion Press, 2015. 536 pages. No price given.

McNulty, Eugene, and Ciarán MacMurcaidh (eds), *Hearing Heaney: The Sixth Seamus Heaney Lectures*. Dublin: Four Courts Press, 2015. 176 pages. £45 GBP.

Obert, Julia C., *Postcolonial Overtures: The Politics of Sound in Contemporary Northern Irish Poetry*. Syracuse: Syracuse University Press, 2015. 237 pages. £31.50 GBP.

O'Brien, George, *The Irish Novel, 1800–1910*. Cork: Cork University Press, 2015. 296 pages. €39 EUR.

O'Connor, Emmet, *Big Jim Larkin: Hero or Wrecker?* Dublin: UCD Press, 2015. 371 pages. €40 EUR.

O'Keefe, Hélène, *To Speak of Easter Week: Family Memories of the Irish Revolution*. Cork: Mercier Press, 2015. 288 pages. €25 EUR.

Ó Riain, Pádraig (ed.), *The Poems of Blathmac Son of Cú Brettan: Reassessments*. London: Irish Texts Society, 2015. 201 pages. No price given.

Ó Ruairc, Pádraig Óg, *Truce: Murder, Myth and the Last Days of the Irish War of Independence*. Cork: Mercier Press, 2016. 384 pages. €19.99 EUR.

Pelaschiar, Laura (ed.), *Joyce/Shakespeare*. Syracuse: Syracuse University Press, 2015. 210 pages. £17.36 GBP.

Rowley, Rosemarie, *Girls of the Globe*. Dublin: Arlen House, 2015. 110 pages. No price given.

Van Der Ziel, Stanley, *John McGahern and the Imagination of Tradition*. Cork: Cork University Press, 2016. 320 pages. €39.

Wallace, Nathan, *Hellenism and Reconciliation in Ireland: From Yeats to Field Day*. Cork: Cork University Press, 2015. 204 pages. €39 EUR.

i re imagining land

Edited by Eamon Maher

The concepts of Ireland and 'Irishness' are in constant flux as we reappraise the notion of cultural and national specificity in a world assailed from all angles by the forces of globalisation and uniformity. *Reimagining Ireland* is a scholarly book series which interrogates Ireland's past and present and suggests possibilities for the future by looking at Ireland's literature, culture and history and subjecting them to the most up-to-date critical appraisals associated with sociology, literary theory, historiography, political science and theology.

Recent Titles:

David Doolin:
Transnational Revolutionaries:
The Fenian Invasion of Canada, 1866
ISBN 978-3-0343-1922-5

Terry Phillips:
Irish Literature and the First World War:
Culture, Identity and Memory
ISBN 978-3-0343-1969-0

B. Mairéad Pratschke:
Visions of Ireland:
Gael Linn's *Amharc Éireann* Film Series, 1956–1964
ISBN 978-3-0343-1872-3

For more information see www.peterlang.com